The
Will
of
Heaven

The
Will
of
Heaven

An Inspiring True Story
About Elephants,
Alcoholism,
and Hope

- Book One -

Debbie Ethell

THE WILL OF HEAVEN:
An Inspiring True Story About Elephants, Alcoholism, and Hope
Book One

© 2019 by Debbie Ethell

Alberta Pearl Publishing
www.albertapearl.com
To contact the author please email authors@albertapearl.com

ISBN: 978-1-7335887-0-6 (softcover)
ISBN: 978-1-7335887-1-3 (ebook)
Library of Congress Control Number: 2019935271

Cover watercolor by Sandra Ethell / Drawing by Debbie Ethell
Cover and interior design and typeset by Katherine Lloyd, The DESK

This book is dedicated to Leslie Simms
and to my family who never stopped waiting
for the flower to bloom.

PROLOGUE

What would Eleanor do? I thought, contemplating the mess I'd made of my life. She had faced insurmountable odds just to survive, including the death of her mother, killed right in front of her, and had gone on to save hundreds of others in similar circumstances. Yet even now there were people who wished her dead.

Eleanor, along with about four hundred others, were wild elephants in Kenya I'd followed since I was eight years old—the age when it all began. Eleanor possessed an incredible amount of courage. *God, I needed that courage now.*

Sitting in the courthouse parking lot, I looked down at the 7-Eleven Big Gulp in the cup holder before me. *I wish I could drink it now.* But I couldn't. Another judge was waiting. They would smell the alcohol on my breath as soon as I entered the courtroom, and I would be doomed for sure. *It was almost time.* With a wave of nausea, I got out of the car and walked into what had by now become all too familiar surroundings.

I checked in at the front desk, and soon a court-appointed attorney was talking to me. He seemed young and unworthy. He talked about something I didn't understand. I made out that I was only to speak two words: "No contest." I sat with him in silence on a hallway bench as a man in a suit approached us.

"Is that Ms. Ethell?" the man asked my attorney, who simply shrugged. I stood to face him. *Now what?*

He began recalling memories I had long forgotten about the evening in question, the evening I agreed was not a contest. Then it dawned on me: this was the officer who arrested me. *Holy shit!* I was paying attention now.

"Do you remember what happened that evening?" he asked, seeming to realize that I really had no recollection.

"Did it involve F-words? I bet it involved a lot of F-words," I joked.

Unamused, he continued.

Over the previous several weeks, I had tried hard to remember. Little bits here and there floated back, but the entirety of the evening remained unknown. I was in my home in Calistoga, California, packing for a trip to South Carolina to see my sister, Carrie, graduate from college. The plan was to head to San Francisco that afternoon and stay with a friend who would drive me to the airport early the following morning. But then someone called and asked me to join them for a quick glass of wine before I left. I agreed. *It was just up the street. What could it hurt?*

Before long, a few more friends joined us, and I talked myself into another drink. Then we went across the street to our favorite dive bar. Suddenly, I found myself wrestling a strange girl in a pool as I sat topless on the back of some guy. *What the fuck?* I jumped off the stranger's back and climbed out of the pool. *What the hell time is it? Where am I?* A clock in the kitchen told me it was nearly 4:00 a.m.

Shit! My flight was leaving in two hours. As I frantically searched for my clothes, I saw a guy watch me from across the room. Richard Prichard. It was a name I could never forget. He seemed genuinely concerned and insisted I not drive. I didn't care what he had to say; my entire family was in South Carolina for the celebration, and they would wonder where I was. *I had to get on that flight.*

When he took my keys away, I let Richard Prichard believe I would stay and "sleep it off," but I didn't tell him about the magnet I had hidden underneath my car with the spare, or that I knew there was a bathroom window large enough to crawl out of. I simply went in and never came out.

The road from Calistoga to Santa Rosa snakes through the Sonoma hills like a river with no guide. It was all I could do to stay on it. I rolled the window down, went slower, and turned the air conditioning on full blast. I *had* to get to San Francisco. The last thing I remember was a clicking sound. *Click-click* … pause … *click-click* … pause. Over and over again.

And then I woke up in jail.

I snapped back to the courthouse conversation. It struck me as odd that the arresting officer was even talking to me in the first place. When I'd been arrested before, no officer had ever come up to speak to me. *What was this about?*

What he said next got my full attention.

"You said something to me that I have never heard in all my years in law enforcement." He shook his head and chuckled to himself as a cold chill began working its way down my spine. *What could I have possibly said that an officer with years of law enforcement experience had never heard before?*

"You don't remember it, do you?" he asked. It was obvious I did not. He told me there had been several 911 calls about a drunk driver on Highway 101 in Santa Rosa. I was silently impressed I had even made it that far. The two officers began making bets with each other as to whether I was going to smash into the median or run into the ditch as my car swerved across the freeway. Every time it seemed certain a crash was imminent, I veered away. *Click-click* ... pause ... *click-click.* I learned later that was the rhythmic sound of the seat belt component as it locked back into place each time I swerved hard to the left.

There were officers ahead of us preventing traffic from entering the freeway while I was still on it, and there were officers behind us keeping what little traffic there was at bay until I could be apprehended. Once they finally pulled me over, the officer now standing before me in the courtroom yelled into his loud speaker to "stay in the vehicle." But I didn't. I opened the door and fell out, dressed in someone else's unmatched pajamas. A few empty bottles fell out with me—as if there was any doubt about what I was doing.

As the officer approached, he began reading me my rights. When he was done, he heard me say something too muffled to understand. When he asked me to repeat it, I grabbed his leg, hugged it, and said, "Thank you, thank you, thank you."

Horrified, I stopped breathing. I heard nothing in that busy courtroom hallway but the sound of his voice as the cold shiver began to feel like the whisper of a threat. I had no idea what was coming but was certain it wasn't good.

"Why are you thanking me, ma'am, I am arresting you," he told me he said. And that's when I said it. Right there on the 101, I said ...

"Thank you for stopping me when I couldn't stop myself."

The officer shook his head once again and looked at me as if he was waiting for my reaction. No one he had arrested had ever thanked him before. Not like that, apparently. I went completely

white and needed to sit down. Before I could deal with what had just happened, we were called into the courtroom, where I got to say my perfect two-word speech.

And just like that I was convicted of another DUI.

Sitting in my car after it was over, I tried to process what happened. It wasn't an actual prison sentence that scared me; it should have, but what had my attention was the fact that for the first time in my entire life, I admitted to another human being that I was completely out of control, that I couldn't or wouldn't stop drinking for reasons even I didn't understand. I knew I was in a lot of trouble but had no idea where to turn for help. And it was to that police officer, *that total stranger,* that I admitted my deepest, darkest secret—the secret I was dying to tell but didn't know how. And I said it to someone I couldn't even remember.

I downed the Big Gulp that waited so patiently. It was a good one, more vodka than orange juice. Slowly my anxiety began to subside, and the feeling of normalcy returned. I had one more fleeting thought of Eleanor. *How was I ever going to get back to her?* All of this craziness that my life had become had to stop, this much I knew. Suddenly, I had an overwhelming sense of courage—*liquid courage*—nothing like the kind I imagined Eleanor had, but it would do. I started my car and headed to my job as a parking valet.

Two blocks from the courthouse, I ran a stop sign and smashed into the back of a nice man's truck.

INTRODUCTION

I was only eight years old when I met Eleanor. She was one of the first known cases of an elephant successfully released back into the wild after being raised in captivity. I first learned about her story on a nature show on PBS, an episode which made time stand still for me. As if a door I didn't even know existed, suddenly opened. A seed was planted that night, and a lifelong obsession took hold.

I didn't know that America's insatiable hunger for ivory was why Eleanor found herself an orphan at such a young age. In 1972, the year I was born, there were approximately 275,000 elephants in Kenya, but by the time I met Eleanor in 1980, that number was in a death spiral due to the awful first wave of poaching, and fewer than twenty thousand elephants remained. Tourism was the most profitable trade in Kenya at the time—without it, the country faced total economic collapse. The powers that be were in a full-blown panic. I did not know then that if I closed my eyes and fast-forwarded forty years, a nearly identical series of events would take place. Only, the second wave would be much larger than the first.

Science had yet to catch up to Kenyan conservationists David and Daphne Sheldrick's hunch that elephants were capable of far more than anyone could imagine. Together they rescued baby elephants in the throes of despair, many suffering unspeakable trauma and cruelty at the hands of humans. They watched the young elephants' wounds heal as they made peace with the past, creating a unique family of orphans brought together under an umbrella of shared pain, suffering, horror, and compassion.

I stalked my subjects in books and research papers the way a hunter stalks his prey. For years I considered my passion simply an obsessive hobby, as I enjoyed reading scientific journals, books, encyclopedias—anything I could get my hands on that taught me more about the magic of elephants. What started out as a tiny notebook with only three elephants during that first episode when I was eight eventually blossomed into a full-blown research project with more than four hundred wild elephants. I knew everything about every single one, and they became my most treasured friends.

By the time I realized I could no longer pretend my hobby was just a silly dream, I was in my mid-thirties with a fifth-grade math education, something I learned is never a good starting point for any scientist. It took six long years to get a science degree that takes most people four, but it transformed me from a curious child into a conservation research scientist.

If I'm being honest, it is still with a twinge of insecurity that I call myself a conservation research scientist, since I don't have a PhD, nor am I considered an academic. I am simply an educated observer with a scientific background. The stories in this book are based on my experiences in life and with the elephants I have come to know. Their stories as well as my own are told to the best of my recollection, as nothing more and nothing less than an educated observer of both.

The truth is that elephants don't have much time. Ten years is considered the long game, and we both know ... *that is nothing.* This is not a book about the lives of elephants but about the lives of my friends—the elephants who saved my life and whose lives I am now desperate to save in return. I am their self-appointed storyteller, because to me these elephants are *everything.* I have no doubt that without them making their presence known in my young life when they did I never would have lived long enough to be able to share our story with you. So I am simply returning the favor and hoping that by some *Will of Heaven* I may be able to extend their lives in the same brilliant way they have extended mine.

CHAPTER 1

I actually have no memory of my first experience with an elephant. My grandmother Pearl took me to visit the elephants at the Woodland Park Zoo in Seattle when I was two years old. I was perched on top of her shoulders to get a better look when she got distracted by something. She didn't notice as one of the elephants approached us from behind.

The elephant stepped up on a curb inside the enclosure so she could reach over the short fence. She gently wrapped her trunk around my waist and began to lift.

Pearl turned around expecting to see one of my parents—but instead saw my tiny arms wrapped around the trunk of the elephant. She screamed. The older elephants screamed. Suddenly all these people rushed towards us. The elephants in the enclosure trumpeted wildly as all hell broke loose. The young elephant quickly let go and ran back to the protection of the herd. People surrounded us to check that I was OK. Throughout the whole ordeal, my grandmother said I remained completely silent. That is, until we started to leave the elephant exhibit. As she pushed me away in my stroller I began to scream, reaching back toward the elephant. She said the elephant followed us along the fence until we became separated by space and time. We had to leave the zoo, as I became completely inconsolable. My father is convinced it was during that visit that elephants were imprinted on me. Thinking about it now, perhaps he is right.

Six years later, I met Eleanor. As the narrators of a nature show on PBS told parts of her story, a whole new world opened up to me. Eleanor was an elephant adopted by the Sheldricks and she would go on to challenge just about everything anyone thought they knew about her species, showcasing behavior that could only be described as ... *extraordinary.*

∞

She was found in the northern region of Kenya in the Samburu Reserve, an area with few sources of permanent water. During the long dry season, elephants, especially those with young calves, find themselves anchored to these regions, which make for a poacher's paradise as they chase herds from one water source to the next.

In 1958, Bill Woodley—Daphne's ex-husband and the game warden of Mountain Parks—was escorting the governor of Kenya and his wife around Samburu after a night of heavy rain when they came upon a sad, pathetic little two-year-old elephant standing all alone in the middle of a muddy plain. Her skin color was wrong, tears rolled from her eyes, she swayed back and forth as if lost in her own world, and her tiny trunk rested on the ground. I would later learn that elephants rarely rest their trunks on the ground, as it is usually a sign of trauma or depression, but Bill knew instantly she was most likely the helpless victim of a poacher. His suspicions were confirmed when he spotted the lifeless body of her mother with a poisoned arrow deeply embedded in her side a short distance away.

The sad screams of a baby elephant bring out the defensive

worst in any herd, and they will protect their young to the death. But Eleanor's frantic cries were met only by silence as she was loaded onto a truck and transported to a makeshift stall in a nearby tourist lodge. She was named after the governor's wife, Lady Eleanor, who had a deep love of elephants.

Eleanor was passed from one facility to the next until Kenyan authorities insisted she be placed in the Nairobi National Park Orphanage, which was simply a zoo full of lost, stray, or orphaned animals. She quickly became the most popular attraction.

In the 1950s David was hired as the first game warden of an unbelievably ugly and enormous parcel of land called Tsavo National Park in Kenya. There were few animals where there should have been many. The idea was to turn the barren wasteland full of colorless scrub brush into a safari destination that would rival the most beautiful in all of Africa. Everyone, including David, thought that was a far stretch.

Occasionally he came across orphaned or injured animals. Each one was brought home to the loving care of Daphne, where she nursed them back to health. Soon their home was a menagerie of all sorts of odd-looking animals raised together in one big happy family.

I sat motionless as the narrator explained that none of the animals David and Daphne rescued were "kept" but instead allowed to go back into the wild anytime of their own free will. Of course, some were too young, injured, or sick, but there were never ropes, cages, or chains holding them back. And each one did eventually choose to go back into wild to be with their own kind. Though many returned for a quick visit every now and then, they all went on to live a life of freedom.

By the time Eleanor turned five, she was listless and overweight.

Rarely permitted to go outside of her cement stall, it was clear to everyone her health was fast deteriorating.

They didn't know at the time that an elephant's life mimics that of our own. Elephants mature at nearly the same rate as a human and can live to the age of seventy or so, just like us. A five-year-old elephant has nearly the same ability to comprehend information as a five-year-old child, so one only has to imagine what that would have been like. Science tells us that if left alone, untouched, a child will die. So will an elephant.

David and Bill worked together and petitioned the authorities for Eleanor's release, and to their surprise it was granted. Just like that Eleanor was handed over to the care of David and Daphne.

When the wary five-year-old elephant stepped off the ramp into the middle of an odd menagerie of animals waiting to greet her, she did so with trepidation. *What must she have thought*, Daphne wondered. Her little belly was distended and grossly large as a result of her inactive lifestyle in the zoo.

Eleanor greeted each orphan that waited for her, which included three ostriches, four buffalo, two elephants, and a baby warthog. Daphne thought she did so with quite a lot of dignity. That memory was one Daphne reflected on later as the actual moment "a legend was born in Tsavo." She didn't know then that Eleanor was literally about to turn the science of elephants upside down.

Soon after Eleanor's arrival, Daphne began to notice how deeply compassionate she was. When two of the young rhinos fought, as they often did, Eleanor would intervene by coming in between them and chasing them off in opposite directions. As David continued to bring home new animals, Eleanor seemed to think they were all gifts for her, and she made herself busy being everyone's mother.

She was instrumental in helping Daphne save orphaned baby

elephants, and as the years passed they felt certain she would eventually find her way into the wild herds that surrounded the compound. And she did eventually ... *33 years later.*

For three decades, Eleanor stayed behind with Daphne, helping her raise and care for *hundreds* of animals. She stayed with Daphne long after David passed away. She stayed while Daphne raised her own two girls to adulthood. And she became the head matriarch of who knows how many elephant orphans—fifty? One hundred? Three hundred? She mourned with the humans when the baby elephants died, and she taught Daphne more about the elephant species than any book or lecture ever could.

By the time that episode was over, I was bawling. It was by far the greatest animal story I'd ever heard.

I kept a journal on those elephants from that very moment to this. I wrote down all of the names of the elephants I met during that hour and every detail I could remember about each one. Every now and then my parents would find something in a newspaper, magazine, or book that talked about Daphne or the elephants, and I painstakingly recorded every last detail into my burgeoning notebook.

I had begun my first research project without realizing it by copying down every detail I could find about each elephant, constantly adding, refining, and hoping that I would one day get a chance to meet them. What started out as three elephants would blossom over the years into thousands of pages of research on hundreds of elephants. But there would always be the one I would never stop searching for. The first one that would capture my attention more than any other. There would be that one that crawled deeper into my heart than all the rest. The first name I ever wrote down.

Eleanor.

CHAPTER 2

*G*etting sober was never my intention. It all just sort of happened that way. Trouble kept finding me everywhere I went, and my luck was running thin. One day a new therapist asked me the same question so many had before—only this time I answered it with absolute honesty, though I have no idea why.

"Debbie, how often do you drink and use drugs?"

Before I could stop myself, it just came out, "Every. Single. Day."

And that was it, really. The beginning of the end. She explained to me that I was addicted and needed to go to "treatment," though I had no idea what that was. I had, by that time, completely run out of options and was living in my car by the beach in Ventura.

Only a few weeks earlier I'd been working as a personal assistant to the famous actress Diane Ladd. I realized the instant I saw the conspicuous ad in the Ojai newspaper that it must be *someone* famous. When her husband arrived at a local coffee shop to interview me, he drove a Lamborghini, and I knew whoever this was—she was big. The following day Diane called me up with her unmistakable Southern accent and asked if I knew who she was. Luckily, I did. I had seen her television series, Alice, where she said a line in a sarcastic tone the entire nation couldn't seem to stop repeating: "Kiss my grits!" I had also seen several of her films and watched as she and her daughter, Laura Dern, made history as the only mother/daughter duo nominated for an Academy Award for the same film, *Wild at Heart*.

She invited me to her house for breakfast and, in that Southern drawl of hers, asked, "Debbie, what is your sun sign?"

I had no idea. I was distracted by a Golden Globe in the living room behind her. After she asked me a series of questions about the month, year, and time I was born, she continued, "My moon sign is the same as your sun sign." She waited for me to respond, but I had nothing. I had absolutely no idea what she was talking about.

"Do you know what that means?" she asked.

"Ummm ... no?"

"It means that you got the job! Welcome aboard!" I thought to myself that if all interviews were based on my sun sign, life would have been so much easier.

I worked for her for a few months, just long enough to meet Laura and her then-fiancé, Billy Bob Thornton. Diane's mother, Mary, lived with her in Beverly Hills where I spent most of my time, and I completely adored her. I didn't exactly know what being a personal assistant to a "star" meant, but soon learned I had very little time for myself. When I was working, which seemed to be every waking minute, there was no time to do anything I wanted to do ... like get high.

There were scripts Diane wanted me to read, stacked on a table in her office. They were sorted by shooting schedule, and the one on top of the pile was for a film called *28 Days*, slated to begin shooting in North Carolina at the end of the following month. Normally I would have loved the idea of traveling and reading scripts, but instead I only felt angry and resentful, so I never read any of them.

Occasionally Diane gave me tickets to various film premieres she wasn't able to attend. Billy Bob Thornton's assistant, Joe, was usually there. He had been teaching me how to be a good personal assistant. Rule number one was *Don't Drink Too Much,* but more than once Joe found me incapacitated, bent over a toilet throwing up, barely able to walk. I found it difficult to keep track of how much I drank at parties where waiters were constantly filling my glass when I wasn't looking. Each time Joe found me, he snuck me out the back door and helped me get into a car so I could leave the party without bringing Diane any unwanted attention.

One afternoon, Diane pulled me aside and began asking me all kinds of questions. I wondered where she was going when she began to home in on me. I knew I would have to act fast to avoid telling the truth.

"What made you come to Ojai in the first place?"

Umm, well … I was running away.

"Why are you here all alone with no family?"

Because they are tired of my drinking.

And my favorite, "How often do you drink?"

I don't know … like every chance I get.

Instead, I lied. "I'm a free spirit, just like you. I love new experiences and living outside the box."

I knew we were at the end. That evening, Diane and her husband Robert sat down with me to make me an official offer as her permanent personal assistant. My three-month trial period was up. Instead, I shocked them both when I said I wouldn't be taking the job.

"Well, why not?" she asked.

"Because I want to be a barista."

"A what? A coffee maker? You want to be a coffee maker?" asked Robert, shaking his head.

"Yep … that's what I want to do."

At the time, it made perfect sense to me. I could learn how to make coffee and smoke pot all day long. No more of this waking up in the middle of the night crap to pick people up from the airport. So I became a barista and was fired within a week for showing up to work stoned. I noticed a "Help Wanted" sign in the bar of the Chinese restaurant I found myself getting wasted in later the same afternoon. But I got fired for drinking on that job too, just a few weeks after that.

Since I no longer had any income, Meg, the girl I was staying with in Ojai before I started working for Diane, suggested it was time to move on. I discovered a parking lot facing the beach located next to a gas station with a bathroom I could use in Ventura. Finally, I could drink and be left in peace without having to worry about paying so many bills. I convinced myself this was just another adventure—my luck would surely turn around.

My parents still had me on their health insurance, so at least I could still see a counselor, even if I rarely told them the truth. I often wonder why I told that counselor the truth on that day. I suspect it had to do with the courthouse conversation with my most recent arresting officer. But as soon as I said those words— *"Every. Single. Day."*—I felt an enormous wave of relief. Little did I know then the impact that saying those three little words would have on my life in the days to come.

After making my first alcoholic admission to a person I could *actually* remember, I coasted down the hill straight into my parking lot. I spent my last $11 on a two-for-one deal on vodka at the local grocery store and couldn't wait to watch the sunset. Even though Meg asked me to leave her home, I knew she worked in L.A. every other week and even more importantly … I knew where she hid the key. On the weeks she was out of town, I stayed in her house, unbeknownst to her, but on the weeks she went back to Ojai I stayed in the parking lot.

The strange thing is I didn't even know I was living in my car until a woman in recovery explained it to me long after I got sober. She said it was called "breaking and entering," though I argued with her at the time because I didn't have to break anything to enter. She replied that if I didn't have actual permission to be inside someone else's house then I was *breaking* the law when I *entered*.

Hmmm …

My counselor startled me by knocking on my window. I was the last client of the day and must not have noticed she followed me when I left her parking lot for my own.

"I am not living in my car," I explained. "I am simply *staying* in it for a night or two … besides, I am no different than Jewel."

This was right around the time the singer Jewel became famous. I saw her do an interview where she told a story about living in her car on the beach before she was "discovered."

Unmoved, my counselor replied, "Yes, but you have no discernible talents whatsoever, so … there is a difference." I was completely insulted by that. Reluctantly, I agreed to meet her the following day so she could show me a treatment center she had in mind.

We headed to Malibu the following afternoon. I was completely hungover, but a drive up the coast sounded nice as long as I didn't have to drive. We arrived at a building with the most startling view of the ocean I had ever seen. The rooms were plush, the pool reminded me of ones I'd seen gracing the pages of Architectural Digest, and there were famous people sitting in circles in what they called "group."

Yes, treatment was exactly what I needed.

I agreed to go immediately and wanted to check in that day, but my counselor explained that I needed to tell my parents first. After a long argument, and a longer drive back to my parking lot, I eventually consented. The other condition of my "release" was that I had to tell them in person.

For fuck's sake, I thought.

My parents had already bought me a plane ticket home for Christmas, but that wasn't for another week or so. I called my dad and begged to have my ticket changed to an earlier flight. I built up the suspense further by telling them I had something that could only be shared with them in person. Looking back, I can see why my call must have scared them. I hadn't been in touch on a regular basis in a very long time. *Was I pregnant? Was it cancer?*

They changed the ticket, and needless to say the visit didn't quite go as I hoped. At the door of the house my dad asked, "So what's your big news?"

OK, so we're getting right into it. "I just discovered something about myself. Something B-I-G!"

"Mmm-hmm," he replied, taking a long puff from his cigarette. That's when I noticed my mother standing behind him, listening to every word. *Was she crying?*

"I'm an alcoholic!" I said. My parents just stared at me, and I could almost hear the silent swirl of smoke floating above our heads.

After what seemed like an extremely long exhale my father finally said, "No shit, Sherlock, me and your mother have known that for years."

It felt like a landed punch. *How was I the last to know about this?* Then they grabbed their coats, got into their car, and left. *I just got here, where the hell are you going?*

I found a bottle of wine and a few beers, downing them to take the edge off as fast as I could. Then I went into my mother's secret drawer, where she kept a "rainy day" stash-of-cash, but found it empty. *That's odd,* I thought. There wasn't anything in her jewelry box, either, and they had hidden the safe I memorized the combination to. *What was going on?* About an hour later, the phone rang.

My dad was on the other end. "You need to talk to Jason."

OK ... who the hell is Jason?

Jason was some friend of theirs I had never heard of. He got on the phone and had a very distinctive Brooklyn accent. He began by asking me a few questions, each one more irritating than the last. How often did I drink? Did I shake when I woke up in the morning?

Yeah ... so? Who cares?

The questions got progressively more annoying until he said, "Have you thought about going into treatment?"

Ahhhh ... there was one I felt like answering. "Yes, I *AM* going to treatment and was just about to tell my parents that before they took off."

Wait. What? Why was HE asking me all of these questions?

My head started to spin and I couldn't tell if it was the interrogation or the beer I downed faster than a college kid at a frat party. He continued the interview until I had enough and hung up. I couldn't shake the unsettling feeling that all these people knew more about my "secret" than I did.

When my parents returned, they sat me down and explained I

was no longer allowed to stay in their home. My mother was definitely crying this time, and she *never* cried. They told me Jason had been guiding them for the past year about what to do about my alcoholism. *Seriously?* I was in shock. They told me if I returned, they would contact the cops and have me arrested for trespassing. *No freakin' way.* In that moment I hated whoever Jason was. *How dare he turn my sweet, codependent parents against me.*

I left, called some friends from my past, and proceeded to get as high as I possibly could. I didn't care what I took as long as it took me to another place. But no matter how much alcohol I drank, I couldn't seem to get drunk and realized I needed something much more powerful. Hours later, having taken anything anyone offered—absolutely nothing worked. I could feel *everything,* and I needed that to stop. I just could not seem to get high no matter how hard I tried.

The earlier conversation I had with my parents replayed in my mind on a continuous loop. I didn't know what else to do, so I called my sister. *Carrie was always someone I could count on.* A few hours later I started to feel like I was going crazy and yet still felt nearly sober. Soon Carrie, along with my close friend Kirsten, put me into a car after a desperate phone call and delivered me to a pathetic-looking cement building in Portland, Oregon.

Not sure what to expect, I was taken inside, but the bright lights hurt my eyes. Someone began asking me a thousand questions. I looked toward the soothing voice and saw a nice-looking man about my father's age. He was wearing a Christmas sweater. *It's almost Christmas? I forgot it's almost Christmas.* I wondered what he would be doing for Christmas. *Probably had a big cheerful family.* I pictured them all sitting around a table with a fire in the fireplace and snow falling outside big, beautiful picture windows.

There were no windows in the room I was in. *He was probably so excited to get out of here. Home for the holidays ...*

He had this habit of saying everything he was writing under his breath. "Patient, Debbie Eth-ell, Date, December 18."

December 18. December 18. Why did that sound familiar? What was December 18?

And then I remembered it—forcing its way back into my consciousness, the memory of that day came roaring back into brilliant view as I felt my heart sink. December 18 was the day the police officer told me about the secret I had shared with him. *That was one year ago today. I was charged with my last DUI one year ago today. My God, how things had changed in a year.*

I had somehow gotten out of most of the charges leveled against me. The man I rear-ended after leaving the courthouse became a good friend. *An alcoholic just like me.* He took pity on me and instead of calling the police he asked me to dinner.

That is the last thing I remember before I slid into what would be my last blackout inside that treatment center. Apparently, the drug cocktail I had taken did work. The sober feeling I wanted so desperately to get rid of disappeared and I became sicker than I have ever been in my life. Since the question as to what I had taken was a big fat blank on the questionnaire, they couldn't give me anything to minimize the symptoms of withdrawal. Instead, my hands were tied to the side of the bed and I was braced for impact.

∞

"Debbie!" a terrifying voice yelled from across the room. "It's time to GET UP!" I tried opening my eyes but could not make out

anything. *Who the hell was that? Where was I? Whoever I had gone home with last night sounded completely terrifying.*

Then I realized I was lying on the cold tile of a bathroom floor. I willed my arms to move, but I was stuck. I couldn't get my eyes to focus. A putrid smell hit my nose, and I felt the nausea return. Then a white tennis shoe appeared close to my face and quickly disappeared. I could hear soft voices. *What were they saying?* The tennis shoe appeared again. *Please don't hurt me,* I thought as I felt myself being lifted. Then I heard the soothing voice of my Auntie Edna. *Thank God ... Auntie Edna.*

The man with the booming voice was huge and lifted me like a feather. I felt like I was floating. *How had I met him?* But I could remember nothing. I felt myself placed in the lap of the soothing voice. Then the water hit me like an ice bath. I tried to get out, but my arms refused to work. Someone was holding me down as I felt the water begin to warm and started to relax. The comforting voice kept talking to me, though I couldn't make out what she was saying.

This was not my Auntie Edna.

But whoever she was, she felt nice. I began to focus my eyes and realized I was covered in vomit. As soon as the smell hit me, I began to throw up again.

The outline of a huge black man with white tennis shoes stood just outside the open door. Right before I was plunged once again into the deep, black waters of the abyss, I recalled that I was in a hospital and these people were not people I met in a bar but were taking care of me. That was the last thing I remember of those five long days.

CHAPTER 3

The river must have looked like a spectacle to anyone who witnessed it. There was Eleanor standing on the bank, watching a menagerie of animals frolicking and playing in the muddy water. There were younger elephants playing with young rhinos. There was a zebra, several ostriches, a few buffalo, and a peacock, all of which had been rescued by David and brought to Daphne.

Suddenly Eleanor lifted her trunk, catching a scent in the wind. An elephant's sense of smell is incredibly powerful, five times greater than that of a bloodhound. A professor would point out to me years later that the two largest holes in an elephant's skull were for its olfactory bulbs—devoted to its sense of smell.

"Anything that has that much real estate dedicated to it must serve an incredibly important function," she said.

A faint chopping sound could be heard in the distance, and Eleanor slowly began walking towards it. Ali, one of the keepers, went with her to investigate as the rest of the animals reluctantly got out of the water to follow their matriarch.

As they rounded the bend, they spotted a poacher frantically trying to hack off the tusk of an elephant he only just killed, the elephant's terrified family off in the distance. The nervous poacher, focused on the dead elephant's relatives, didn't notice Eleanor sneaking up behind him from the opposite direction.

His eyes grew wide as he suddenly took notice not just to Eleanor's proximity but to the odd assortment of animals trailing close behind. As Ali apprehended the poacher, Eleanor investigated the dead elephant. She slowly ran her trunk up and down its lifeless body as if taking meticulous notes. Then she gently placed one foot on its skull and, with a sickening twist, removed each tusk from its socket. After carefully examining each one, she dragged the tusks a short distance away before tossing them deep into the brush. Ali and the poacher watched her in awe.

It was the only elephant carcass Eleanor had ever been known to encounter, other than that of her mother. Yet her behavior suggested she knew the reason behind the elephant's senseless death.

No one realized then that Eleanor's behavior with the tusks of a fallen elephant would be repeated time and again by hundreds of elephants in the years to follow. And it was the one elephant behavior that haunted me more than all the rest ... that the elephants seemed to understand *why* they were being hunted.

∞

I had nightmares about it often and did so again right before I woke to the sound of rain. I was in a room I didn't recognize, surrounded by things I didn't know. As I moved on the hard bed I heard a loud, scratching sound. *What was that?* I looked down and picked up the edge of the sheet. It was plastic. *What the ...* As I looked around, my head began to throb like I was about to have a stroke. I slowly got up and looked out an enormous window, onto a courtyard with a tree. It looked massive and lonely and barren, devoid of all color and life. The branches were intertwined in their own misery and seemed somehow intimate with the rain falling between them. It was dark, gray, and miserable-looking outside. I found it comforting in an odd *I-know-how-you-feel,* sort of way.

Everything on the bed was plastic and made a loud, raspy scratching sound each time I moved. The pillow, the sheets, the blankets ... all of it was plastic and disposable. I went into the bathroom and caught sight of myself in the mirror. I was instantly horrified. My hair was matted together in a most unusual arrangement. I picked up one section, and like a perfect uncivilized dreadlock it stayed right where I left it.

I felt like I had awakened from a deep coma. Back in my room, I picked up a plastic blanket and sat in a chair overlooking the courtyard, trying to remember everything that happened. Suddenly my door opened and a booming voice yelled, "Debbie! It's time to GET UP!"

The toe of a white tennis shoe appeared through the crack in the door.

"I'm here," I said.

The man froze. "Oh, I didn't realize ... that ... you were ... get dressed and meet me in the hallway in ten minutes."

"For what?" I asked.

"Morning walk. It's mandatory. Be outside your door in ten minutes." And he left. I never saw his face. *Morning walk? In this weather?* I'd forgotten that it rains in Oregon all the time, so this was not unusual. I put on some clothes but forgot about my dreadlocks until I saw the look on the nurses' faces at the desk down the hall.

"Can I get some aspirin for my headache?" I asked.

They all stopped what they were doing and stared at me.

"Sorry," said one of the nurses finally, "but we can't give you anything."

Oh God, my hair. It suddenly dawned on me what they were staring at.

"Does anyone have a hat I can borrow?"

One of the nurses broke from her trance and tossed me a hat that lay on a desk.

I waited patiently in the hallway for the man to return, hoping to get some answers about where I was and what happened. Eddie was an impressive sight when he came around the corner. A huge black man, he stood well over six feet and spoke with the deepest booming voice I ever heard. It sounded vaguely familiar to me. He told me to follow him, so I did.

"Where is everyone else?" I asked.

"There is no one else. You're it." He chuckled as he held a door open for me.

The fresh air filled my lungs, and I stood there for a second, taking it all in.

"Keep up," Eddie yelled from across the parking lot.

God, how had he gotten so far away already? I had to practically jog to keep up with him. Each one of his steps felt like three of mine.

"Keep up," he repeated.

"Is this a hospital?" I gasped as I caught up to him. My head was pounding.

"No," Eddie replied. "It's a detox treatment center."

"What's that?"

"A place where people detox off drugs and alcohol. You were checked in nearly a week ago."

"Wait a minute! A WEEK AGO?"

"The nurse assigned to you is Karen."

"But … " I couldn't remember what I wanted to say as I struggled to keep up the pace.

"The rules are pretty simple. The doors are never locked from the inside, only the outside. If you leave for any reason, you will not be let back in, and you are free to leave anytime you want."

"I get it, it's like jail."

"It's not like jail if you can leave. There's no salt, no caffeine and— "

"What do you mean there's no salt? What does that even mean?" I stopped in the middle of the sidewalk, bending over to catch my breath. We were less than a block away from the treatment center and I felt like I'd run ten miles.

Eddie turned to face me. "No salt, no caffeine, no sugar, and no nicotine. You can't have anything that alters your mood or contributes to cravings; that includes salt."

"Wow, you guys really know how to party," I said, rolling my eyes as we continued our journey.

Eddie went on to tell me about how he found me passed out on the bathroom floor on the third day of my stay, and how Nurse Karen had given me a shower when I was covered in vomit. The foggy memory suddenly floated back—parts of it, anyway. I began to feel a giant wave of relief. I asked where everyone else was and he told me they were all in "group."

"What's group?"

"You'll find out."

Upon our return, I entered a room full of people sitting in a circle, reminding me of the treatment center in Malibu, where I was supposed to be. There was one vacant chair for me. The teacher, or whoever, was explaining something about emotions.

I couldn't concentrate. The room was awful. There were water stains on the ceiling and curtains that looked like they hadn't been updated since 1972. Clearly there was no infinity pool. *Who were these people?* They all looked pretty normal. I sized up each one, wondering what brought them here. They wanted me to speak. I didn't want to, so I just introduced myself, and the teacher asked me to stay behind after they all left a few minutes later. Everyone seemed very excited—too excited.

"What's going on? Why are they so amped up? " I asked as soon as they were gone.

"Christmas," she said.

Shit. That's right—Christmas. "What day is today?"

"December 23."

"December 23?" I asked, my voice panicked. "Like two days before Christmas, December 23?"

That day was the first day since checking into the treatment center I could remember every single, awful minute, from the beginning all the way to the end, and that is why December 23 became my sobriety date. I never thought I would live to see the age of thirty, especially as I got older and harsher consequences were handed out like candy. In a way I was right. The old me *didn't* live to the age of thirty. She lived to the age of twenty-six and her new life began on December 23, 1998. It is a day I celebrate today as my *actual* birthday, and I look forward to it more than anything else every year. It is a day when all my friends, hundreds of them, come together to give me a living funeral—a day where an unexpected death turned itself into a most remarkable journey.

CHAPTER 4

I found Eleanor's compassion for animals other than her own species extraordinary. Late one evening, Eleanor was inside the stockades with the other young elephants when they heard a group of lions attacking an animal not far from the compound. Eleanor bolted into the darkness, leaving the others behind. Hours later, when daylight broke, the keepers saw her guarding an old buffalo who had been gravely injured in the attack. They were surrounded by lions, but Eleanor held her ground and would not let the lions near the injured buffalo.

As the veterinarians began to move toward them, Eleanor simply stepped to the side to let the men approach without fear of intervention by her—as if she had been waiting for them all along. She continued to chase the lions away as they examined the buffalo. It was obvious that the animal would have to be put down, his injuries were too severe. But this scared them. What would Eleanor do if *they* then killed the buffalo? If she wouldn't let the lions do it, what would she do if they did?

But she did nothing. As soon as the buffalo was put down, she calmly walked back to the stockades where the younger elephants were waiting, as if she knew the outcome all along, as if she couldn't handle his suffering at the jaws of the lions, so felt she must intervene. *Was she consciously aware of this? Was she directly making these choices?* I wondered about this all the time.

∞

It was Christmas Eve, and I felt like hell. I just wanted to retreat to the comfort and solitude of my room, which I did in the middle of yet another "group" I decided I now totally despised. A young perky nurse came looking for me. She was probably my age, had gorgeous blonde hair, and had a huge wedding ring on her left hand. I hated her instantly.

"Are you ready to come back and join us?" she asked in her annoying *I-love-my-life* voice.

"Fuck off."

"You know, things will get better," she said.

How? I wondered. *It's Christmas fucking EVE.* "Yeah … how do you know that?"

"Because it always does."

Oh, how insightful. Her words made me want to gag.

I was sweating again, my stomach hurt, my head pounded, and my irritation level was rising. I had been to see the doctor earlier, and when I told him about the obvious need for an exterminator with all the bugs flying around, he just laughed. *Why was that so funny to everyone?* He ducked as I swung at one that nearly landed on his head.

"There aren't any bugs, dear," he said.

"The fuck there aren't. That one almost landed on you."

"You are experiencing the symptoms of withdrawal. With alcohol there are usually bugs, but they are, in fact, simply a figment of your imagination. A normal part of withdrawal."

Not possible. OK, I get it, they think I'm crazy. I put my hands under my legs to resist any further temptation to swipe at the buzzers dive-bombing us from above.

"This too shall pass," he said, denying me anything for my headache or the bugs.

No caffeine. No salt. No aspirin. This was hell.

Young Perky reminded me of a bug I wanted to smash. As she tidied my room, she began telling me about how things would be different one day and how these were only symptoms of withdrawal. *God, I wish people would stop saying that.*

"Do you know what it's like?" I asked.

"Well, no, not personally, but I've seen lots of people—"

That was it. I'd had enough. I didn't want any more stories from textbooks about cases like mine. I was *done.* She wasn't even an alcoholic; she didn't know what it was like. *Fuck her and her stupid fucking husband and perfect goddamn life.*

I picked up the first thing I could find and threw it at her. She shrieked this perfect little pip-squeak shriek as she made a mad dash for the door, but I had a book in my hand aimed at her perfect little head. She didn't know that I used to be a fastpitch softball pitcher, that I had gone to college on a full-ride pitching scholarship. Aiming that book at her head was like walking for me. I could do it in my sleep. The book landed right where her head would have been had she not closed the door in the nick of time. But when she peeked back in I threw my second round. It landed right on target. I knew this would cost me, but for a moment I felt good.

I slid down a wall to the floor, waiting for retribution. *What could they possibly do to make me feel any worse?* The door opened, and a nurse I hadn't seen before walked in like she owned the place. Honestly, I had no energy left to fight. I was sweating profusely and exhausted. As I sat silently on the floor in the corner of that dark room, the nurse picked up an overturned chair and pulled it up to the window. Then she turned on a soft lamp and did something remarkable. Without addressing me in any way, without asking me to go back to "group," she did the simplest thing only someone like her could do—she just started talking.

At first I was confused but soon realized she was telling me her story. And just like that time stood still. I can't remember any of what she said—it wasn't even that her story was all that remarkable, but she told me things I *never* imagined she could have done. She seemed so grounded, like a perfect college mom. Yet she *did* things. Awful things like I had done. She didn't seem racked by shame, either, which was odd. I was ashamed, so deeply ashamed, by the things I had done. She said she had fourteen years sober, which at the time was impossible for me to believe. *Why would anyone EVER choose to do something like that?*

I didn't know then that the nurse was doing something I've done a million times since. Only an alcoholic can work with another alcoholic, because we speak the same language. *Only an elephant can truly understand another elephant.* What Eleanor said to the traumatized survivors in their silent transmissions we will never know, but I felt certain it was similar to what this woman was saying to me, making me feel more comfortable in this awful world to which I had just awakened. She helped me see the way forward. The shame, the guilt, and the undeniable fear wrapped itself around me like a boa constrictor sucking the life from its prey. She knew what she was doing when she entered my room, but to me it changed everything I thought I knew about ... *everything.*

When she was done, I had forgotten about how I felt an hour

earlier, and my headache was gone. She told me her name was Karen. Nurse Karen. *NURSE KAREN!* That was the nurse with the soothing voice who washed me in the shower that day. *No wonder I loved listening to the sound of her voice.* Then she asked me the strangest question:

"What do you want for Christmas?"

"Wait, you're joking right?"

"No."

"But I will be *here* for Christmas."

"Indulge me. Tell me three things that you want for Christmas."

"Seriously?" I thought this was ridiculous, but she clearly didn't feel the same.

"Yes, I want you to tell me three things, and they can be *anything*."

"OK, fine. I want it to snow on Christmas," I said, rolling my eyes. "I want my Auntie Edna. And I want prime rib because when I used to eat solid food, I enjoyed it."

She laughed, wished me a nice holiday, and let me know she would return the day after Christmas. After she left I sat in silence for a long time before I crawled into my plastic sheets and had my first good night's sleep in what felt like forever.

∞

I woke up to blinding light. As my eyes adjusted to the brightness, I thought someone had left the lights on. I turned to the window thinking the sun must be shining full blast. As I got closer, total shock set in. *Was that ... snow?*

It *never* snows on Christmas in Oregon. As far back as I could remember—and I was born and raised in Oregon—that had never happened. Suddenly, Eddie was at the door yelling at me to get up.

"Eddie! Do you see it's snowing?"

"Yes, I see. Dress warm. Ten minutes!!"

On our walk, Eddie said the snow was in fact a Christmas "surprise." No one had predicted it. The weather guys were wrong, as usual. Since we weren't allowed to watch television, I relied on him for all the details. It was supposed to melt by noon, and indeed it did, but it actually *snowed* on Christmas.

Holy hell, I thought, *we're off to a good start.*

I wondered why Eddie was even here on Christmas. *Must not have any family*, I thought. Nope. He told me he had a wife and several kids and would be going back to join them as soon as the walk was over.

I came to a screeching halt. "Wait, you just came this morning to walk? What about everyone else? Why doesn't anyone else walk in the morning?"

"I don't care if there is one patient or twenty patients, Ms. Ethell. My job is to get them exercise by walking every morning, so I come in and do that. Today is no different just because it's Christmas. I need my exercise and so do you. Let's go."

"But I thought you said it was *mandatory* that everyone show up."

"I just say that to get someone to walk with. Once newbie's been here for a few days, they usually figure out nothing happens if you don't show. But I usually get a couple, and I need my exercise ... so keep walkin'."

It turned out Eddie was in recovery himself. He had also "done time" at the very same treatment center. Now a licensed drug counselor, he enjoyed walking with the "newbies" in the mornings. Years later, I happened to stop in at a meeting I had never been to. Eddie was celebrating twenty years of sobriety, and it was a *huge* celebration. Everyone laughed and told stories about Eddie and his past. It seemed as though I'd walked right into the middle of *It's a Wonderful Life*. He didn't recognize me, but I got to thank him after the meeting for all those morning walks; I never missed one and enjoyed them immensely.

When we got back to the center, I had to do my daily check-in with the nurse. Blood pressure had to be checked—that type of thing. I didn't know the nurse who was waiting for me, but while she was filling out a chart, I noticed her name tag and froze. It said "Nurse Edna."

I instantly felt a lump forming in my throat. *Two of my three wishes.* My eighty-eight-year-old Great Auntie Edna was my grandmother Pearl's older sister and the matriarch of our family. I adored her as much as both my grandmothers, each of whom had long since passed away. She had an amazing flair for fashion and taught me to always dress up when preparing for any sort of confrontation.

"Never," she would say, "*never* forget to put on lipstick." She was convinced that a woman who looked good always got the advantage of a sneak attack.

She was waiting with my family when I didn't get off the flight to South Carolina to see Carrie graduate from college and was devastated when she learned the reason was that I was in jail for another DUI. She had been terribly worried about me, and now more than ever I wanted to see her. I knew she was spending Christmas with my family, but I also knew I couldn't go anywhere near them.

There was no one left in the treatment center but me. Everyone had a pass to go home for the day. It felt oddly quiet and peaceful. I went to the gym and played basketball by myself. I realized I hadn't played like this in—well—I couldn't even remember the last time. But it felt good.

I went to the cafeteria when it was time for dinner. I was the only one there besides one kitchen employee. I hadn't really eaten anything solid since checking in. My stomach was still recovering. But when I picked up my plate in the cafeteria, the woman behind the counter wrote "Merry Christmas Debbie" on a label on top of my plate. She winked when I looked up in surprise.

"What's the special today?" I asked.

"Prime rib." I couldn't move. *Wish number three.*

I sat in my room that night and looked out the window from under my plastic blanket. The snow had been replaced by rain, and I felt the strangest feeling. *What was it?* I couldn't put my finger on it for the longest time, but it returned time and again, like a butterfly tossing in the summer wind. I contemplated my three wishes. It was all completely surreal to me. Then it hit me—that strange feeling I couldn't shake as the night closed in, that unfamiliar feeling I almost didn't recognize. *Hope.*

I imagined all the things I wanted in my life, each seeming more impossible than the one before. What would my life look like if I stayed sober? That was almost too hard to contemplate. What if I met a man who was sober like me? That was almost too hard to contemplate. But more than anything, I wanted to get back to the elephants and find out what happened to them. I fell asleep as I had awakened; dreaming about elephants.

The next day, I tracked down Nurse Karen and could hardly breathe as I blurted out what happened with the three wishes. She stopped, put her hand on my shoulder, and said without skipping a beat:

"Welcome to recovery."

CHAPTER 5

As my mind began to clear, I started to think about my future, something I hadn't done in a long time. On the surface it looked quite bleak, even I had to admit that. This whole treatment thing did not look good "on résumé." But as the fog began to dissipate I started to think about who I was and who I wanted to be before my addiction completely took over. It had been so long since I thought about any of that.

When I was little and my life spun out of my control, I did the one thing that calmed me down like nothing else could. I wrote about the elephants. As night closed in, I stared at the lonely tree overlooking the courtyard and felt the familiar whisper of fear. I thought about David Sheldrick, someone I deeply admired, who had an enormous amount of courage, and tried to distract my mind.

He was always someone who fascinated me. Brought to Kenya as a baby, he was raised on an expansive coffee plantation near the region of Mweiga in Central Kenya. His father built the famous Treetops Hotel on a section of the land. The hotel would solidify its place in history as the location where a Princess became a Queen. The future Queen Elizabeth and her husband, Philip, the Duke of Edinburgh, were vacationing there when she learned of her father's death in 1952.

David followed in the footsteps of his father, who served

honorably in World War I. Drafted to the military at the beginning World War II, David rose through the ranks relatively quickly. He was both a talented athlete and incredibly handsome: on top of that, his predecessors noticed he had a gift for working with people, which immediately led to his being the youngest officer (at twenty-six years old) ever appointed to major.

After the war, David worked for local safaris in Tanzania as a professional hunter and quickly became known as the "white hunter," hired to kill Africa's most majestic wildlife—until one day he just couldn't bear to do it anymore. He knew he could no longer be responsible for the removal of something so beautiful and necessary to the African life he loved. Each time his bullet took the last breath of an animal he admired, it felt like a part of his soul went with it. I understood that inner turmoil. I understood what it was like to go down a road I knew deep down was not the one God intended for me.

In 1948, at the age of twenty-eight, David was hired to be the first game warden of an enormous parcel of land called the Taru Desert. He was given the monumental task of turning the newly renamed Tsavo National Park, roughly the size of Maryland, into one of the world's most beautiful African safaris, though at the time he could scarcely imagine how. The park was, and still is, considered massive in scale when it comes to protected national reserves.

Standing on top of Mazinga Hill, David looked over the vast wilderness. There was nothing but scrubland as far as the eye could see. No beauty. No elephants. I pictured myself standing on top of Mazinga Hill looking at the scrubland of my life. No beauty. No elephants. He wondered how he would ever make it look beautiful again. I wondered the same thing. The task in front of both of us seemed nearly impossible.

Without thinking, I went back to the one thing that brought me peace so many years earlier. I grabbed a notebook and a pen and starting retracing the steps of ghosts of my past. Wide awake and suffering from insomnia, I went all the way back to the beginning and stopped only long enough to retrieve a memory buried deep beneath the rest of my shattered dreams.

∞

Tsavo was divided along the Mombasa/Nairobi railway into two sections: East and West. Tsavo West, considered the prettier half of the two, encompassed roughly three thousand square miles. Years before he rescued Eleanor, Bill Woodley worked as a game warden along with David. The two remained friends for most of their lives—even after Daphne divorced Bill and married David. When the time came to appoint someone he could trust to run the west side, Bill was the only one on David's list. But that left David with the scrubbier, 5000-square-mile section to the east.

Together they walked from one end of the park to the next, camping together for months to get a better understanding of what they were up against. But something tickled David's brain in the same way learning about Eleanor tickled mine. He had been to the most beautiful safari parks in all of Africa. Teeming with wildlife, they all seemed to have one thing in common: *elephants.*

At the time, he wasn't exactly sure the role they played in an ecosystem, but whatever it was he knew it was important. As they continued, they saw far fewer elephants than they expected for a park that size. They noticed that the few animals they did see were more skittish and afraid of humans than either of them remembered in other regions of Africa.

David learned why one day as he spoke with a tribal leader of the Wakamba, one of the many tribes that inhabited the vast park.

"Do you know why they named this park Tsavo?" asked the tribal leader.

"No idea," replied David.

"Because *tsavo* in our language means *slaughter* in yours."

David shuddered as he heard it, thinking about the enormous number of scavenged carcasses he and Bill had come across. They were both shocked to realize the large-scale poaching going on inside the park. It wasn't just the elephants being killed, but a multitude of other animals poachers ate and traded along the way. It made sense why the few animals David and Bill did come across ran at the first sight of humans, and why the elephants only appeared under the protective cover of darkness.

The Wakamba were not considered as fearless as their rivals to the south, the Waliangulu, who were quite dangerous even though they were a fairly small tribe of game hunters who hunted elephants with precision and hid out inside the thick bush. The Wakamba preferred to hide high up among the rocky outcrops so they could see any person or animal approaching from a good distance.

The Wakamba, like the Waliangulu, wielded the most powerful weapon in the region: one of the deadliest poisons on Earth called ouabain, derived from the Acokanthera tree. Ouabain poison, at the height of its potency, can drop a large bull elephant in mere minutes. Arrowheads dipped in the rubbery mixture are kept wrapped inside hides, as the men usually traveled a good distance before using it. David admired the courage of the men of both tribes; after all, a drop that touched the skin was the end of any man who carried it. Yet the two tribes had used the poison as a weapon for centuries against both man and animal and were as comfortable carrying it as they were a piece of fruit.

One day, as David walked across Tsavo East on a routine patrol, he noticed large impressions in the ground. He was intrigued by their various sizes as well as their presence across different areas of the park. Some of the impressions looked like small indentations, yet others were deep, extremely large holes.

"What on Earth could possibly make holes so large I could drive a lorry into one of them?" he asked Daphne one evening "I've never seen anything like it."

"Perhaps they are made by man. Maybe someone is making them using an earth mover of some kind," Daphne wondered aloud.

"I looked for tracks and couldn't find any. Besides, I was a good three-day drive away from any civilization that has that capability. And if that were so, what would they be using them for? I found no clue as to their function."

"What about weather?"

"I don't know," he said, shaking his head in frustration. "I suppose anything is possible at this point. Once I come across another group of them I will camp out to see what I can find."

As the weeks passed, David became increasingly perplexed by the strange phenomenon. When he finally came across another group of impressions, he set up his camp behind a large rock out-cropping, hidden from whatever made them below.

Under the light of the full moon he waited. Hours passed and he saw nothing. He got up to stretch his arms and thought he heard something. He crept up slowly to the edge while he scanned the landscape, searching while he waited for his eyes to adjust to the dim light. Suddenly, out of the pitch blackness, he began to see gleams of white, first one pair, then another. He realized it was elephant tusks reflecting the light of the moon. He thought he could hear the sound of digging but couldn't be sure. It went on for hours until he finally heard the unmistakable sound of water. *The elephants were digging for water.*

Amazed, David watched them for hours. Then, just before dawn, the elephants returned to the cover of the bush, and a wide assortment of animals—from baboons to birds, antelope to lions—entered the long slope to have a drink for themselves.

David knew that on some level elephants were the key to the ecosystem of the park, but to what extent he simply wasn't sure. Not until he witnessed elephants digging for water did he realize that elephants were the missing link upon which so many animals depended for their own survival.

At that moment, David understood the importance of elephants as the largest land mammal on earth. The other animals depended on them for water, simply because only something the size of an elephant could carve a waterhole big enough for every single creature to fit inside without fear of being trapped. Suddenly it all fell into place; animals didn't just follow the elephants, they *relied* on them for their own survival. Without elephants there were very few animals, and that was the reason why Tsavo East was so barren.

David discovered in that one evening what it would take science another thirty years to prove. Like the most important stone in a carved archway, the keystone is the one that holds the rest together. If the keystone is removed, the entire arch collapses. David recognized in that moment elephants were the key—the keystone of an ecosystem that was collapsing without them. He knew there was only one way to save Tsavo East and turn it into a safari destination and that was to bring back the elephants.

The only question was … *how.*

CHAPTER 6

*E*ach evening at the treatment center, all the patients
were loaded into white vans and taken to meetings
of Alcoholics Anonymous, otherwise known as AA,
across town. It was a surreal experience and not one I can say
I appreciated. But something inside those rooms grabbed my
attention. The laughter caught me off guard from the moment
I stepped inside that first room, as well as the lack of shame
people seemed to feel as they shared sometimes-awful things
about themselves, things I would never say out loud, let alone in
a group of people. There were anniversary cakes, coins, and balloons, and I honestly didn't get what all the fuss was about. But
the people seemed genuinely happy, and they looked normal—
not like the group of hairy, disgusting old men I had envisioned.
Instead, they were all ages, all ethnicities, and all walks of life.
I couldn't imagine any of them actually being friends in the
"wild," but inside the meetings they seemed to truly enjoy one
another's company.

A woman named Yvonne approached me after a meeting and
asked if she could be my sponsor. I had no idea what that was.
I grew hopeful when I thought it meant she would support me
financially, but she explained it meant only that she would work

the twelve steps with me and teach me, the same way she was taught out of the basic text called the Big Book.

How disappointing, I thought.

We spoke every day by phone, and I began to look forward to seeing her each week at the meeting. Slowly, without even realizing it, I also began to miss those people and their laughter that echoed throughout the massive room.

One afternoon at the treatment center, I noticed a book on the library shelf, a book I used to treasure when I was a kid. I couldn't believe it was just sitting there staring at me: *Elephant Memories,* written by the great elephant researcher, Cynthia Moss. It was the book that taught me my first basic research skills. I sat down and immediately began reading it again, retracing some of my long-forgotten footsteps until it jumped out at me. Something so extraordinary it took me a moment to catch my breath. Right there in plain sight, on page 36, it read:

" … the first family we ever photographed in 1972 was called the 'AA' family."

I thought how odd it was to read that right after I had been introduced to *my* first AA family. Even though Cynthia and her team were naming elephant groups "AA," "BB," "CC" as a way to catalogue their research—it felt like a sign.

A few days later, I got called into the "principal's office."

"You're out," he said.

"What? Why?"

"Insurance ran out," he said. "You have to leave tomorrow."

"But how can this be? Where am I supposed to go?" I hadn't even thought about where I was going next. I didn't want to leave and suddenly felt terrified at the prospect.

"This is a detox. Typically patients get cleared for a week. You've been here nearly three. If you don't have anywhere to go, we can probably figure something out." *Thank goodness. They had a plan for me.* I was so relieved.

A cab arrived the following morning. I sat next to my duffel bag, all of my worldly possessions in the back seat, and turned back to watch the pathetic-looking cement building disappear as we drove away. Eddie was outside smoking a cigarette, and the last thing I saw was him waving as I left.

"Where are we going?" I asked the cab driver, anticipating any number of answers.

"Women's shelter," he replied. *That is NOT what I expected.*

"Wait! Women's shelter? No ... there must be a mistake."

"I'm taking you to the women's shelter. There's no mistake."

I started to shake. I felt like a caged animal sitting in the back of that cab. I had never been what I considered "homeless," but now that I was officially on my way to an *actual* women's shelter, it seemed the label applied. I was terrified of the people I would meet and who I would have to share a room with. I closed my eyes and prayed, though I had no idea who to pray to since I wasn't religious. I ripped open my duffel bag and grabbed my notebook, flipping the pages frantically as I looked for the perfect elephant story to calm me down, but they all blurred together. As my mind raced, I prayed to the only versions of a higher power I ever had: David, Daphne, and Eleanor. I thought about what each one had gone through, and how they continued to put one foot in front of the other even when it seemed the odds were stacked against them. Slowly, I felt my panic subside and my heartbeat slow just enough to catch my breath.

If they can do that, I can do this. Just breathe, I thought to myself, closing my notebook as the cab pulled up to an unmarked building.

After my tour of the facility, I must say I was pleasantly surprised. It wasn't anything like I thought it would be. It was clean, nice—almost nicer than the treatment center I'd just come from. There were no water stains on the ceiling and the curtains ... well, they could still use some updating, but they weren't nearly as distracting as the ones in rehab.

At the end of my check-in, I was given a key to my locker. While trying my key to make sure it worked properly, I started to laugh. Suddenly everything seemed hilarious.

I didn't have a key to a car or a key to a house. I was now the proud owner of a key to my very own ... LOCKER!!!

Locker 42 to be exact. I just couldn't seem to get a grip and started laughing so hard tears streamed down my face. It felt so good to laugh for a change, even if it was just incredibly sad ... and fucking hilarious at the same time.

"Oh God," I finally said to the woman checking me in, "it just can't get any worse, can it?"

"Hmmm," she said without looking up, "you'd be surprised."

I shared a room with some woman I hadn't met yet, but the other women seemed normal, clean, and nice. Even though the facility was better than I expected, I definitely didn't want to stay any longer than I had to. I decided to walk to a meeting, so I grabbed my notebook and two recovery books I had in my duffel bag and headed out.

When I returned, my eyes were drawn to the bank of lockers. One door was left open. As I got closer I could feel my stomach sink. It was *my* locker. As I pulled the door back, it was empty. Apparently, in all my hilarity, I had forgotten to use my new key, and now my duffel bag with every last possession I had left in the world was—*gone*.

"Shit! I forgot to *lock* my locker," I yelled, and then I noticed the woman who checked me in sitting behind the counter.

"Told ya," she said, laughing quietly as she flipped through the pages of a magazine. "Things can *always* get worse."

God dammit! How could I be so stupid?

I slid down the wall to the floor beneath the locker door.

What was I going to do?

"Don't you know anyone who's sober?" the woman finally asked.

"No. I don't. I've been living in California for the past few years. Everyone I know here uses like I did."

Think, dammit, think.

Suddenly I remembered someone. Years earlier, I worked at a disgusting car dealership, one of those dealerships that consider the word "shiesty" a compliment. I worked as an assistant on the weekends, and it was one of the few places that didn't ask why my breath smelled like alcohol when I interviewed. My shift started at 7:00 a.m., which meant I was usually drunk from the night before. Bob, one of the salesmen, was the first sober person I'd ever met. He homed in on me the very first day.

He was an enormous man with an even bigger personality. Bob seemed excited just to be alive. It seemed like he loved watching the sun rise because he talked about it all the time, and asked me about my drinking constantly. No matter what I said, he would follow it up with something like, "Man, it is a *GREAT* day to be sober!"

Despite his annoying questions about my drinking habits, there was something that attracted me to him. Not in a romantic way, but in an I-wish-I-loved-life-as-much-as-he-did sort of way. He asked me to go to an AA meeting once. I told him I would never be caught dead in a meeting. I learned he spent many years in prison. I couldn't imagine Bob ever having been to prison—he seemed too full of life to be an "armed robber." But it was in there that he met sober people who taught him how to live a better life clean.

One day he brought me two books. They were both books about recovery and both had been written by a man I never heard of named Bill Wilson. I never opened either one, and God knows how many times I had moved since that day, but somehow those two books followed me everywhere I went.

As I sat on the floor, the two books lying beside me came into focus. *The same two Bob gave me years ago.* I took them with me to the meeting because I knew they were about recovery, and I wanted to look like I fit in. If someone saw me holding them, they would think I knew what I was talking about.

"What's his last name?" asked the girl after I told her the story.

"I don't know. I can't remember."

In all the time I owned those books, I never so much as opened the cover, let alone read anything inside. I grabbed one, opened it, and scribbled on the inside cover was the name Bob L. A memory suddenly came floating back: *You won't ever forget my name, because it's Robert E. Lee, just like the general.*

"Bob Lee," I said, getting up, "His name was Bob Lee."

As I approached the counter, she tossed a phone book at me and set a phone on the counter. I flipped open the book to the "L" section. The pages were covered with "Lees." Bobs, Roberts, Robs with every middle initial in the alphabet. I had no idea where to begin.

"What am I supposed to do? Call every single one of them?" I laughed.

"What else do you have to do?" she said, unwavering.

She had a point.

I flipped back to the first page, and instead of going in order, I decided I would just select them randomly and check each one off as I went. I closed my eyes and my finger landed on one of the hundred Robert Lees.

The phone rang in my ear. The girl behind the counter popped her gum. I started to sweat.

What was I even going to say? That I'm some random girl you haven't seen or heard from in, I don't know, five, six years? Oh, and by the way, I'm in a women's shelter downtown and have like two weeks sober?

I couldn't figure out what to say when a scary voice suddenly answered the phone.

"What!"

OK ... this guy sounds mean as fuck.

I blurted out that I was looking for a man named Bob Lee, and we worked together a few years earlier, and my name was Debbie, but before I could say anything else he cut me off.

In a gentler voice he said simply, "I've been waiting for your call."

I froze. *What did he just say?* I was so shocked I couldn't breathe. Unable to speak, I started to cry. *What the hell was happening?*

The girl stopped popping her gum and shoved her ear close to mine to see if she could figure out what just happened.

"Where are you?" he asked.

"I'm ... I'm ... in a women's ... shelter downtown" I croaked.

"In Portland?"

"Yes," I said between sobs, and I gave him the address. He said he would be down to see me the next day. When we got off the phone, the gravity of the situation hit me. *How had that just worked? How could I possibly have found him after dialing just one number?* After every single possession I owned had either been left in California or stolen from that locker—how was I standing there holding those same two books, neither of which had been opened until just that moment?

Later on, when asked if I believed in a power greater than myself, I would reflect on this moment, certain that something somewhere was leading me, laying bread crumbs down a trail I could not see. Because of moments like this, I knew there was something bigger than myself up there guiding me down here, something holding my hand, leading me to a destination ... to where I didn't know. All I could do was hope that my dreams and my destiny would collide at some point. Until then, I would take it only as far as I could see—one step at a time.

CHAPTER 7

*H*ow can I learn more about a species that only comes out at night and is terrified of humans?" David asked Daphne one evening.

He knew elephants held the key to a lock he could not open. For six years he worked tirelessly in Tsavo East, carving out roads, digging waterholes, and working to understand the people that lived in *the land of slaughter*. He came across countless animals that would have died without his intervention, and he brought each one back to the healing hands of Daphne. Yet all of the elephants he came across that were still alive were either too injured or sick to be saved.

In 1954, a drought hit the region hard and forced all of the remaining animals to beg for mercy. A dam was constructed as a way to store water. When a debate ensued as to what to name it, a Waliangulu man hired as a laborer said simply, "Aruba," which means *elephant* in the Waliangulu language. A few months later, the Aruba Lodge was constructed a short distance away and soon filled with tourists.

As the drought reached its height, the tourists complained about having to watch the large number of emaciated and starving animals wearily making their way to the waterhole day after day. It was not uncommon to witness exhausted elephant herds, walking with steely determination, arrive at the waterhole with a weak and dying baby trailing far behind.

One morning a jeep pulled up to David's office. "You must come, *bwana*."

"What is it?" David asked.

"There is an elephant at the lodge. A baby with no family. Come! He is waiting for you."

David gathered a team of men with rope and jeeps but was reluctant to get his hopes up. An angry elephant mother could easily flip their jeep with one swoop of her trunk. But after watching the youngster for several hours, they were convinced the baby elephant was likely abandoned by his desperate family. They had seen other families abandon young calves that were too weak to keep up. Yet the young elephant wasn't as weak as they thought. Instead, he seemed to only want to stay in the water. It was possible that the family was forced to leave when the stubborn youngster refused to follow. The cool water must have been a refreshing break from the pounding heat.

With the help of several men, they captured the young male and brought him back to David's compound. At two years old, he was large enough to kill any man, but thankfully the young elephant's strength was depleted by lack of food.

The next morning, just as David was getting used to the idea that he finally had an elephant of his own to study, the same man from the previous day pulled up to his office again.

"You must come, *bwana*."

"What is it?"

"There is another elephant at the lodge. Another baby waiting for you."

"Again … another elephant?"

"*Sawa, sawa.* You must come."

By that evening, an exhausted David had two baby elephants to raise instead of one. Another stall was built for the young female they named Fatuma, next to the one they had just built for the young bull named Samson. The possibility of rearing an elephant in hopes of learning more about the species as a whole was exactly the opportunity he had been waiting for.

David studied everything he could about the duo in hopes of unlocking the secret he longed to answer. He noticed almost immediately how completely different the two elephants were from each other. Fatuma seemed to have a natural mothering instinct, inserting herself into the middle of the orphaned gang as "caretaker." Samson became fascinated by a group of recently rescued ostriches. More than once David had to reprimand him for grabbing them around their necks and dragging them unwillingly into the daily mudbath. Samson formed a close bond with David and visited his office regularly throughout the day.

While Fatuma doted on all of the orphans, Samson made friends with a young rhino named Rufus. It soon became apparent, however, that Samson's sheer size was too much for the smaller Rufus, so he lost interest. Sensing this, Samson came up with a new strategy and began kneeling down to the ground to level the playing field. This absolutely delighted Rufus, and the two began to play for hours.

The kneeling behavior of larger elephants to encourage the smaller ones was something David and Daphne would witness again and again throughout the years. They were convinced the elephants had a clear understanding their enormous size intimidated younger elephants, so they knelt or lay down, signaling to the younger, smaller ones that it was safe. It never failed to excite the smaller elephants, who climbed all over the larger ones the way young children climb a sand pile.

By the time Eleanor arrived, Samson and Fatuma were twelve years old. She joined the menagerie along with the three ostriches, a few more buffalo, and another baby rhino. Samson immediately took a special interest in Eleanor, and she seemed relieved to be placed in a stall directly next to his. It was obvious she had not been in the company of another elephant in a very long time, and being around one so much older and wiser seemed to put her at ease.

Each morning, from the comfort of their bed, David and Daphne could hear the familiar creak of the stall door being opened from the inside as Samson led Eleanor out into the bush for another day of adventure and mingling with wild herds of elephants. It made Daphne smile each time she heard it, thinking how vastly different Eleanor's life was in such a short amount of time.

A few weeks after Eleanor's arrival, Samson went off on his own and returned with a young elephant. David went with several men to investigate and found two dead female elephants a short distance away. How Samson understood that the youngster needed David and Daphne's help, they never knew. Once the newcomer was delivered to the loving care of Fatuma, Samson simply walked away, seeming to congratulate himself on a job well done.

One afternoon as Eleanor and Samson made their way back to the stockades, she became transfixed by suckling sounds coming from a stall at the far edge of the compound. Instead of waiting for Samson, who seemed lost in his own thoughts, she peeled off and headed straight for a stall full of keepers with another baby elephant they were working desperately to save. At first she watched from the other side of the stall, but soon she unlocked the gate as Samson had taught her, let herself in, and began to rumble gently to the baby. Daphne noticed immediately how different Eleanor was from Samson and Fatuma and wondered if the fascination with the new babies was due to a familiarity between her own experience and theirs. I wondered about that too.

∞

In order to make any headway with the poachers of Tsavo, David knew he would have to gain the trust of the Wakamba tribe. The Wakamba, armed with poisoned arrows, were skilled elephant hunters and were easily hired by American trophy hunters who wanted a "quick kill." He worked to find a delicate balance, since Wakamba hunters had lived on the land for centuries and passed down their well-honed hunting skills for generations.

One day a stroke of luck changed everything when he apprehended a notorious Wakamba poacher he had chased for many years, a man named Wambua Mukula. Instead of arresting him for his long list of poaching crimes, David made him a deal. He offered to waive all charges against him in exchange for information on other poachers. At first Wambua refused, but once he discovered that a friend from another tribe had in fact turned him in, he had a change of heart. By the end of that week, Wambua became a member of David's staff as an official paid "informer."

By the time Wambua was introduced to Samson and Fatuma, who walked freely around David's office compound, he was convinced David had special powers.

Wambua stepped out of the offices one day when he first saw the two elephants a short distance away. Terrified, he yelled, "*Nzou! NZOU!!!*" meaning Elephants!!! in Wakamba, before running back inside.

Suddenly David appeared and walked straight toward Samson

and Fatuma with treats in hand. Wambua peeked around a corner in disbelief. The elephants didn't run away, flap their ears angrily, or retreat. Instead, they met David halfway and extended their trunks. He seemed completely at ease while Wambua, covered in sweat, watched in wonder.

"Come outside, Wambua," said David.

"No!"

"Samson and Fatuma, I'd like you to meet Wambua. Wambua, this is Samson and Fatuma."

David continued to coax him until Wambua gingerly stepped outside. He had only seen elephants up close, when they were charging him and his fellow poachers. He had never experienced one looking so calm in the presence of humans.

"Breathe, Wambua," said David, placing a hand on his shoulder. "It's OK, they won't hurt you."

"What do you mean they won't hurt me?" Wambua hissed "They could kill me with one swipe."

"Yes, they could, but they won't," he said as he led Wambua to them. "Samson is extending his trunk to you. This is an elephant's handshake." He showed him by breathing into Samson's outstretched trunk. "Now you do it."

"No, no, I can't," Wambua said, closing his eyes. Samson gingerly took one step forward, reached up to Wambua's face and touched it gently. As his trunk dropped to Wambua's shoulders, Wambua slightly opened one eye.

"He wants you to breathe into his trunk," coaxed David.

With one very shaky hand Wambua slowly reached out for Samson's trunk and quickly blew into it.

"Good, that's it," smiled David. "Now he will know you forever."

David knew elephants, and knew they *never* forget.

From that day forward, Wambua listened as David taught him the intricacies of elephant behavior. Within a few weeks, Wambua became as accustomed to Samson and Fatuma as they were to any of the men walking around. It wasn't long before Wambua decided to use the elephants as his allies when dealing with the poachers they arrested.

Wambua lingered patiently next to the stalls holding the most recently apprehended poachers until he spotted Samson lumbering along, looking for David. Samson normally walked in front of the holding cells that lined the walkway leading to David's office. Like Wambua, the poachers they arrested had never seen a living elephant up close either—other than one that was trying to kill them. Wambua waited until a hush fell over the men as they crouched in absolute terror, watching Samson. Then he planned his entrance just as Samson made his and made up all kinds of stories to scare them into talking.

"This elephant knows you have killed his family, and now he is looking for you!"

Sometimes Samson would extend his trunk to the men locked in cages, who would jump to the very back of the stalls shaking in fear. Wambua got more men to admit to their crimes than any other interrogator.

As the years passed and poaching escalated, David must have wondered if what he was doing was actually changing the minds of men like Wambua. Did they fear elephants any less because the men understood them more, or did learning about elephants and their behavior simply teach the men new ways to kill?

∞

Bob showed up at the women's shelter the next afternoon as promised. He brought his girlfriend who also had long-term sobriety,

and they took me to a meeting. At dinner afterward, he told me he had turned his home into a halfway house for sober people like myself to help them transition back into the real world, *whatever that was*. Apparently his last three "inmates" had just relapsed, so the house was now empty except for him. He had a furnished spare room I could use if I wanted, free of charge.

"What's the catch?" I asked. I didn't know Bob *that* well and hadn't seen him in years. *What if this was a trap? What if this was setup of some kind?* My stomach began to hurt.

"The catch is you have to put yourself in a meeting every day. You have to be part of an ongoing, outpatient treatment program, and you have to submit to a drug test anytime I ask. If you fail, you're out. If you lie about anything, you're out. Understood?"

I moved in the next day. Bob gave me a backpack and bus pass. I had never taken the bus before. He showed me the pad of paper on the refrigerator where I could write down the food I wanted and he would get it. And he had a cat named Asia I fell deeply in love with.

Wrong continent, I thought, *but she'll do.*

My fears about Bob's intentions dissipated shortly after I moved into his house. He was serious about recovery. He introduced me to every sober woman he knew and became someone that I trusted deeply. Bob never once acted inappropriately and always treated me with respect.

If I wanted cash, I was expected to get a job; he would not give me any money. I was allowed to just focus on my recovery, and he did not pressure me to find work right away. His last and final rule was, "No sitting on the furniture when it gets dark."

"I don't get it. Why?"

"Shootings," he said, a bit too nonchalantly for my taste. He explained that a few blocks from our house was a nightclub called the Copper Penny, notorious for Asian gangs and criminal activity. When Bob wasn't home, I rebelled and sat on the furniture anyway. After a few weeks, I was convinced he simply exaggerated.

One evening, as we sat on the floor and watched a movie, we heard the unmistakable sound of gunshots. They were close—too close. Suddenly, one of the windows burst and glass went flying everywhere. Soon the living room was lit up like a Christmas tree with what seemed like a hundred police cars stacked up in front of the house. Bob simply swept up the broken glass and went back to watching the movie as though it were the most normal thing in the world. I was dumbfounded.

The next morning, I could see the unmistakable chalk outline of the man killed just feet from our driveway. The caution tape was still hanging loose from the shrubs, reminding me of when I was a teenager and we toilet-papered someone's house.

And that's why they call this neighborhood "Felony Flats," I thought as I walked to my bus stop. I never sat on the furniture again.

CHAPTER 8

I kept my word to Bob, enrolled in an outpatient drug treatment center and went to meetings every day. I hated my drug counselor, Mark, the first time I met him. He sat in the group circle, quiet and unassuming, but it was a trick. The group would talk about their day, or their week, or whatever; I rarely paid much attention. Then, as if on cue, someone would say something that sounded completely absurd to the rest of us. We would attack like a pack of rabid dogs until Mark interrupted. Then, instead of jumping on the bandwagon as we expected him to, he would shift to something another person in the group had said, which shifted our attack. It was all perfectly enjoyable until they went after me.

"OK, I get it. I went a little off the deep end with alcohol, but shrooms are, like, my thing." I knew I suffered with alcohol, but I simply could not imagine never taking a mushroom again.

"So," Mark said, his piercing blue eyes reminding me of a wolf homing in on its prey, "You're still holding out then? What about pot or cocaine?"

"What about them?"

A few members of the group laughed quietly and I got uncomfortable.

"Do you believe that you have a disease?" Mark asked.

"Obviously, that's why I'm here." I rolled my eyes.

"But you still want to take psychedelic mushrooms when you go on camping trips?" Mark said as he raised his eyebrows.

"That's RICH!" interrupted a guy named Toby. He explained earlier that his face went completely crooked every time he drank, so I decided not to take *anything* he said seriously. Mark continued to stare at me as the others jumped in.

"You're crazy if you think that's a good idea," said Sarah, the subject of the previous attack. She had just explained how she instructed her ten-year-old daughter to "watch Mommy" every time she went shopping to make sure she didn't buy any alcohol. I pounced all over that one.

"I'm not fucking crazy," I erupted to the group "I'm addicted to alcohol, I get that, but it doesn't have anything to do with a shroomer here or there." Everyone burst out laughing. Clearly, I had just made things worse for myself.

"Addiction is a disease," said Mark after the group calmed down, "and your brain doesn't know the difference between mushrooms, alcohol, cocaine, or heroin for that matter. It just craves alteration of whatever kind it can get. If you are truly holding out for a mushroom here or there, then relapse is imminent for you, I'm afraid."

The conversations we had in that room haunted me in my sleep, making me question if I was, in fact, the crazy one. I thought all my decisions were perfectly normal and clear, but what if, to the outside world, I was just walking incessantly in circles. I was struck by the thought of Aitong, another elephant who touched me deeply, partly because she couldn't stop walking in circles either.

∞

Aitong suffered an awful head injury thought to have been caused by a group of stampeding buffalo. No one knew what happened to her mother, and she was found trying to attach herself to another family of elephants clearly not her own.

At one month old, she came down with a severe case of pneumonia on top of everything else. Pneumonia is usually a death sentence for an elephant. By the time the symptoms are recognized, it is often too late. Elephants don't have the ability to cough, so the only indication is the tell-tale sign of a steady, clear liquid stream seeping from their trunk. It is almost always a sign that death is near.

Daphne knew Aitong's chances were poor. Eleanor went straight to work and hovered over her for days while she stood at the brink between that world and this. When she finally did get up, she walked continuously in circles, revealing the severity of her head injury. Emily, an orphaned one-year-old elephant attached herself to Aitong immediately. She seemed especially concerned about her inability to walk straight.

When Aitong was unable to join the others on their daily walk, Emily stayed behind with her along with her nursery mate, a young bull named Imenti. Soon two other young elephants began to hang back, too. One day, Aitong grabbed one of the young elephant's tails and tried to follow behind her as she moved forward. But she was unable and veered to the left. This happened a few times before the young elephants appeared to understand what Aitong was trying to do. Emily stood on one side of her while Imenti braced Aitong from the other side. By leaning into her, Emily was able to get Aitong to take her first few straight steps.

The small group of elephants worked with Aitong each day until she was completely exhausted. At first she managed to walk only a few wobbly but straight, steps. A few days later, she took several more. Within only a few weeks, Aitong was finally able to join the others in the bush. Though it would take the young group quite some time to go a short distance, the progress they made was unmistakable. The compelling kindness and patience, not to mention the power of perception and compassion shared among the young elephants, moved Daphne and the keepers beyond words.

∞

I felt the same way as Aitong. I didn't know how to walk straight, either. All my great ideas involved some sort of criminal activity. Based on my earlier conversations in the group that day, I, too, realized there was something wrong with my head. When I first learned that alcoholism was a disease, I laughed. But when I considered some of my choices, I thought there might be a shred of truth to that. And even though I desperately wanted to stop, I just couldn't do it on my own. It felt like a form of possession in a way.

I thought back to what Mark said, "A disease is an abnormal condition that causes pain *(check)*, dysfunction *(check)*, distress *(check)*, and social problems *(double check)*." I had all of those. I slowly came to the realization that I had something I could recover from, but it would take an enormous effort and tremendous compassion from the people around me, leaning into me like Emily had with Aitong to get me to walk a straight line.

The following afternoon, when the group had once again latched on to some stupid thing I said, I lashed out at Mark, "No one has ever been so rude and disrespectful to me before, and just so you know, *NO ONE* has ever spoken to me like that before, either."

"Based on what you've shared with us about your past, I highly doubt that," he sighed, closing a notebook as he stared at me.

Infuriated, I stormed from the room, but instead of leaving, I waited in the lobby. I knew if I left I would be violating my agreement with Bob.

The receptionist was a nice man named Lowell. He had a soothing voice that always calmed me down and a way of sharing a perspective that always made sense to me. He worked in Mark's office, not because he needed a job but because his wife was an alcoholic who never got sober.

"I come here so that I can see the miracle of recovery work in others, and that makes me have hope for her," he told me one day.

I doubted I was the miracle he was looking for, but his story touched me. That morning, after I told him what happened and what a dick I thought Mark was, he just laughed. Clearly, I wasn't the first person who found herself venting to Lowell in the lobby. Then he asked me if I thought anything Mark or the group said might be true, even if only a little bit true. His gentle way of asking me questions without any judgment allowed me to see the possibility of such things.

My conversations with Lowell helped me see the truth about myself. Eventually, I realized that what Mark was saying was, in fact, just the truth, however hard to hear. And it *was* hard to hear, but since I had hurt so many people along the way, the truth wasn't something I really wanted to focus on. Now I knew that if I wanted to be free of the demons of my past, I had to. Somehow, some way, I just had to.

CHAPTER 9

*H*e didn't see her right away, but after a few passes in the air with his plane over the carcass of another dead elephant, David spotted a young female elephant standing next to the body of her dead mother near Sobo Rock. David called for help to rescue the young elephant while he went to inspect the bullet-ridden body of her mother.

Eleanor couldn't have been more pleased to have another baby to look over. Sobo, as the young elephant was named, was devastated by the loss of her family. This happened sometimes with young survivors. Like gentle children, some form attachments so strong that the trauma of losing their family puts them in a tailspin even the most gifted are not able to pull them out of.

But Eleanor tried anyway. She hovered over Sobo, just as Sobo's own mother would have, touched her constantly, and never let her out of her reach or sight. She rumbled lovingly to her, and once again Daphne watched in wonder. Sensing Eleanor's preoccupation, the other young elephants kept each other company, allowing Eleanor to focus on saving Sobo.

Sobo continued to deteriorate as her depression got worse. Daphne prayed for a miracle, which showed up the following morning bundled in a blanket carried by one of the keepers. Gulliver, as the baby elephant was named, was placed on a soft bed of hay in the stall next to the one Eleanor and Sobo were in. He was on death's door, and like so many before him, he was also another poaching victim. No one knew exactly what happened except that when they found him he had been wandering all alone with no milk or nourishment for days. He collapsed right before the men rescued him, but they quickly scooped him up and brought him to the only person that had any chance of saving him.

Daphne and the keepers went straight to work. Sobo became interested in the noise happening in the next stall and peered through the slats to investigate. Then she gently slid her trunk through, touching the edge of Gulliver's blanket. Suddenly she shoved past Eleanor and walked out of her stall straight into his. The men parted to let her through as she got closer to investigate the baby elephant clinging to life.

Eleanor remained just outside Gulliver's stall and did not follow Sobo. Instead she stood back and watched the scene unfold before her. Sobo examined Gulliver with her trunk, lightly touching his wounds, until she began inspecting his face. He surprised everyone by opening an eye, which got steadily wider as he realized it was another baby elephant touching him and not a human.

A few hours later, when Gulliver tried to get up on his wobbly legs to take the bottle Daphne offered, Sobo quickly got behind him and tried to lift. When she was not able to, Eleanor, who had been waiting outside patiently the entire time, gently entered the stall, nearly filling it with her massive frame. She put her huge trunk underneath Gulliver's little body, propping him into a position in which he could take milk easily. Daphne had to force herself to concentrate as tears clouded her eyes. Eleanor was so essential to her work saving elephants, Daphne often wondered what she ever would have done without her. Together they always shared the same goal.

From that point forward Sobo remained next to Gulliver's side, taking care of him just as Eleanor took care of her. Even more surprising was Eleanor's willingness to let her. It seemed she understood that letting Sobo comfort one that was worse off than herself was "just what the doctor ordered."

Sobo appeared to pull out of her depression. Once Gulliver became her main focus, she looked as happy and attentive as any of the elephants. Even though initially it appeared Gulliver's health was improving, as the weeks passed, it was clear he was getting sicker. His love for Sobo was strong, and when she encouraged him to do something he tried with everything he had. But soon even his love for Sobo couldn't pull him back.

Sobo and Eleanor kept vigil inside his stall when he was no longer strong enough to get up. Daphne watched as the hollows in his cheeks became more pronounced and his face began to take on the sunken appearance of starvation. Daphne had little success raising an elephant still dependent on milk. A diluted mixture of cow's milk and glucose was given at regular intervals, but she didn't know then that cow's milk was, in fact, poisonous to elephants.

After losing several elephants under the age of two, which were too young to survive without the nourishment of elephant's milk, Daphne decided to experiment using various recipes for an elephant milk formula she was given throughout the years. Eventually, she discovered that coconut oil was the missing ingredient. Once that replaced the deadly cow's milk formula, her baby elephants thrived. Scientists from all over the world who had been trying to find the missing ingredient for themselves stood back in wonder when she finally made that discovery. Even they had to admit ... *that was impressive.* The Queen of England was so moved she honored Daphne with a damehood for her finding, and hundreds upon hundreds of baby elephants under the age of two were saved as a result.

But that story wouldn't reveal itself for many years.

As the days passed and life slipped away from Gulliver, Daphne took comfort knowing at the very least that Gulliver died surrounded by two elephants and keepers who loved him deeply. David, Daphne, and the keepers, who had also grown quite attached to him, held a funeral. Just before he was lowered into the ground, Sobo came forward and gently touched Gulliver's lifeless body with her trunk, inspecting him slowly, as if trying to find the reason he was gone. The keepers held Gulliver above ground until she was finished. Instead of leaving with everyone when it was over, she stayed behind at his grave, still refusing to leave his side. Eleanor tried to coax her away, but Sobo wouldn't budge. Instead, a keeper set up a lawn chair covered in a sleeping bag nearby to keep a watchful eye on her as night closed in. There she stayed until the early hours of morning.

Sobo became severely depressed once again. Nothing Eleanor did seemed to pull her out of it, and just as before Daphne feared the worst. Each evening, as the line of orphans walked single-file back to the safety of the evening stockades, Sobo peeled off and headed to Gulliver's grave, where she could be found night after night by Eleanor and her keeper, who each waited patiently as she continued to grieve. Elephants die of broken hearts just like humans, and all Daphne could do was hope she would find something to live for.

Eleanor did everything she could to comfort Sobo, but she displayed the same signs she did on that first day after her rescue. She stayed just outside the circle of orphans, rocking slowly back and forth as if locked in her own world of sadness and grief. Her trunk rested on the ground as Daphne voiced her concerns to David, but he knew unlocking the mystery of elephant behavior was something they hadn't yet mastered.

A few weeks later, after the first rains of spring, the keepers led the orphans to a different waterhole. It was the elephants' favorite time of day, as they loved splashing and playing in the mud. David and Daphne sat atop Mazinga Hill looking down on the scene when a trumpet scream suddenly caught their attention.

"What's going on?" Daphne shielded her eyes from the sun as David stood to get a better look. Sobo, trumpeting wildly, ran around the edge of the waterhole.

"There—in the distance," David pointed in Sobo's direction. Daphne could see the herd of wild elephants with their trunks raised in the air. She looked back to see Eleanor slowly leaving the waterhole with her own trunk raised, detecting the scent of the strange herd approaching.

"What is she doing?" Daphne murmured, wondering why Sobo acted so strangely. Sobo ran straight at the wild herd, still screaming. All they could do was sit and watch the scene unfold.

Suddenly, the herd all began trumpeting, urinating, and defecating at once, something elephants do when they are extremely excited. Sobo ran straight into the middle of the herd and was greeted by a sea of trunks that seemed to be coming at her from every direction.

"Oh my God, Daph," David said, but the tears were already streaming down Daphne's face. "She's found her family. By God, she's found her lost family." David shook his head in disbelief. They both stood and watched in awe, but the scene unfolding below them was unmistakable. It was an epic elephant reunion.

"Oh ... Eleanor," Daphne whispered. There she stood, unmoving, at the edge of the waterhole with her trunk in the same position, raised high in the air. The temporal glands on the sides of her face were seeping liquid, the only indication that Sobo's reunion had affected her too.

As Sobo eventually walked away with her family, disappearing into the distance, Eleanor remained glued to the ground next to the waterhole, trunk still raised, as though trying to catch one last scent of her before she disappeared.

"We have to go, it'll be dark soon," David sighed.

"What about Eleanor? I don't want to leave her." Daphne replied.

David stared at Eleanor for a moment, "She's just trying to make sense of it all, just like we are."

Daphne knew they had to get back; one didn't risk being caught in lion country in the dark of night. The orphans had been led back to the compound by one of the keepers, but Eleanor remained glued to the waterhole's edge. Daphne wondered what Eleanor must be thinking as they left, and dusk turned to night. She hated leaving her behind, but she also knew there was nothing they could do to make Eleanor join them if she didn't want to.

David and Daphne talked into the night about what they had witnessed. By some miracle, Sobo found her long-lost family, a family that had somehow managed to survive not just Tsavo's devastating drought, but also the poaching incident that killed Sobo's mother. It would have been very likely they were with her, since elephant females stay together for life. There are only two things that separate them: human intervention and death.

The following morning, Daphne raced to the kitchen window where she could see the stockades and, to her relief, there was

Eleanor, waiting patiently outside for everyone to get up. Daphne stayed up half the night waiting for her and breathed a sigh of relief as soon as she saw her. For the next few days Eleanor threw herself into her matriarchal duties for all the other orphans, but every now and then she stopped what she was doing, turned in the direction Sobo disappeared, and lifted her trunk as if searching for any sign she left behind.

As I thought about the reunion between Sobo and her family, I wondered if the reunion between my family and me would be nearly as spectacular.

CHAPTER 10

*E*very Thursday, I journeyed across town to a group meeting of people in recovery called Sunset, the same meeting the treatment center's white van took me to. Although it took me two buses to get there from Bob's, I went every Thursday no matter what. It had been a long time since anyone asked me to come back anywhere except for this meeting. Even though I met Yvonne there each week, I mostly kept to myself and tried to be invisible even though I attended for months.

One night, a woman named Barbara asked me if I would come early the following week. I was instantly offended. No one had *ever* asked me to come early unless I was in trouble for something. She was from New York and could be hard to read, but from the look of her I could tell: she wanted to fight.

Fighting was a big part of my story. I fought so much growing up I can't even remember the first time I got suspended for it. Even though I told myself I never picked fights, they always seemed to find me, except when it came to ones with my boyfriends—but I justified picking those because they usually deserved it. Now I can see I was the common denominator. I learned early on that once someone was screaming in my face, I was going to get hit anyway, so I might as well hit first. It was my one and only strategy. Hit first, get suspended. Hit first, get suspended. The whole ordeal exhausted my parents. My earliest fist fights started in middle school, but they continued throughout high school and even into adulthood.

∞

Taft College was my last stop on a tour of softball scholarships. I turned down their initial offer in high school because I thought Taft, just outside Bakersfield, California, was uglier than an armpit. Now they were all I had. I begged to get on the team, but they made me try out with a hundred other girls on a hot July day. Luckily, I made it as a fastpitch pitcher.

Two years later, as I sat in a boring history class, I became distracted by a strange clicking sound coming from a girl next to me. She was new, and I was surprised when she showed up in our dorm room a few nights later at one of our epic parties. We were all on full-ride softball scholarships, and the only thing we did better than play softball was party. As a joint was passed around, she introduced herself and said her name was Tawana. A few moments later I heard it again—that same clicking noise I heard her making in the class.

"What is that? What is that clicking sound?" I asked. Instead of answering, she spit out a razor blade.

"What the fuck?" said Janice sitting next to us, eyes nearly popping out of her head.

"Why do you have a razor blade in your mouth?" I asked as more people leaned into the conversation.

"It's so you can slice someone who's coming at you," said Tawana. She had just moved to California from Tennessee, and as she explained, "All the girls in Tennessee fight with razors." And like her, they got used to storing them in their mouths alongside their cheeks.

Janice was beside herself. "How? Why? Demonstrate!"

Tawana grabbed the edge of the razor she held between her front teeth with the knuckles of two fingers, swiping backwards with what appeared to be deadly accuracy. I definitely wouldn't want to be standing behind someone who had that ability.

I had never seen anything so unbelievably creative. It opened my eyes to a whole new reality, and I imagined the damage I could inflict.

"Give me some of that joint and I'll show you how to braid them in your hair." She inhaled as we smashed the razors used to shave our legs and peeled out the delicate blades embedded inside. Once my roommate Julie wove my long hair into a French braid, Tawana showed Janice, step-by-step, how to intricately weave the blades into my braid without cutting my hair. Since girls always grabbed the hair during a fight, I thought this was nothing short of genius.

A few weeks later, I found a girl I had to fight. Ana lived directly across the dorm from me. She was Mexican and I found the idea of fighting her familiar, since I had grown up getting my ass kicked by them. Those girls were born knowing how to fight, so I knew I had to prepare.

Ana got together with my ex-boyfriend, "Killer," only days after we broke up. In other words, Ana didn't know the code. Part of the fun of breaking up was getting back together. "Killer" was the only football player that all of the upper classmen warned me to stay away from. When I asked why, they explained he was dangerous, was known for hitting girls and just an all-around bad seed. I became his girlfriend by the weekend.

I moved on to my next boyfriend, and we were together for most of the following year before we broke up. Within a few days, Ana was *his* girlfriend. The final straw came after I did some laundry. My roommates and I took turns doing each other's and it was my week. When I came back to check on them, all the white clothes were bright pink. Further investigation revealed a distinct vial of red lipstick as the culprit.

Tawana had been with me in the laundry room, and now she was Ana's roommate. I walked straight into their dorm room since everyone was at dinner and found Ana's makeup bag with the same brand of lipstick. I tracked down Julie and Janice, told them my plan, and together we smashed our razors.

I secretly hoped Janice paid attention to Tawana's razor-braiding lesson at the party. Following Auntie Edna's advice, I made sure to apply a perfect layer of beautiful red lipstick before gulping down a bottle of Mad Dog 20/20. It struck me that applying lipstick for an occasion like this was not exactly the kind of confrontation Auntie Edna had in mind, but I didn't care—I was going into battle.

The alcohol replaced the fear I had for the fight with the pure, unadulterated rage I felt for Ana. It was the first fight with a girl I deliberately picked. The plan was to jump her as she came out of class. There was a trail on campus between the buildings and the dorms. Just before the entrance to the dorms was a covered picnic area with tables. That's where we waited.

I wasn't prepared for all the people getting out of class at the same time, as an enormous crowd came around the bend with Ana tucked somewhere in the middle. I called her over, and she seemed to know relatively quickly what was happening. I threw my drink in her face. The fight was underway. A chain of guys formed a circle around us to stop anyone from breaking us up. Instantly we were on the ground.

"Watch out for her rings," I could hear Janice yell from the sidelines.

The rings—I had forgotten about those. Ana wore spiky rings on nearly every finger, and if landed in the right spot she could slice my face as clean as any razor blade.

Tawana was right. Ana went right for my hair. I heard Alfred yell, "Let 'em fight, come on, let 'em fight," as people tried to break us up, but Alfred knew. I spent hours with him crying on his shoulder about how much I hated Ana. He, Mike, and an enormous football player named Pringle were regulars in our dorm room parties. They all knew how much I hated Ana, so the three of them built up a defensive wall to let us go at it until we were through. The more Ana hit me the more enraged I felt. It was as if all of my frustration from my whole life came pouring out of me in that one fight. I couldn't feel a thing and had no idea if any of her punches were landing. We fought until we were absolutely exhausted.

I got up first and did a quick mental check through. I felt pretty good, and when I touched my face there was no blood. Ana sat on her knees, looking down, her face covered by her long brown hair.

"Are we done?" I asked, out of breath, standing over her.

She nodded.

"You owe me for the laundry … and stop dating all of my ex-boyfriends." Slowly she looked up, and I could see the blood on her face. Then I looked to her hands and it was clear the razor blades had done the job. Her hands were shredded.

"Holy shit," whispered Janice, noticing it when I did. "Let's go."

"Are we good now? Is there anything else?" I asked Ana.

"No, we're good," she said as her friends helped her up. "We're good."

Just as Ana's friends closed in around her, mine surrounded

me. As I went to take my first step, we all heard a loud, sickening *craaaaacccckkkk.* I stopped, frozen in place.

"Was that … was that your leg?" Janice asked, wide-eyed and horrified.

"I … I … don't know … I think so," I said. A moment earlier, when I was speaking to Ana, I stood on my other leg, not the one that just made that awful sound. Just then, I felt a giant wave of nausea mixed with a touch of woozy. I needed to sit down, but it was a long walk back to the dorms.

"Here, let me help you," said Alfred.

"No, let me just lean into you. I don't want them to see me limping."

With each step I could feel the adrenaline of the fight subside and the pain in my leg grow. I only made it a few steps before I had to be carried back to my dorm room. As soon as I was placed in a chair, Janice and Julie went to work unraveling my hair.

"Four in and four out," said Janice.

Thank goodness all of the razor blades were retrieved, I thought, but the pain in my leg was too unbearable to focus on anything else.

"Let's take off your boot and see how bad it is," Julie said. I had worn my favorite pair of combat boots. I bought them at a secondhand military store, and they were lined with steel reinforcements. It seemed like a perfect wardrobe choice as I prepared for the fight, but as Julie began to unlace them, the pain increased to a massive level. All of a sudden I was freezing, even though it was warm outside, and incredibly thirsty.

"We should take her to the hospital," Janice said "I think she's going into shock."

Without taking my boot off, I was loaded into Julie's car and taken to the local hospital. The look on the nurse's face said it all, and I was whisked into my own room surrounded by a curtain. The nurse wanted to wait for the doctor to take off my boot to see the full extent of the damage.

Once he did, my entire leg swelled up like a big, fat, green balloon. There was so much pain I could hardly breathe. Julie and Janice held each hand, and I wondered what it would have felt like if the doctor hadn't given me a heavy dose of painkillers a half hour earlier. I was stunned to learn that my leg was not at all sprained as I'd hoped, but was instead broken in five places, including a shattered ankle, everywhere it seemed not protected by the steel inside the boot. I knew my time at Taft had ended, which was confirmed a few hours later when Coach Bandy showed up to let me know I was kicked off the softball team. He was angrier than I'd ever seen him and explained how deeply disappointed he was in my actions, but I felt nothing. I was completely numb.

After everyone left for the night, a nurse accidentally pulled open the curtain surrounding my bed when it got caught on a table she was pushing down the hall. There was Ana, staring at me from across the hall with two bandage-covered mitts. By that time my leg was in traction, hanging from the ceiling. There wasn't anything to do but stare at one another, so finally we began to talk. By the end of that night, in a strange twist of events, we became friends.

A week later, we received our disciplinary notices. It was official, we were getting kicked out of school too. On the morning of the hearing, Ana and I made other plans. Our strategy was to drop out when the administration office opened, an hour before the hearing, therefore preventing the incident from being added to our records. We knew it was brilliant, so we decided to meet at the cafeteria and grab some breakfast beforehand. Neither of us expected what happened next. She wasn't able to open the doors because of her bandaged hands. Each time I tried, the heavy door got stuck on one of my crutches. We looked like a pair of stooges until someone noticed and ran over to hold the door for us. As we entered the cafeteria, a hush fell across the room. Everyone seemed to be staring at us, including the kitchen staff. Suddenly someone stood and started clapping, then the entire room broke out in a frenzied standing, screaming ovation. It was ridiculous and heartwarming at the same time. It seemed an oddly inappropriate way to end my time at another college, but I loved it nonetheless.

Little did I know then it would be an *entire year* before I could walk again without the use of a crutch or a cane. My leg had to be re-broken multiple times, and the pain I experienced over that year was like nothing I have experienced before or since. Yet I'm still amazed that it never once dawned on me that the fight, or the circumstances leading up to it, had anything at all to do with my drinking.

∞

I waited in the parking lot until I couldn't stand the cold any longer. With no coat, there was only so much I could take before I found the elements unbearable. The meeting with Barbara was all I could think about in the week leading up to it. I braided my hair that morning but with no one help me, I left the razors behind.

It was already dark outside by the time I opened the door to the warm, well-lit room. To my surprise, Barbara was already there waiting for me. But as I entered, I saw two more women, and one of them was Yvonne. *I can handle one of these women but not all three*, I thought. And I knew I could never fight Yvonne: she was one of my only two friends.

"Thank you for coming," said Barbara as she walked over to me.

"What's going on?" I asked, agitated. "What do you want?" Eager to get whatever was about to happen over with as soon as possible.

"Well," said Barbara, looking back at Yvonne and Sue, "we see you show up here every week in the same clothes."

I wasn't sure where she was going, but the instant she said it, I felt a wave of shame. I knew my predicament, having only one set of clothes—the ones I was currently wearing—but tried to think about it as little as possible. I wasn't paying attention as Barbara continued talking, until the three of them moved to the side and pointed at a table in the back of the room.

"What?" I asked not seeing it at first "What's that?"

"Those are clothes … for *you*," said Barbara as I took a step closer.

I stood there in shock for a few minutes before everything came into focus. The table was piled high with all kinds of clothes. There were sweaters, pants, and even raincoats and gloves. That's when I realized these women weren't here to fight me—they wanted to help me. I could not believe what I was looking at as I felt a lump form in my throat. For an *entire* week I thought we were going to fight. It had been so long since I could remember anyone going out of their way to be nice to me—at least someone who didn't want something in return.

Since my duffel bag was stolen at the shelter, all I had left were the clothes I was wearing, my notebook, and those two recovery books. Bob stuck to his word and never did give me any money, and to be honest, I didn't even care anymore. It had been nearly nine months and I had bigger things to worry about than my lack of makeup, hair products, or a change of clothes. Just surviving felt overwhelming on most days. I was someone who always prided myself on the clothes I owned, the color of my hair, and how well put together I was. Nothing could have prepared me for the fact that all of it would be stripped away, leaving me bare and ugly.

Yvonne approached me, wrapped her arm around my shoulders, and led me to the table I couldn't seem to make it to by myself. She reminded me of Eleanor the way she mothered her own newcomers, making them feel less alone and safe. That day something changed inside me. The kindness and generosity of those women changed me. And just as I felt at the treatment center the previous Christmas Eve, that unfamiliar feeling flittering around my room, I felt hope again.

Months later, after finding a good job, buying a fancy car, dyeing my hair to perfection, and putting on some fancy clothes, I went to Sunset dying for them to see the "true me." I wondered if they would even recognize me. Instead, something even more shocking happened.

No one mentioned a *thing*. Not a single person.

Ted was still the door-greeter, and when I approached, he gave me a massive bear hug as he always did and told me to "keep coming back." He said nothing about my fancy clothes or my hair color. My resentment grew as each person came up to hug me, as they did every week, but said absolutely nothing about my appearance.

I whined to Yvonne about this later when she gently grabbed my face in her hands, "It's because they have already *seen* you."

"What do you mean?"

"There wasn't anything for them to recognize. They didn't notice your hair or your clothes because those are only decorations on the vibrant soul underneath, which they have already *seen*."

Thinking back on that moment, I can see how the universe had a perfect plan. Everything in my life was exactly the way it was supposed to be. The only way I could have learned that powerful lesson was by removing everything I had an attachment to. I had to be stripped of everything I judged in other people, allowing me to be less judgmental of myself. I learned to never ask someone if they are hot when they are wearing long pants on a summer day, or if they may be cold only wearing a shirt with no coat in the winter. It may actually be that they are wearing every last piece of clothing they own.

Whenever I'm asked why I dress up all the time, I answer simply, "Because I can." And I know what it feels like not to be able to. I wish I could say it was my last lesson in humility, but God, as usual, was just getting started.

CHAPTER 11

*D*avid, along with Daphne and a fellow scientist named Malcolm Coe, decided to research everything they could about the elephants in their care by meticulously taking notes on everything they did—including the enormous amount of poop they expelled.

When David broke apart the balls of dung, he was shocked to realize how many tiny seeds were embedded inside each one. It wasn't until the rains fell later that year that the importance of this began to make sense. Suddenly, every dried ball of elephant dung began to sprout as the seeds buried inside came roaring to life. The Sheldricks' house looked like an oasis in the middle of a barren desert with so much elephant dung sprouting up everywhere.

My father, a horticulturist, explained that a dormant seed simply sleeps, and only water will wake it up. That is what happened in any landscape that had elephants. The countryside of sleeping seeds woke up, and what once resembled a barren wasteland suddenly morphed into a lush garden. David realized that the ball of elephant dung acted as a perfect incubator to the dormant seeds sleeping within. Since elephants could travel an enormous distance, they deposited new seeds along the way, planting vegetation everywhere they went. Before this, researchers thought birds were the main transporters of seeds. No one had yet made the connection that elephants could carry much larger seeds, farther than any bird ever could.

Then they discovered that dung beetles, which carried off balls of elephant dung, were in fact burying them deep beneath the surface. At a depth of up to four feet, the buried elephant dung acts as an invigorating fertilizer to the plants seeking nourishment from above. The pieces of the puzzle started to fall into place as David began to realize the full extent to which elephants play in an African ecosystem.

Daphne became David's lead research assistant, and they began collecting samples of every plant the elephants ate, as well as those they avoided. But there was a problem. In order to adequately do the research required, they had to get close enough to wild herds of elephants to study them.

One afternoon, while walking beside Eleanor, Daphne was lost in her own thoughts when Eleanor suddenly stopped. Daphne cautiously looked over Eleanor's back to see they had accidentally walked right into the middle of a wild herd of elephants—a dangerous thing for any human. Eleanor seemed to sense the danger and shifted her body to position herself between Daphne and the wild herd of elephants. Daphne waited for the herd to notice her and raise the alarm, but they went about what they were doing as if a human among them was a normal part of their day. Daphne watched the wild elephants with awe and realized she had never been so close to one before. She took out her notebook and began taking notes, using Eleanor's back as a makeshift desk.

Each day after that, Eleanor walked with David or Daphne into the middle of a wild herd, positioning herself between them and the wild elephants they were studying as if she knew what it was they wanted. The wild herds didn't seem to mind the presence of humans as long as Eleanor was with them. In any other situation, a human would have good reason to fear for their life. Together, David and Daphne, accumulated more data on the wild behavior of elephants than any other researchers had before that time. The Sheldricks discovered numerous species of plants and animals that had never been catalogued before in Kenya, and each one was meticulously collected and sent to a lab in Nairobi for further analysis.

∞

Two years after Eleanor's arrival, Fatuma took the young elephant Samson rescued (whose name escapes me) and went off with a wild herd. The two had been spending more and more time with the wild elephants, and when the herd finally decided to move on, they left with them. David, Daphne, Samson, and Eleanor were all sad to see them go, each mourning their absence in their own way until the inevitable rescue of yet another desperate orphan yanked them back to the present.

At seven years old, Eleanor took over the head matriarch role that Fatuma had vacated, as if she had been in the position all along. Daphne realized the incredible power of one elephant working with another early on. A baby elephant had an infinitely better chance of survival if Eleanor could get to it right away. Yet she was incredibly gentle, never possessive, and let Daphne feed it the nourishing milk she could not provide herself. It seemed that each elephant David rescued came in more traumatized than the last. Daphne often wondered what horror they witnessed, but one didn't have to look far. On a daily basis, David battled poachers entering Tsavo from all sides, a conflict that would crescendo into one of the bloodiest elephant massacres in Kenyan history—one that would ultimately drop Kenya to her knees. All they could do was hold on, keep saving the precious few they came across, and pray for a miracle.

A few years after Fatuma returned to the wild, Samson was finally forced from the compound. At age eighteen, he was older than most elephants when they left to join groups of young bulls. Though Samson tried and failed several times over the years, it soon became apparent that if he was going to have any hope of living wild and free, David and Daphne would have to help him. Occasionally he would disappear for months at a time, and just when they felt certain that Samson had indeed joined a wild herd, he would return with wild bulls in tow. This led to some rather uncomfortable situations when the staff accidentally encountered wild elephants lingering right outside their sleeping quarters, and David quickly realized that it was likely a disaster waiting to happen if he didn't intervene.

They began using flash bombs to scare Samson away. Daphne swore she could see confusion on his face when he returned again. It ripped their hearts out to have to chase him away, but they knew if they didn't, he was bound to be killed by some situation involving human conflict. Their attempts to banish him from the compound worked, and he wasn't seen again for a long time.

David was sad to see him go, as they had grown enormously close over the years. He had saved Samson's life more than once. A few years after his rescue, Samson fell deathly ill. David set up a vigil outside his stall and even had water trucked in for a makeshift waterhole just feet away—because a good mud bath was always something that made Samson feel better. But Samson was too weak to do anything but lie down in the mud bath. Without hesitation, David crawled in with him and coated his feverish body with the cool mud mixture in hopes of bringing his temperature down. It worked, and Samson made a full recovery.

Watching Samson go back into the wild, David knew there could be no other way, no matter how hard it was or how much he loved his first rescue. He and Daphne had given him their best shot. Even though he stayed back longer than any other elephant—nearly nineteen years—they were grateful at how quickly he seemed to adapt to his new life.

Months later, Daphne was inside doing dishes when she heard her youngest daughter, Angela, talking to someone. Drying her hands, she went out on her front porch to see a massive bull elephant looming over her five-year-old daughter, who was reaching up to touch his trunk. Instant fear gripped her heart until she realized it was their beloved Samson, who always had a special place in his heart for Angela. Just as his trunk touched the top of her little head, he noticed Daphne standing just off in the distance. He quickly flared his ears and began a hasty retreat for fear of another flash bomb. Daphne watched without moving as he walked a good distance away before he turned back once again and looked at them. All Daphne could think of to do was to wave as tears streamed down her face. She knew he had come back to say one final farewell, and it broke her heart that he couldn't be a part of their family anymore.

Years later, when they spotted Samson again, he had grown to an impressive size. Standing on top of their station wagon, they watched him through their binoculars, relaxing in the shade of an acacia tree, hanging out with a herd of female elephants. Always recognizable by his two broken tusks, he looked in their direction and raised his trunk in the air to catch their scent. He didn't approach, and the Sheldricks didn't call out, but the recognition was apparent.

In his daily work as a game warden, David was forced at times to kill animals, though saving the ones he could became far more important. He grew to love many of them deeply, including a civet cat named Old Spice after the aftershave David loved. The cat made a home in one of David's slippers. Other friends included Reudi, an orphaned rhino that required milk feeding throughout the day and night, and a bird named Gregory Peck that regularly perched himself on David's shoulder, accompanying him everywhere he went.

Together, David and Daphne worked tirelessly to save them all. And when some would inevitably succumb to their injuries before they could return to the wild, they felt relief in the fact they had, at the very least, given each one a chance. Humans killing animals for sport was something that bothered David deeply, but it wasn't until one fateful day that he realized just how much.

David was flying his plane on a routine patrol over Tsavo when he spotted a massive bull elephant with a badly injured back leg that looked about three times its normal size. He decided to land the plane to have a closer look. He could see a poisoned spear lodged in the bull's knee. It had clearly been there long enough for a severe infection to set in. As the bull hobbled over to a water-hole, David followed on foot.

He was hiding behind a rock when the large bull suddenly rumbled long and deep, obviously aware of his presence. David moved from around the rock to get a better look. The bull had sunken eyes and loose skin all over his skeletal frame. With such a devastating injury, he was clearly starving. The injured leg was unbelievably swollen, and the bull kept touching it gingerly with his trunk.

David suddenly felt a cold chill run down his spine as it hit him. *Two broken tusks.* The rumble wasn't one of alarm, but of recognition. It wasn't a stranger looking back at him; it was his beloved Samson. As a youngster, Samson had broken both tusks showing off to the rhino, Rufus, by lifting a log much too big and heavy for such a young elephant. As David slowly walked to the other edge of the waterhole, he knew without further investigation there was nothing he could do to save him. Not this time.

They spent nearly two decades together, and David couldn't bear the thought of Samson suffering any more than he already had. After saying a few comforting words, he slowly raised his rifle and gave his friend one last parting gift. As Samson's body crashed down with a deafening thud, David ran to his side, cradled his face in his hands, and sobbed.

David stayed with Samson's body for a long time, reflecting on all the years they spent together, flooded with sadness and memories of his old friend. Did the man who threw the poisoned arrow know that this elephant had been raised and loved by humans? Did he know that Samson once cared for an orphaned mongoose named Tickle who slept in an empty pipe in his stall and rode around on his back? Did he know that when Tickle finally left to join her own kind, Samson was depressed for weeks? Could the killer have known Samson was so gentle toward orphans smaller than himself that he knelt on the ground so they wouldn't be intimidated by his enormous size? Had he any idea the remarkable story this precious elephant had to tell?

It would be a long time before David was able to tell Daphne the events that unfolded that day, but she knew the instant he came home something was terribly wrong.

David wondered what it was all for: Elephants by the hundreds of thousands killed for a trinket. *Trinkets of nothing more than pain and suffering.* Samson had suffered for days if not weeks, and it would haunt David for the rest of his life. Yet ivory owners in America and Asia defended those trinkets. "Oh, this was taken from an elephant that died over a hundred years ago" or "This was from an elephant that died of natural causes," as if there was actually someone walking around the African bush documenting the slaughter. As David said, those excuses were just a fancy way of smothering reason with a hopeful wish. To admit it was anything else revealed the owners of the artifacts were no different than the poachers themselves.

Samson was as special to David as one of his own children. When David's sadness finally turned to rage, he dug out the poisoned arrow to find some sign of ownership and make whoever killed Samson pay. But he found nothing. He would later reflect with Daphne that ending Samson's life "was quite simply the hardest thing I ever had to do."

When David finally returned, he instructed his employees to go to Samson's body and remove his tusks lest they fall into the wrong hands. All tusks were placed in the stockpile room to be sold later at auction, but David couldn't bear to have Samson's placed among so many ghosts. He chose to have them set aside, in a corner of his office, where they remained for years, untouched but never unloved.

Something changed in David that day. It reminded me of the change that was taking place inside me. A switch was flipped, and David's life was never the same. He began to fight with the poachers who were killing everything he loved, with a vengeance no one who knew him had ever seen before.

CHAPTER 12

*D*ereck and Beverly Joubert know elephants well. I followed the work of these African conservationists and filmmakers for many years, and, while working together on an elephant project, Dereck sent me this confirmation of thoughts that had haunted me for years:

> *We followed tracks of three bulls that removed the ivory (and watched them take the ivory) which they took 2km before dropping. There are cases of elephants wedging ivory in trees and we have, on film, elephants standing on the tusks removed from a skull. On one occasion I filmed a bull elephant investigate a carcass thoroughly until it "found" the cause of death: a bullet hole in the forehead. At that point the elephant lifted its ears into an alert posture, spun around and ran away from the waterhole and carcass.*
>
> *This was a regular visitor (daily) but after this the elephant did not return to the area for 4 weeks. There is, in my opinion, very clear evidence that elephants are aware of death in a way that is different from the way they are aware of life ...*

The story of Eleanor ripping the tusks out of a dead elephant continued to trouble me. I was disturbed by the idea that elephants seemed to know, at least on some level, what was happening to them—they knew *why* they were being hunted.

Nightmares about elephants began to hit me hard again during that first year in sobriety. Night after night, I woke up in cold sweats, unable to get my bearings. I had no idea what to do or how to help the elephants I cared so deeply about. I knew I was bound to learn horrific details about the experiences my elephant friends were going through. If I didn't want to be at the continuous mercy of my own post-traumatic stress, I needed to find a way to deal with the loss I felt sure was coming and the anxiety and helplessness I felt at not knowing what I could do to help my friends halfway around the world. But sharing that secret with anyone seemed somehow ridiculous to me at the time. Instead I began to get more depressed, and my anxiety grew. This eventually forced me into the chair of another new therapist, who encouraged me to seek forms of meditation.

Meditation changed my life. It took me awhile to figure it out, and I sought out different ways to do it, but one day I found myself so lost in space that time came to a complete stop. I knew I finally found the zone everyone talked about. I joined a meditation group, and we built up to meditating for two hours in one sitting once a month. I made a commitment to meditate every single day for a year, and I found the peace I was searching for.

∞

December 23, 1999, my one-year sobriety anniversary, is a date I will never forget. I kept a calendar at Bob's, each passing day marked with a big red "X." I flipped through the calendar that morning, looking at the 365 red X's that marked my journey. I could hardly believe I had done it. I had stayed sober for 365 whole days! It felt like a minor miracle, considering before that year I couldn't remember staying sober for a single day.

There was one celebration after the next. I started my day with my early-bird meeting at 6:30 a.m. Mark gave me a pass from my outpatient treatment so some friends from the meeting could take me out for breakfast. I couldn't believe how many people showed up to celebrate. As we left, someone pointed to the sky as a massive meteor streaked across the brilliant sunrise. It felt like another sign.

"Congratulations," Mark said when I told him how it went. "Now you don't have to go to meetings anymore."

"Wait … what? That's not what everyone says. You have to go to meetings forever and ever" I said, rolling my eyes.

"No you don't *have* to go to meetings anymore. You *get* to go now."

Over the course of that year, Mark became one of my most trusted friends. I spent hours in his office working on one problem after the next.

A few months earlier, Lowell informed me that my insurance had expired and it was time to transition out. I panicked. I couldn't imagine not being there; it was the one place I had grown to love. I talked to Lowell nearly every day, and Mark had become as important to me as any of the sober women I knew. Then Lowell pushed the paperwork aside and soothingly offered to set out another chair in the group room if I wanted to "hang out" for, say, another three months. I was beyond relieved and gave him a hug so hard he had to ask me to loosen it up.

Later that evening, I took my usual two buses to Sunset for a celebration I will never forget. The front table was packed with

gifts, potted plants, and metallic balloons. It was the same table that only a few months earlier was stacked with free clothes. It seemed like the entire town came out to celebrate, and I was completely overwhelmed by the generosity I felt in the room that night. There were people packed in to listen to my story, including my sister, Julie, my roommate from Taft, Nurse Karen, and even Eddie from the treatment center.

I knew then I found my home. The laughter and the joy I experienced that year was like nothing I ever felt. It was also the hardest year of my life, no doubt, but I learned so much about myself in that short period of time. I knew I still had a long way to go to be able to really spend any time with my family of origin. But leaving the meeting that night made me feel as if all things were finally possible.

One day I walked into a new meditation recovery meeting. I arrived late and sat in the very back, where I couldn't see the person leading the meeting. His voice sounded oddly familiar, with a very distinct Brooklyn accent. I was lost in the cadence of it when I first noticed the hair begin to stand on the back of my neck. *What was it?* I began looking around for what was setting me off. *What was it?*

And then, as the person finished speaking, the room said in unison, "Thanks, Jason."

Jason, it didn't register ... *Jason*, it still didn't register ... *JASON!* It registered. It was *The Jason* that had guided my parents through the year before I got sober. *The Jason* I hated to the very core of my being the day before I checked into rehab.

Only now I didn't feel anger. I was beyond grateful and suddenly dying to meet him. I could hardly sit still through the entire meeting. Everyone was so zen, breathing deep breaths, and I could barely contain myself. Then my mind raced, covering all the things he might expect me to say. After all, I wasn't very nice to him when we last spoke. In fact, I wasn't nice at all. Maybe I had an amends to make? I decided I would check in with my sponsor later, but for now I would do what she always told me to do: "Just tell the truth and watch the miracles unfold."

I stood in line behind a group of people waiting to thank him for leading a meeting I paid little attention to. Finally, it was my turn.

"I'm Debbie Ethell. My parents are Ray and Sandra, and I just wanted to thank you for ... *everything!*"

His eyes grew wide as I told him I just celebrated one year of sobriety. I showed him my coin, and he burst into tears, which was not at all what I expected.

We went to coffee, and I got my chance to thank him properly for what he had done for me and my family. A few Christmases later, when Jason fell in love with a new man he spent the holidays with us at my parents' farm. He became a very dear and trusted friend, someone I looked up to and admired. We never lost touch again.

I began seeing my family the year after I got sober. Not at their house—I didn't feel *that* comfortable. But I would meet them at various restaurants across the city. My sister was my rock during that first year. She came to Bob's and visited me at the half-way house. Because she joined her own support group for family members of alcoholics soon after I got sober, she understood what was happening and would act as a go-between for me and the rest of our family.

It was especially difficult for my mother. She was convinced that my alcoholism was her fault, that she must have done something wrong and "made me an alcoholic." I tried to explain that it didn't work that way, but I couldn't seem to convince her. It must have been terribly difficult for both my parents at the time, but I was so focused on just getting from one day to the next that there was little I could do to make them understand except to just stay sober and hope that time and patience would help to heal some of those wounds.

Mark and I would get into long talks about whether I was born an alcoholic or whether I had become one based on the circumstances of my life. I never believed the latter; I knew I was born an alcoholic. My family was riddled with them. The circumstances of my life might have led me to the bottle sooner, but I knew they didn't make me an alcoholic. In the end, I agree with my friend Wayne B., who says, "My childhood didn't make me an alcoholic, but it did put a definite spin on my personality."

CHAPTER 13

I was standing at one of my usual bus stops when Bob pulled up to give me a ride home. He showed up like that occasionally; sometimes it was to take me to get an impromptu drug test or to see if I was lying about where I said I would be. This time he wanted to know if I was interested in going to a movie. He said it starred Sandra Bullock, and since she is one of my favorite actresses, I was all in.

The name of the movie didn't even occur to me until we were partway through the film. Surrounded by darkness, I felt another cold chill wrap itself around me before I could put my finger on what was happening. My mind began to race. Sandra's character was a woman trying to get sober after being sent to a treatment center for 28 days, which was also the name of the film. *28 Days ... 28 Days ...* and then it hit me. It was the movie that Diane Ladd had starred in—the film we were all getting ready to fly to North Carolina to shoot right before I quit working as her personal assistant to become a "barista." *28 Days* was one of the scripts she asked me to read, and for some reason I thought it was a film about being on a ship stuck out at sea. Since I never read any of the scripts she gave me, I had no idea. But the coincidence took my breath away.

As if on cue, Diane suddenly appeared on the big screen as

one of the patients in the treatment center sitting in the familiar circle of "group." I could hardly breathe as I watched her. While she was in North Carolina shooting this film, I was in my own "group" circle surrounded by real-life drug addicts, myself among them. And just as I was contemplating the twist of fate, Steve Buscemi, another great actor, came onto the screen as the head drug counselor in the treatment center, and the plot thickened.

Several years before I went to work for Diane I met Steve too. He flew out to Portland to meet the cast and crew of a film I was in called *The Mortified Man*. It was based on a true story about a man who fell into the pit of an outhouse and got stuck for three days. I played the man's girlfriend, Sabrina, who had sex with him moments before he fell in. The film attracted a lot of attention at the time due to the disgusting subject matter. I reflected back on that film and how, in some ways, it mirrored the insanity of my own life. After Steve saw the film at a film festival in Europe, he flew out to Portland to meet us for dinner.

It was my last attempt at acting, though I had worked at it for a few years. I landed several bit parts here and there, but the pressure of everything only made me only want to drink more. Soon I couldn't show up to anything without having several drinks beforehand. Somewhere along the way, I lost control and began showing up to auditions completely bombed. It wasn't long before word spread and I became "that" girl. I gave up soon after. The truth was that acting was never really my thing. I hated the repetition of it all.

"What's going on? Why are you so quiet?" Bob asked as he drove me home.

I couldn't explain it to him or even to myself at the time. Watching Diane work with Steve on that film made me wonder what it would have been like had I been there behind the scenes with the two of them. I wondered what I would have thought had I found out it was a script about a treatment center, even then I knew deep down it was somewhere I desperately needed to be. And I couldn't decide if the life I had now was actually better than the life I left. It certainly didn't feel like it, but I had no other options, so I stayed quiet and forced the thoughts of my current life out of my mind.

∞

Eventually, I grew restless living at Bob's and wanted a place of my own. I began working a part-time temp job, but it didn't pay nearly enough to cover rent on my own. I wailed about this one day to my new sponsor, Shelly, as we sat down to coffee.

"I'm so tired of living in Felony Flats," I cried "I just want my own place and the freedom to do what I want whenever I want."

"So move," she said.

"There's no possible way I can move on the money I make."

After awhile I could tell she had had enough. "Debbie, I want you to start acting *as if.*"

"I don't even know what that means."

"It means you are going to the section of town that you do want to live in, regardless of the cost, and you are going to act *as if* you can afford it. I want you to come up with an amount that if you were working full-time you could afford—something reasonable. And then I want you to go find an apartment in that price range."

"This doesn't even make any sense."

"Are you willing to try?" She always nailed me with that one. Even though most of the time I was only 51 percent willing to follow her suggestions—and rarely happy about it—I was at least 1 percent over the mark of where I needed to be.

That Saturday I took the bus into northwest Portland and began searching for apartments. It was an area where you could walk to all kinds of shops, restaurants, meetings, and, most importantly, it was within walking distance of Mark's office.

I did as Shelly suggested and came up with a figure I thought I could afford if I landed a full-time job. The only problem was that northwest Portland was a swanky place to live, and rents for even some of the crappiest apartments were higher than I thought I could afford.

Finally I found a place that I didn't hate. It was a basement apartment with one small window covered by bars. There was an enormous spider hanging out in the corner, and it smelled only slightly damp and dingy. But it was better than everything else I looked at it in the price range, and I could picture myself living there.

The apartment manager explained that, once my application was accepted, I needed to put down a small deposit by the following Friday, and then she could hold the unit for me another two weeks. Even though the deposit was all the money I had to my name, I reluctantly agreed since it was also part of Shelly's suggestion, which still seemed completely ludicrous. At least I had a few weeks to try and figure out how I could afford it, or at the very least I would simply have to start over. Before I left, I made an appointment to meet her again the following Friday to pay the deposit.

On my way home, I ran into a blind friend of mine on the bus. Patrick, who I knew from meetings across town, began asking me about my day, and I told him about my search for apartments in the area.

Suddenly this little old lady butted into our conversation and began asking me all sorts of questions about my apartment search. I was tired and thought she was rude. I just wanted to speak to my friend and not to every last lonely stranger on the bus. Instead, I kept my answers short and tried to continue my conversation with Patrick in spite of her annoyance. Right before we pulled up to a bus stop where I needed to transfer downtown, she shoved a business card into my hand.

"You need to contact him," she nodded toward the card "He will help you."

"What do you mean?" I asked.

"He owns properties in Northwest, and he is like my surrogate grandson. Tell him I sent you, what you are looking for, and he will help you." But right as she said it, everyone raced off the bus to make their next connection. And just like that she disappeared into a sea of people.

"But what is your name?" I asked under my breath. She was gone before I could even get it. I wondered for a moment if she might be a ghost. When I looked down at the card I was holding in my hand, I got hit with the sensation that it was another sign.

I contacted the number on the card the next day. When I didn't receive a call back, I tried again the following day, and again the day after that. On the fifth day, after leaving as many messages, a woman named Alexis called me back. She asked me to come in and speak with her the following Friday.

I met her in a beautiful Victorian house in northwest Portland. When she brought me back to her office, I thought she wanted to show me a list of available apartments, but instead she informed me that she wanted to interview me for a job. *A job?* Since I had been so persistent in my phone calls to the owner, calling every day, they thought I would make a good leasing agent for the company. I explained that I had absolutely no experience, but she insisted they would train me.

"Do you want to walk over and see the building you would be in charge of leasing if you take the job?" It was only a few blocks from the office, and it was a beautiful, sunny spring afternoon. The walk felt nice, and we were lost in conversation before I realized where we were.

"Here we are," said Alexis, pointing at the building in front of us.

I instantly became aware of my surroundings and stood back in shock as I looked up.

"What's the matter?" she asked.

"It's nothing … it's just that … this is the apartment building …"

"Yes, it's the building you would be in charge of leasing."

"No, I mean—Greenway Apartments is the building that I'm already renting an apartment in. I have an appointment to meet the manager in an hour to pay the deposit."

"Really, which apartment?"

"Number 31."

"Ewwww," she cringed, "the basement apartment?"

"It was all I could afford," I said quietly.

"Would you like to see the apartment you get if you take the job?"

"Wait … the job comes with an apartment?" I couldn't believe what I was hearing.

"Yep, come on and I'll show you."

We walked up three flights of stairs and she opened the door to the brightest studio apartment I'd ever seen. It had an entire wall of windows and an absolutely stunning view of Mt. Hood. There were beautiful wall-to-wall hardwood floors and even an enormous window in the bathroom shower. It was the most beautiful apartment I had ever seen and definitely not one I could ever have imagined myself living in. It was magnificent. As I looked around, I didn't notice that Alexis was holding a wad of cash until she handed it to me.

"If you take the job, you not only get this apartment, but you also get a signing bonus."

I took the job on the spot. When I called Shelly and told her everything that happened, she said simply, "Welcome to recovery," just as Nurse Karen had in the treatment center.

Within three weeks, I had every unit in the building rented and was soon hired by the owner of the company to do all of the accounts payable for twenty-three more of his apartment buildings. Soon after I started, the little old lady from the bus came walking into my office. Her name, I learned, was Cora, and I discovered she wasn't a ghost but simply an angel.

The truth is that I would have been thrilled with the dark, damp basement apartment in that building. If I'd had my way, I would only have reached that far. But I learned another powerful lesson—that if I turned my will over, I would be given the penthouse apartment full of light with a magnificent view of the mountain.

"Sometimes," Shelly told me later, "when you reach for the stars, you catch one."

CHAPTER 14

*H*ow old were you when you had your first drink?" Mark asked in a private session after our group one day.

"Twelve," I said "It was at a slumber party."

"How did alcohol make you feel?" he asked.

After thinking about it for a minute I said, "Like I had been touched by an angel."

∞

It was the first slumber party I had been invited to in years. My mother thought I was depressed. That was an understatement ... *if you had been through what I just had, you would be depressed too,* I thought. I had just turned twelve, and now that everyone was convinced the cloud of darkness that surrounded me the past year was lifting, I was invited to rejoin a group of friends I had known since preschool.

I felt as though I just buried both my best friends, and in a way I had. *One week ago today I buried Eleanor next to my beloved dog Jake.* There in my backyard under the raspberry bush my dad planted when I was little, I put the charred remains of my elephant notebook into a hole next to a cross with the word "Jake," and covered it with dirt. Then I sat there and cried until there were no more tears. I went on about my life and made everyone think I was OK, but they didn't know my obsession to be buried next to Jake and that notebook continued to grow.

Renee's mother was gone for the evening, so we decided to make ourselves a drink. The five of us began mixing all the hard alcohol into what we were convinced was the "perfect concoction." It wasn't. But it did the trick. Soon we were all drunk, I more than the rest. The party ended when Renee fell through a window, leaving a gaping wound in her arm. By the time she was taken to the hospital, I was throwing up in the church flowerbed next door. I'd never had so much fun in my life.

The next morning, everyone was hungover, but for me everything seemed pinker, brighter in some way. Despite throwing up half the night, the feeling I had when alcohol entered my system was one I had never experienced and could hardly wait to get back to. I didn't feel as numb from losing my elephant notebook as I had only one day earlier. I was still incredibly sad, but alcohol gave me the hope I so desperately needed. I know now that discovering alcohol on that night saved my life. Without it I likely would have found a way to bury myself under that raspberry bush.

I had just come through a year of intense bullying by a gang of Mexican girls at my middle school. I loved school, but each day at lunch they would find a way to pounce. I tried talking to the teachers, but it didn't work. When I stuck up for myself, it only made things worse. I made the mistake of wearing the same jeans two days in a row in what I now know is the kiss of death for a teenage girl.

Lunch became a game of cat and mouse. They seemed to find me wherever I went. If I sat with someone at one of the lunch tables, the gang would threaten whoever was next to me. They would sit at a table next to mine and taunt me while I ate lunch by myself. I was terrified all the time. One girl I had been friends with since kindergarten explained to me that she couldn't be my friend anymore because they would come after her. I understood. With each ring of the bell changing to yet another class, my stomachache continued to worsen until the Hour of Hell, the lunch hour, arrived.

I couldn't take it anymore, and one day I ran out the back door as soon as the lunch bell rang. To my relief, no one saw me run into the woods behind the school, where I sat for a long time by a creek. Everything was so peaceful there. My stomach hurt just thinking about going back. I tried to tell everyone about the bullying, but my teachers and my parents all thought I was exaggerating. I knew the woods would eventually become the same as those that wound their way behind our house, so I carved a perfect four-mile trail from the school to my backyard.

That was my new routine over the next several weeks, and it worked beautifully. The gang couldn't find me at lunch, and I was finally left in peace ... until one day a survey crew worker spotted me sitting by a creek. Too scared to make up a lie, I told him where I lived, and he took me home. My parents were furious, but a long interrogation revealed everything. My father insisted on taking me back to school that afternoon.

"I'd like to see her attendance records," he said to the vice principal, Mrs. Brown, "I want to know how long she's been skipping school."

Mrs. Brown laid book after book on the table that showed my perfect morning attendance, but every afternoon was blank.

"Where are her afternoon attendance records?" he demanded after flipping through each book.

"Well they should all be right there," Mrs. Brown said as she took a look for herself, but each page staring back at her was blank.

"I—I ... don't know what to say."

"Why are all of her afternoon attendance records blank? Do you even know how long she has been missing school?"

It was clear she did not.

My mother grabbed the book to look for herself. She turned the pages until she found the first blank afternoon.

"Six weeks?" she asked "This shows she's been skipping school for six weeks?"

They were furious. Mrs. Brown began to flutter.

"You mean to tell me that she hasn't attended a single class in the afternoon for nearly two months and NO ONE EVEN NOTICED?" I could feel the wall shake as my father's voice boomed.

People began appearing in hallways, and the principal, Mr. Overfield—or as the students called him, Mr. Overfed—came out of his office wanting to know what the problem was.

Soon everyone was whisked behind a closed door. Glued to my bench in the front office, I could only hear bits and pieces when their voices rose high enough. The secretary offered me a lemon drop from a bowl that resided permanently on her desk. Grateful, I popped one in my mouth. Finally, the door flew open and the group surrounded me.

They wanted the names of the girls bullying me. I refused at first but couldn't find a way out, so I eventually gave in despite knowing things were about to get much worse. The Mexican girls would kill me once they found out I snitched. But the adults insisted it had to be done this way. Mrs. Brown explained from that point forward they were going to instruct the teachers to keep their doors unlocked during the lunch hour so that when the gang would try and corner me in the hallway, I could go into a teacher's room. No one was getting suspended. No one was getting kicked out of school.

I was dead. My stomach churned like an angry ocean before a storm.

The next day, the Mexican girls chased me down a dead-end hallway. Just like I thought, they were angrier than before. But I knew Mr. Valcheck, my math teacher, always ate lunch in his classroom, so I chose the dead-end hallway for that reason. As they closed in, I went for his door only to find it locked. *Didn't he know the new rules?* I pounded on the window, but he just looked up and waved me away. Right there, outside of Mr. Valcheck's class, I took yet another beating. Later, as I sat in his class with a split lip, he asked me what happened with a smirk. Without waiting, he just winked and walked away. It felt like even the teachers taunted me.

A week later, I crept into a girls' bathroom, thinking for certain I hadn't been followed. I had already learned bathrooms could be tricky. Always a dead-end. If I got caught in one, there was no hope of escape. I learned to go hours and hours without peeing. I chose that specific bathroom because it had a door to the locker room where Mrs. Albie was always in her office, even though she was known for ignoring bullying. I thought if I needed her she would surely help. Just to be sure, I kneeled down to check that all the stalls were empty.

As I sat down, I thought I heard a giggle. I held my breath and sat perfectly still. *Did I just hear that?* After a moment, when I heard nothing more, I breathed a sigh of relief. And that's when I heard the unmistakable *click* of the door locking from the inside.

My heart sank. I knew what was coming. I could hear them stepping off the toilets and opening the stall doors one-by-one. I slowly opened my door to see the five of them staring back at me.

Something happened to me that day. It was the first day I decided to fight back; after all, I knew what was coming if I did nothing. What difference would it make if I hit back for once? I found that as soon as I started swinging, I got madder and madder—all of my anger and fear poured out. I didn't notice the pain, I didn't notice the blood, and I didn't notice they had knocked me out until I realized I was lying motionless on the floor. I awoke to the sound of their laughter as they left the bathroom

After I pulled myself up, I got a paper towel and held it to my nose. There was a growing lump on the back of my head. I looked at the door leading to the locker room. I didn't have to try to open it. I already knew it would be locked, but I tried anyway. Just for good measure, I yelled, "Mrs. Albie," and she yelled back, "Go away." I knew she must have heard the fight.

I was afraid to tell my parents what was happening even though they noticed I was changing and getting more depressed. There was already an enormous amount of stress at home, and I didn't want to be responsible for contributing to it any more than I already had. But there were other reasons I couldn't divulge the full truth to my parents.

My dearest dog, Jake, had just died, and my whole family was devastated by the sudden loss. He and I had the strongest connection I've ever had with anyone or anything except for the elephants. The truth was that I always felt more comfortable in the company of animals than I ever did with people. As far back as I can remember, I felt different, unsettled when it came to relating to humans, but animals brought me a peace nothing other than alcohol ever could.

"Jake," was the first word I ever said. As I sat in my high chair my parents took a bet, each coaxing me to say either "Momma" or "Dadda," but instead I stretched my arms over my head, pointed my toes, and screamed at the top of my lungs: "JAKE!" They were stunned, but Jake was thrilled as he excitedly licked my face.

Growing up, Jake herded me like the perfect border collie he was. When I wandered down the sidewalk he ran after me, grabbed my diaper, and pulled me back into the yard. Night after night my parents found me missing from my crib only to find me curled up underneath their bed, wrapped tightly around my best friend.

Jake knew all about the elephants. One-by-one I shared each story with him, and he listened as patiently as I imagined any close friend would. He went to the vet one day while I was at school for a routine check-up, and when I came home he was gone. Bladder cancer, they said. I never got a chance to say goodbye and secretly prayed I could have offered him comfort in his final moments the way he comforted me. I missed him terribly, and his absence left a gaping hole. We never really spoke about him again. Though I realize now my parents were grieving just as I was—they couldn't speak of him without bursting into tears themselves—but at the time it felt like a void as wide as the Grand Canyon.

I was incredibly angry at my parents, though, for another reason. Besides Jake, I had a rescue rabbit named Petie. Even though we learned after I named him that *he* was a girl, the name stayed. She had a cage in the back yard that was always left open so she could leave and roam the yard whenever she pleased. Every few months my father took her away for a day or two for what he called "a routine check-up," and a month later we had baby bunnies.

Petie tried to attack anyone who got near them, but I could

hold any one I wanted. Petie and I also shared a special bond. As the babies got older, my father loaded them all in a box. He explained they were going to other young girls like me who would adore them as much as I did.

One day I went with my dad to the farm where he worked as a horticulturist. I always liked going there because I could wander wherever I pleased. While my dad went into the office, I decided to have a look around. I heard some noise coming from the farm manager's house. Bruce and my dad were good friends, and we visited with him each time we went there.

As I rounded the corner, I saw something strange. Bruce was standing over a table covered in what I thought was berry juice. He had a large ax in his hand, and just as the scene came into focus, he swung the ax hard onto the table. I heard high-pitched screaming and then all these tiny balls of fur began bouncing off the table. As I got closer, I recognized my bunnies and the horror of the situation began to sink in. He was chopping the heads off of all my baby rabbits.

"Stop!" I screamed through my terror "No ... STOP!!!"

I ran toward Bruce determined to save the ones I could. As soon as he saw me running toward him he panicked and threw all of the bouncing balls of fur into a box with his ax and ran into his house.

"Shit!" I heard my dad yell from behind, but he caught up to me before I got to the scene. He grabbed me, still screaming and crying, threw me over his shoulder, and took me back to the car. I pounded on his back to put me down but he wouldn't. Bruce reappeared and yelled, "I'm sorry. I didn't know. I'm so sorry."

"Stay there!" My father shouted angrily as he plopped me in the back seat before he walked back to speak with Bruce.

I was numb with shock by the time he returned. He explained that Bruce was supposed to have "harvested" the baby rabbits the day before, but he got busy with something else. He didn't know we were coming to the farm that day, and the whole thing was just one big "unfortunate accident."

"Is that where you take all of Petie's babies? None of them ever went to homes with girls like me, did they?"

"I'm sorry," he said quietly as he lit a cigarette, but that only made things worse. I sobbed the whole way home.

We were poor, this much I knew. My father made all of our furniture that wasn't handed down by a relative, and my mother, an artist, painted all of the artwork. We had lamps and tables made out of driftwood and paintings depicting scenes of peaceful forests. But I never realized the extent of it until we sat down to dinner a few weeks later.

"Are these baby chickens?" my little sister asked as a dish of chicken was passed around the table. As soon as she said it my mother looked at me. I knew instantly that this was no chicken.

"It's them, isn't it?" I demanded. My parents both looked down and refused to answer.

"Who is *them*?" asked wide-eyed Carrie.

"You are disgusting!" I screamed "How could you make me eat *them*?" I was beyond mortified. It was horrifying enough to watch my baby rabbits get their heads hacked off weeks before, but to find out that I was now eating my *friends* ... my *babies* ... it was more than I could bear.

"Put it down," I screamed at Carrie "Don't touch it. It's the rabbits ... it's the baby rabbits, not CHICKEN!"

"That's enough," said my father. But when I wouldn't stop, he stood and yelled, "THAT'S ENOUGH!!!"

I stood with him and continued to scream until he slapped me so hard I saw stars. Everyone went silent. Stunned, I ran to my room and slammed the door.

There were explanations about why we had to eat the rabbits. It never occurred to me that most of the food we ate came from one farm or another. I never thought about what happened to the cows, sheep, and chickens I befriended once they were no longer waiting for me in the field. The whole idea of what happened to them turned my world upside down.

I didn't care and wasn't interested in any more explanations. It only made me close off more to a world I already felt disconnected from. I couldn't trust my parents to tell me the truth, and now that Jake was gone I felt more alone than ever.

The bullying at school was just the icing on the cake. The only thing that seemed to make any sense to me after that was suicide. At night, after everyone had gone to bed, I would steal a knife from the kitchen and sit in my bedroom holding it to my chest. I thought about how hard I would have to press to get to my heart, but each time I tried, the pain was so intense I couldn't do it. Eventually, I gave up the knife but began thinking of other ways to kill myself. When I realized I just didn't have the courage, my depression got worse. I began to pray for other ways to die. For God, or whoever was up there, to take me anytime.

I get hit with a nostalgic familiarity when I see a headline that yet another kid has taken a gun to school and killed a bunch of students. I looked for my dad's gun but couldn't find it. Had I found it, I wonder where I would be now. I remember thinking jail would be a blessing if it meant I would finally be left alone. I am saddened when I hear of a kid killing his bullies, but I understand that pain too. The stories of the elephants were the only thing that brought me relief. When I closed my eyes and thought about them, I felt calm and at peace.

I retraced David's footsteps in my daydreams and stood with him on Mazinga Hill, overlooking the landscape. As he flew his plane on regular patrols, I was in the seat next to him, looking for injured animals. Sometimes we saw lions, buffalo, or an ostrich. If I concentrated extra hard, I could almost smell Africa, feel the wind blowing in my hair and the hot sun on my skin.

When I read that Jane Goodall said, "I traveled to Africa long before I actually went there," I knew exactly what she meant. With every orphaned and injured elephant David brought back to Daphne, I was there, recording every last detail of the event in my notebook.

Everything I could find about the elephants and their stories was pasted and written into that notebook. I would read about them over and over again, each time discovering something new. I had eighteen elephants in my journal now compared to the three I had started with when I was eight. Night after night, I turned the pages of Daphne's books, read about Eleanor and the elephants, and then I prayed for my life to end.

CHAPTER 15

My salvation came while I was sitting in that prick Mr. Valchek's math class. The smoke alarms started going off and we were all paraded into the schoolyard, thinking it was a drill. Only this time we saw real fire trucks pulling up in front of the school. Although it was cold and I didn't have my coat, I was excited; I hated Mr. Valchek and his stupid class.

The fire was small, and they got it handled right away, but soon after we were let back into our classes, an announcement came over the loud speaker: "Will Debbie Ethell please report to the principal's office." Before I even got up from my desk, there was Mrs. Brown with a stern look on her face, opening the door of my class. I thought it was strange that she didn't say a word as she escorted me to the main office; she was usually very nice. As we entered, there was a small group of people, including firemen, who stopped talking and stared as soon as I walked through the door. Mrs. Brown led me down the hall to Overfed's office.

I wasn't paying attention to anything they were saying at first; I was confused and didn't understand why so many people were crammed into the tiny office. When they told me that my locker was the starting point of the fire, that I was probably going to be charged with arson ... they had my *full* attention. I didn't know what arson was but knew it wasn't good. And they mentioned the word "authorities." This meant that my dad was going to be called and would probably leave work early once again. I was in for it, that was clear. I knew immediately that the Mexican girls had ramped up their game, but no one would listen.

As I sat down on the hard bench once again, waiting for the arrival of my parents, the secretary gave me a stern look before she grabbed the bowl of lemon drops off the counter. It was clear she wasn't going to offer me any candy. Somehow that stung worse than anything.

When my parents arrived, they left me sitting on the bench while they went down the hall to meet with the same group of people. When they came out, I could hear my dad insist on seeing my locker. Overfed didn't think it was a good idea, but relented when my dad said, "Show me the goddamn locker, Rick!"

As we walked down the hall, the smell of smoke grew stronger. It surprised me that my locker door wasn't red anymore but black. When they opened it, I was shocked by what I saw. Scribbled all across the inside of the door were the unmistakable words "Bitch," "Slut," and "Whore." Most of the books were burnt to a crisp. I knew my parents would have to pay for them, and I secretly wondered how, since we were already eating our pets.

"Let me get this straight," my dad said, folding his arms across his chest "You think she lit this locker on fire, but before she did, she scribbled those words about herself?"

Overfed started to squirm. "Well, you know kids these days. They do all kinds of crazy things … "

My father stared at him and said nothing. I looked from my dad to Overfed and could see his large belly heave up and down.

Finally, after what seemed an eternal stare-down, my father

said, "This is the third goddamn time I've been called to come to your school to clean up a mess you refuse to. We don't even get so much as a phone call letting us know that our daughter has been skipping school for weeks, and when you tell us that the bullying has stopped, we have this. Now, do you want to rethink that answer?"

Overfed choked. Soon their attention turned to me, and once again I told them everything.

"See? Like I said, now that we know all the facts, we can easily work things out," Overfed stammered as I stared back at him. He turned to look at my father, but my parents were already halfway down the hall to the main office. They were disgusted, I could tell. Overfed quickly turned and ran as fast as his little peg legs could carry him. He reminded me of an enormous water tower set on top of tiny stilts. No one noticed that I wasn't with them when they left.

I stared at my charred locker and began removing the burnt books. One by one they tipped out and fell to the floor, scattering ashes with a "thud." Then a small notebook came tumbling out and I recognized it instantly. *Oh no! OH NOOOOO!!!* It was my journal of elephants. It had been wedged between two of my schoolbooks when I was reading it the night before. I never took it to school with me, so it was a surprise when I noticed it that morning as I took my books out of my bag. I grabbed it and flipped through the burnt pages as I began to sob.

When my parents found me they thought I was crying because Overfed said he was going to charge me with something. But I knew the Mexican girls had just destroyed the only part of my life that remained good and untouched. They tried to reassure me that I was not going to be in any trouble, but I couldn't explain how devastated I was that all of my elephants were gone ... *all of my elephants and their stories were gone.* When they tried to take my notebook from me, I cussed at them for the first time in my life. Instead, my mom found a plastic bag for what was left of it, and we took it home where I buried it next to Jake.

All the Mexican girls were expelled. Mr. Valchek and Mrs. Albie got into trouble, and I was told to stay away until the school officials sorted everything out. When I returned, I was given a new locker and everyone stared at me. I sat by myself at lunch like I always did, but this time no one taunted or bothered me. I didn't mind being alone, I just didn't want to be picked on. That's when a girl named Devorah asked if she could sit with me. She was the new kid who moved to the school right before the fire, and she became my first friend in a long time. The following week, Devorah and I were invited to Renee's slumber party and the night that changed everything.

Alcohol became the *relief* I so desperately needed and found just in time. Whenever I got a chance to drink after that, I did. And because I puked nearly every single time, I became quite popular in the middle-school drinking circles. For a long time, alcohol replaced the gaping hole left by the loss of my elephant notebook. But as the years passed, it turned against me in the most horrible, awful way, leaving me once again begging for mercy.

∞

By 1989, elephant killings were at an all-time high. Dr. Richard Leakey, the son of famed anthropologist Louis Leakey, became the new head of the Kenya Wildlife Service, tasked with the mission to stop the killing. The Kennedy of Kenya, as I referred to him, knew that without elephants, there would be no Kenya, and he began to systematically root out the corruption that had many politicians by the throat.

There were warehouses stuffed to the gills with ivory and a wealthy Asian buyer ready to pay millions in cash for every last piece. I came across a *New York Times* article that disturbed me to the core. It described a plane full of tourists flying over Tsavo East National Park, vying for a glimpse of an elephant habitat; instead, all they saw was an elephant graveyard. The red soil of Tsavo was full of ivory tusks bleached white by the sun as far as the eye could see. My stomach churned as I wondered what David would have thought had he been the one flying the plane. What had been a haven for nearly fifty thousand elephants in the 1960s was now estimated to have fewer than five thousand.

My heart sank.

The sale of that ivory could have pulled Kenya out of its debt and done an enormous amount for the people of that country. But just as the sale was about to go through, Dr. Leakey came up with another plan. He wondered how selling the country's stockpile of ivory would do anything to stop the killing. He knew it would only drive the price even higher, and the price per pound of ivory was already the highest since anyone started keeping track. He also knew that selling the ivory would only escalate the death of Kenya's people. If tourism dried up, as it surely would with no elephants, then the country's largest source of income would be gone. Dr. Leakey knew that selling the ivory was only a short-term deal; it was the future he had his eye on.

He made a decision that sent an ominous chill down the spine of the Asian buyer. Instead of selling it, he decided to burn every last piece down to the ground. Dr. Leakey must have known the statement it would make as the leaders of the world tuned in to see what would happen next. An event unlike any other took place on July 19, 1989, as the leader of Kenya, President Moi, along with Dr. Leakey, held a torch to light pile after pile of the ivory of dead friends past. I sat, transfixed in front of the television once again, watching as if it were happening in my own backyard. In a final farewell to everyone who fought so hard for the lives of elephants as well as their freedom, a wisp of smoke not only reached heaven but the ivory markets, as well.

One day went by and nothing happened. Then two. On the third day after the tusks of Kenya were set ablaze, the entire ivory market came crashing down. What once sold for nearly $1100 per pound dropped to less than $3. The gun shots ringing out in Tsavo stopped literally overnight, and vultures that once feasted on carcasses of dead elephants began to starve.

No one had any clue the magnitude of what would happen after the ivory burn, least of all Dr. Leakey, but his idea had worked *brilliantly*. Elephants that had only been coming out under the cover of darkness slowly began peeking around corners during the day. I felt an enormous relief that my elephant friends had been spared for the time being.

CHAPTER 16

Softball took over my life the same summer I discovered alcohol. I became a fastpitch pitcher along with Carrie. We practiced every single day. My parents switched off catching for both of us, but they soon realized the best chance of getting either of us a college scholarship would require someone with pitching expertise. They found one of the best fastpitch softball pitching coaches in the state, Wayne Smith, and he didn't charge a dime.

He coached only the most talented girls and didn't believe in charging if that meant some talent would be left out simply because they couldn't afford it. The only problem was that he was booked solid. My father contacted him over and over again but always got the same answer: *No.* One day we realized Wayne would be giving a pitching clinic at a school about ten miles away. It was already full and there was no way we could get in.

"Get your mitts and get in the car!" Dad shouted.

"Why?" I wailed. *What difference did it make if we weren't even able to get in?* It made no sense. On the car ride over, he asked us if we remembered Nadia. Of course we remembered her. Nadia Comăneci, the Olympic gymnast, was like royalty in our family. So was her coach, Béla Károlyi. We were mesmerized as we sat glued to the television, watching her perform in the 1976

Olympics, when she became the first gymnast in history to score a perfect ten and again in the 1980 Olympics in Moscow, when she won two gold medals. We knew her whole story, forward and back.

An unfortunate glitch led to the disqualification of Béla's gymnastic team at the National Championships in Romania and they were not allowed to compete.

"But you *are* going to compete," he told Nadia. She was by far the most talented gymnast he had ever seen. "You just make sure you are warmed up and ready to go when I call for you."

"Why? I don't understand," she said.

"We will find our opportunity," he said. "You may not get a score, but you will win this competition! You just need to act *as if* and be ready when I call you, yes?"

She nodded.

The stadium was packed, and no one noticed when Béla spirited Nadia to the side of the floor mat where another competitor was performing a floor exercise routine. Nadia watched her and knew she had better skills than the gymnast currently grabbing everyone's attention.

Béla intently watched the judges, waiting for just the right moment. He told Nadia to remove her warm-up gear and to get ready. Nadia had no idea what was about to happen, but suddenly an opportunity emerged, and Béla screamed at her, "Go NOW! GO, GO!" as he lifted her onto the floor.

Nadia raced into the middle of the floor while everyone was distracted, as the judges added up the previous competitor's score. She launched immediately into her first tumbling pass. A quiet hush came over the room as she did flips unlike anything anyone had ever seen. Nadia made one tumbling pass after the next, each one more perfect than the last, to an absolutely mesmerized crowd.

By the time she returned to Béla, the roar of the crowd could be heard miles away. Everyone was on their feet. No one had ever seen anything like her. From that point forward, Nadia Comănechi was a household name in Romania, long before she and Béla defected and came to America. Our family talked about their story often.

∞

Carrie and I began warming up together outside while our father went in to see if there was any room for us. One of the doors to the gym was open, and we could hear the distinct pop, pop, pop of softballs hitting their intended targets. He told Wayne where we were, but Wayne explained once again that the clinic was full. Our dad told him we would be outside pitching anyway, and if he had a chance to come and take a look.

Sweat was pouring off my forehead by the time I realized Wayne was standing in a doorway, watching us. Everyone else had gone, but we were just getting started. After watching for a few minutes, he slowly walked over and began to coach us. When the session was over, he asked if we would be willing to work hard every day on our skills and not talk back. We both agreed and ran to the car as our parents hung back to speak with him privately. When they joined us, they were so excited they took us out for ice cream. It was as if Béla Károlyi himself had agreed to be our coach.

Wayne and his wife, Alice, became an extension of our family. For the next several years, we spent three nights a week working with Wayne on our pitching skills, with only one month off per year. I worked harder at pitching than I ever had at anything.

Softball became a most welcome distraction, replacing the time I'm sure would have otherwise been spent pursuing drugs and alcohol.

By the time I entered high school, I had become popular, partly because of my talent as the varsity pitcher and partly because of Anisa Nielson. I met her over the summer, only a few weeks after my locker was burned, when I got hired at a local farm tying hops. We hit it off immediately, and since she was already in high school, she didn't know a thing about my past. My braces came off and my hair was no longer the spiky mess it was a year earlier.

Anisa, a cheerleader, taught me about fashion and how to apply make-up. She gave me all of her hand-me-down clothes, which were nicer than anything I could afford. I couldn't believe my good fortune. She introduced me to all of her friends, who I had no idea at the time were the most popular in school, and I began dating the quarterback on the football team. I got to experience what it was like to be on the other side—going from one of the most hated kids in school to one of the most liked. I discovered both sides made me equally uncomfortable, partly because they were based on perceptions and not on the reality of who I was.

When voted in as princess at various school dances, I always asked the most picked-on boy to be my date. One day I went to Tad's house so his parents could take pictures of us before the dance. After we took several pictures, I was surprised when his mother asked to speak to me alone in the kitchen.

"Is this a set-up of some kind?" she asked.

"What do you mean?" I was stunned by her question.

"Why would someone like you ask my son to be your date?" I could see the pain in her eyes. I was shocked, but suddenly realized she didn't know a thing about me or my past. How could she have known I was also once bullied relentlessly?

"Because I know what it feels like … to be the underdog." And that was the truth. I told her how I had made friends with Tad when he offered to help me in my math class. I couldn't stand the pain of watching him get picked on the way I was, and when I saw the boys in my class bullying him, I fought with them to leave him alone. When the leader of the pack made it known he wanted to be my date to the school dance, I asked Tad instead.

By my junior year of high school my parents seized an opportunity to sue the school system over a Title IX violation. According to the law, the girls' teams were supposed to have everything the boys teams did. But everything from the girls' sports funding to the maintenance of the fields was much less than the boys'. Our softball fields were full of dirt clods, while the boys had brand new sod brought in each season; our uniforms were tattered from so much use, while the boys got new uniforms each year; there were lights on the football and baseball fields and no lights on our dilapidated fields. When my dad brought up the issue at a school board meeting, he was practically laughed out of the room. But my parents were civil rights activists in the sixties and used to bigger confrontations. No one laughed when an attorney who agreed to take the case for free showed up to challenge such obvious violations.

"The girls don't even play softball games at night," screamed one of the boys' parents, furious that the school was required to put lights on our softball field just like the boys baseball team had on theirs.

"Well now maybe they will," my dad yelled back.

Later that year, under the bright lights on our brand-new, perfectly manicured softball field, our team made it to the state finals for the first time in our school's history, and college scouts began showing up to our games on a regular basis. It wasn't long before games and tournaments were scheduled nightly on that field, now known as one of the nicest softball fields in the state. Even now, when I drive by and see the lights shining bright at night, it makes me proud of my parents' willingness to fight for the underdog too.

My sister and I rose through the ranks of the softball community, each of us landing coveted pitching spots on the only two national teams in Oregon. We were on the road every weekend during the summer, going from one tournament to the next. In our entire softball career our parents never missed a single game and were with us every step of the way. Carrie landed a top pitching spot at the University of South Carolina with a full-ride scholarship, and I got kicked out of my first school before my scholarship even had a chance to kick in. Wayne fired me more times than I could possibly count for talking back, but like the surrogate father he was, no matter how frustrated he became, Béla always took me back.

∞

Mishak was working as a night watchman in Nairobi in 1987 when he heard about a job opening for a "keeper." When he arrived for his interview, he wondered where everyone was. Other than a few people working in a kitchen, the place seemed almost empty. He secretly wondered what it was that they were "keeping." He told one of the people he was there for an interview.

"Take this food to the men," said a man in the kitchen.

"*Sawa*. Where are they?" Mishak asked.

"Follow the trail, there you will find them," the man nodded in the opposite direction.

Mishak looked back to a trail he hadn't noticed before. It

wound behind the compound and must have gone into Nairobi Park. He knew the park was full of animals, including lions, but when he looked back, the man in the kitchen impatiently waved Mishak away.

"Go. That way."

Mishak picked up the wheelbarrow and started down the path. Soon he smelled a campfire and saw a wisp of blue smoke, indicating he was close. As he rounded the corner, he stopped and stared at a group of men talking quietly on the other side of some trees. Something didn't seem right. The group of men huddled around the campfire, and in between them were a group of baby elephants. *It must be a poaching gang,* he thought.

Mishak had never seen a living elephant before, but his village had killed plenty. The elephants where he was from were known to be deadly and aggressive; he was taught to avoid them at all costs. But these men didn't appear to be afraid of these elephants, and the mini-herd of elephants didn't seem to fear the men. That's when he noticed the blankets. Each baby elephant was covered in a brightly colored blanket.

What is this place?

"*Bwana! 'Bari gani* ... bring the food over here," one of the men shouted as the others turned around to greet Mishak. He slowly brought the wheelbarrow to the men. He couldn't stop staring at the strange scene as the men giggled, sensing his confusion.

"You wonder what we are doing in this place, ah?"

Mishak stayed silent. He needed a job but knew that killing animals for a living would not be something he could sustain. "Why are those blankets on them?" he asked.

"We are filling in, as their mothers who were killed by poachers. The blankets keep them warm, just like their mothers would."

Mishak could hardly believe what he was hearing. *Mothers ... ?*

"I'm here for the interview for a keeper," Mishak said.

"Yes," said one of the men, "you are being interviewed right now" He nodded to Mishak's left, where a tiny gray trunk snaked its way up his side. The trunk slid up his arm to his shoulder, his neck, and then his face, inspecting Mishak as she went. The elephant's soft touch tickled, so he closed his eyes but remained completely still. By the time Mishak opened them again, a quiet hush fell across the men watching from the warmth of the fire.

Mishak was surrounded by a small group of baby elephants as one after the next approached him and inspected him with its trunk. He seemed at ease until he turned around to see Eleanor's massive frame approaching from behind. Terrified, he quickly looked back to the men, gauging at which point he should run, sure that they, too, would run for their lives at the sight of a full-grown elephant walking directly toward them. But they didn't move. Instead they kept talking and stoking the fire as if it were the most normal thing in the world.

Mishak started to sweat as he heard Eleanor's gentle footsteps approach. He closed his eyes again and stood completely still while he waited to see what fate would bring. The baby elephants parted to let Eleanor through. She extended her trunk along his back and slowly moved around to Mishak's front. Her trunk worked its way slowly up and down his body as she took in his scent. When she finally got to Mishak's face, it tickled him so much he began to laugh. The men at the campfire chuckled watching him. After Eleanor finished her inspection, she stood back and rumbled long and deep. Mishak warily opened one eye to see what was about to happen. As Eleanor slowly walked away, the baby elephants closed in on Mishak, again reaching out to him with their trunks.

Daphne, who stood in the brush nearby, watched in awe along with the rest of the keepers. She looked back to Eleanor and wondered if she knew something no one else did.

"It seems like you passed your interview," said one of the men. But the brilliant, wide smile on Mishak's face said it all. He couldn't stop watching them. They were simply extraordinary up close, and it was clear that the elephants were as fascinated by him as he was by them. From that point forward, wherever Mishak went, there was a long line of elephants following his every move.

I wondered what David would have thought had he learned that fate had brought him another Wakamba man, one that became known as an actual *elephant whisperer*; a man from the same tribe as the poacher-turned-interrogator Wambua Mukula, with whom David worked all those years ago. But this Wakamba man was one who had "the touch," who could make any elephant that came into his care trust him as much as its own mother. His skills became known as "Mishak's Magic"—because there simply wasn't any other explanation for it.

Whenever a seemingly hopeless case was rescued, Mishak was summoned. With a voice as deep as Barry White's, he could gently coax the youngster to take milk in a half an hour, something that would take days for anyone else. Perhaps Eleanor had known just how special he was the first time she met him. I like to think so.

CHAPTER 17

Only days before Kenya's great ivory burn, on my seventeeth birthday, I used my fake I.D. to sneak into a beer garden at the Hubbard Hop Festival, our town's annual celebration of summer. Since it was such a small town, everyone knew me and how old I was. I was politely asked to leave.

My father didn't realize I wasn't in my bedroom when the cops knocked on our front door. Furious, he walked a few blocks to bring me home as ordered. After depositing me back in my room, he locked the door, and I waited a few hours before sneaking out again, convinced I wouldn't be recognized if I snuck into the same beer garden. By the time I was turned away for the second time, I was in a blackout and didn't notice I was being followed by two police officers as I stumbled back to my car. They waited for me to drive all of three feet before arresting me, and I woke up in jail early the next morning. After calling a friend to bail me out, I climbed back through my bedroom window only minutes before my father opened the locked door to check if I was still where I was supposed to be.

The following evening, suffering from an awful hangover, (I convinced my mother I simply had a bad case of the flu), I watched Dan Rather report on the Kenyan ivory burn as he stood in front of a massive pile of burning tusks. The day after the ivory markets crashed, I got caught illegally climbing the town's water tower. When confronted by another police officer, I was shocked.

"How did you even know it was me?"

"Because, Einstein, you spray-painted your initials at the top for the whole town to see."

My blackouts were cramping my style. A few weeks later I got caught stealing a carload of merchandise from the local mall, and days after that, a hit-and-run car accident. Hubbard only had one judge, and by the end of that summer we were on a first-name basis. Finally, exasperated with my last appearance, he sentenced me to six months of weekends in juvenile hall.

A few months later, just as I decided it was time to turn my life around and focus once again on my softball career, country after country agreed to stop killing African elephants. And in December of 1989, the international coalition called "The Convention of International Trade of Endangered Species" (CITES) made it illegal to sell any ivory from African elephants killed after that date. Thankfully the elephants were given another reprieve.

∞

Little did I realize then just how big the year 1989 would turn out to be for the elephants. A renowned whale researcher named Katy Payne decided to come to Oregon that summer to spend time with some fellow researchers at the Oregon Zoo.

Katy and her husband, Roger, made the groundbreaking discovery that whales communicate using infrasound: long, low sound waves that travel over great distances below the human range of hearing. They noticed a strange sensation underwater when recording the whales. It felt as if a shark, or something dangerous, were sneaking up behind them. After experiencing it multiple times, they began to wonder if it was their organs vibrating slightly enough to induce the sensation. Only something like infrasound, which act like the smallest earthquake, has that capability. They experimented using a recording device, playing it back at different speeds. If infrasound was indeed present, they would be able to hear it on a slower playback. To the stunned scientific community, infrasound was *exactly* what it was. As long as whales had been studied, they were always thought of as solitary creatures. Researchers could see only one whale where they couldn't see any others; no one had any clue that whales were indeed communicating with each other across vast oceans until the Payne's remarkable discovery. Once they realized that whales were in fact corresponding using infrasound, they discovered whales were *anything* but the solitary creatures they were previously thought to be. The whale was literally transformed overnight from what scientists thought of as a solitary loner to an outgoing cheerleader gossiping with all her friends.

While Katy was watching a small group of female elephants in an indoor enclosure at the zoo, she noticed one of the females resting her head against a concrete wall, the only wall facing the outside. Then she felt it … ever so slightly. She thought to herself she would have missed the feeling had she not already experienced it underwater with the whales. Katy felt once again as if someone were sneaking up behind her. On instinct she went outside to see what was on the other side of that concrete wall, and to her surprise there was a male elephant resting his head in the same position as the female on the opposite side.

Katy grabbed a recording device, and later that afternoon she discovered that the largest land mammal in fact communicated the same way as the largest marine mammal … *using infrasound.*

Prompted by her findings at the Oregon Zoo, she went to Africa to determine just how far elephants could "hear" one another using infrasound. Her research showed that African elephants were able to detect infrasonic communication up to two miles away. Since calculating the actual distance an infrasonic sound wave can travel is tricky and difficult to prove, another group of scientists decided to undertake the same experiment not long after Katy's.

The way science determines whether elephants actually hear one another is if the elephant receiving the communication responds. But imagine standing in a massive parking lot when someone yells out a name from the far side. You might stop and look, but since the name you hear isn't your own, you don't respond. It isn't that you didn't *hear* it—the communication simply wasn't intended for you. Elephants typically hang out in groups: they aren't usually by themselves like the whales. The trick was to find two elephants, then, by monitoring the receiver's response, determine if they were indeed communicating with each other. Their research proved elephants could hear infrasonic sound waves up to *six* miles away.

Then, in 1995, another extraordinary coincidence happened when a "bug scientist" named Dr. Caitlin O'Connell went to Africa while traveling with her boyfriend, who was working on an unrelated project in Namibia. Each day she found herself observing a group of bull elephants in nearby Etosha National Park until she noticed something eerily familiar. Dr. O'Connell had done her master's thesis on ground vibration communication between plant hoppers, and something about the way the elephants were moving around struck her as oddly similar to the behavior of her bugs.

When a male plant hopper was placed on a stem and a female

call was played back, the male would "freeze." He would then change course slightly, moving in the direction of the female. Bugs are able to pick up the slightest sound vibration in their legs, a sensation that allows them to find and locate females.

As Dr. O'Connell watched the bull elephants, she noticed the same type of "freezing" behavior discovered in her plant hoppers. After a brief stillness, the bull elephants changed direction slightly and walked a short distance until freezing once again. She began to wonder if elephants were indeed picking up vibrations in their feet the same way bugs did. Soon another experiment was underway, and what she discovered changed *everything*.

Elephants were not only able to "hear" through their feet, but the distance from which they could receive, as well as make these seismic vibrations was … over twenty miles!

Twenty … freaking … miles.

It wasn't until a giant tsunami hit Asia in 2004 that people really started paying attention. Reports began to surface that elephants all over Thailand reacted to the tsunami long before it hit. A group of elephants were with their *mahouts* (trainers) and a group of young schoolchildren on a beach in Phuket, Thailand, a city that took a direct hit. Stories emerged about those elephants suddenly breaking from their mahouts and running away from the beach, gathering children as they fled, right before the tsunami hit. One of the more famous stories involved a young British girl named Amber Owen who was saved by an elephant named Ning Nong.

Tsunamis also create infrasound, similar to earthquakes, tornados, and hurricanes. If elephants have the ability to detect these vibrations in their feet, then it makes sense that they knew a tsunami was coming long before anyone else. Dr. O'Connell's research was revisited and finally began to get the attention it deserved.

When I first read about this discovery, it brought me to tears. It proved what many scientists, including David and Daphne, had long suspected: elephants were able to communicate with one another over an enormous distance. Daphne witnessed the freezing behavior between Sobo and Eleanor when they traded off watching over Gulliver. It appeared as though they seemed to know when one was coming and the other was going. Their actions suggested they were communicating in a form neither David nor Daphne could hear but knew was there.

The very fact that one researcher who studied whales and another who studied seismic communication between bugs were able to identify just how elephants were communicating between one another seemed like divine intervention. I was struck again by how little we truly know about these magnificent creatures, and I was dying to learn more.

∞

As we came home in the dark of night from another long softball tournament, I sat in my usual seat in the back of the bus. Everyone slept, but I was wide awake with a book in hand and a flashlight in my mouth, transported to Africa once again as I was introduced to another great elephant. He would actually change history—or the history that had up to that point been written about the life and behavior of bull elephants—by doing things no one had ever seen elephants do.

He was the seventh calf of Emily, sister of the famous elephant, Echo, from the EB family study group in Amboseli, and the subject of a documentary filmed by a group of Japanese filmmakers. Echo, as well as the rest of her family, had been studied for well over twenty years by elephant researchers Cynthia Moss, Harvey

Croze, and their team. I devoured the books Cynthia wrote about them: *Elephant Memories* and *Echo of the Elephants*.

Emily, along with a few members of her family, began to visit an open garbage pit, something that upset everyone. Once an elephant gets used to foraging for food in garbage pits, it inevitably dies—rangers will kill the elephant when it gets too close to people, or it will eat something impossible to digest. Garbage pits are sometimes used illegally in order to attract animals for tourists to see. As is often the case, Emily ate nondigestible items such as glass and plastic, and by the time the Japanese film crew returned, she was already gone.

An elephant's death causes overwhelming grief to its family, but there are few things more devastating than when the matriarch dies. Cynthia Moss and her researchers discovered this firsthand with the death of Emily. For months after Emily died, they witnessed Echo's family visit the site where she died over and over again. It isn't uncommon for elephants to visit death sites for years, and they're one of the few mammals, other than humans, known to have a sophisticated ritual around the death of a loved one.

After Emily was gone, the film crew returned to find the remaining members of Emily's herd, including her youngest calf, with Echo's herd. She was already a seasoned matriarch in her own right. Emily's daughters appeared to do what they could to provide for the calf, but they couldn't provide the one thing he needed most: elephant milk. Even though Echo was still lactating from her last calf, it had been a dry year, and she didn't have enough nourishment to feed two babies at once, something Emily had done years earlier when she fed one of Echo's babies along with her own. The crew noticed how weak the little calf became. They couldn't bear to watch the tiny bull they had fallen in love with starve to death in front of their eyes, so they called Daphne, who put a rescue team together in order to give the baby one final chance at her elephant nursery several hundred miles away.

Even though the young calf was only six months old, he was incredibly strong. The researchers worked with Echo and the rest of the EB Group of elephants to try and separate the calf from the herd. Even though they were a group of wild elephants, they seemed to understand what the researchers were trying to do. By the time the keepers got to the young bull, he was too weak to fight off the six men and was easily loaded onto the truck.

But as the truck pulled away, the calf overpowered the men with a sudden surge of energy, pushed open the back door, and ran deep into the bush. Unable to find him as night closed in, they abandoned the search until morning.

The next morning, he was found once again among his big sisters, cousins, and Echo, who had kept him safe throughout the night. The men watched from a distance as the sun faithfully took its place in the morning sky, until the young bull collapsed, startling his cousins. They tried to lift him and get him to his feet, but he was too starved and exhausted.

By the time the men approached for the second time, the herd seemed to understand the seriousness of the situation and moved a short distance away, allowing the keepers to approach without fear of interference. It reminded me of the way Eleanor stepped aside to let the keepers approach the injured buffalo she'd protected from a pack of lions during the night. It seemed there were clearly situations in which elephants understood when humans were trying to help and when humans intended only to kill.

The young calf was named Edo in honor of the Japanese film crew that contacted Daphne. Edo was the original name of Japan's capital city until it was changed to Tokyo, the film crew's home. The Edo Period was a time in Japan's history that signified growth and stability, something everyone wished for the young bull.

Daphne knew Edo's chances weren't good. By the time an elephant collapses, either from exhaustion or starvation, their hours are usually numbered. Eleanor went straight to work, hovering over the tiny elephant, touching him lightly with her trunk, and rumbling reassurances. Edo remained in a collapsed condition, barely able to even open an eye. He had IVs hooked to his ears as he was laid on a soft bed of hay and covered with a blanket. Mishak comforted him with his deep voice, and just when they thought Edo had passed the point of no return, something remarkable happened.

Another newly rescued elephant orphan named Dika suddenly came into his stall. Dika, who was also only six months old, had been rescued three months earlier after his mother was shot and killed by poachers. He only survived by running through an acacia thicket, a route the poachers were unable to follow. When he reappeared, he was covered in hundreds of acacia thorns (similar to those of a porcupine) that had to be individually extracted over a period of several long, agonizing days. Dika suffered from a terrible infection after the removal of the thorns, but that wasn't what scared the keepers. It was the deep depression he sank into over the loss of his family that made them nervous. But Daphne and Eleanor had seen it before with Sobo.

Day after day, Dika stood apart from the others. Tears rolled endlessly down his face, less common for elephants than for humans. He swayed back and forth, his trunk on the ground. Daphne knew the situation was hopeless unless Dika found something to live for. If she and Eleanor couldn't find a way to bring

Dika out of his depression, then he had little, if any, chance of survival.

The curiosity young elephants exhibit around elephant babies seems similar to the way young children are transfixed by a human baby—as if they are completely lost in their own world of wonder and fascination.

Dika suddenly appeared behind the legs of the keepers watching over Edo. He rumbled gently as the men parted to let him in. He began to softly touch Edo's face and mouth with his trunk. Edo slightly opened one eye. When he realized that it was in fact another baby elephant and not a human touching him, he tried to get up. Dika remained in constant contact with him. Unable to stand, Edo watched wide-eyed as Dika took a bottle from a keeper. Dika stopped only to rumble quietly before he began sucking on the bottle again. Edo watched Dika intensely, and when a bottle was offered to him, he took it as though he had done it a hundred times. The men watched in wonder, and Eleanor stood completely still outside the stall, just as she had done when Sobo discovered Gulliver. Daphne knew to never underestimate the power of communication between elephants and thought Eleanor must be communicating with the pair in ways she couldn't hear.

Dika, who had been on death's door only one day earlier, suddenly threw himself into helping Edo, leading him out on walks as he regained his strength with Eleanor always close by. Dika stayed close, constantly touching him with his trunk as a sign of reassurance. He had been given a welcome distraction, and everyone knew it had likely saved his life. Once again, Eleanor stepped aside, seeming to understand that taking care of Edo was the one thing that could save Dika. From that day forward, the two little bulls remained glued to one another's side.

CHAPTER 18

I spoke with Laura about the elephants often. She knew all about Eleanor, Edo, Daphne, and David. She loved the stories and was the only one who knew about my secret obsession. I met her one day when, soaked to the bone, I walked into a small meeting I'd never been to before. As soon as the bus doors opened, a torrent of rain pummeled me as I looked for the address. Finally, I saw the telltale sign placed outside of a meeting on the church door, and I entered a room with a small circle of chairs. As a puddle formed beneath me, someone moved a chair slightly outside the circle in hopes that I wouldn't drench anyone.

She was a beautiful woman, and I was shocked when she introduced herself to me and gave me her phone number. I instantly loved the sound of her voice and the way she spoke with her elegant, well-manicured hands. Her blonde hair was dyed to perfection, something I envied the moment I saw her. She was half Valley girl, half socialite, and I didn't know anyone else like her. She scooped me up that day and didn't let go. With fewer than thirty days sober when I met her, I loved the fact that she never asked why I always wore the same clothes. I went to her home and met her husband, her kids, and her dog. She had the perfect life complete with a white picket fence built around a stunning home.

She discovered meetings a few years before I did, when a nice policeman grabbed her right before she jumped off the tallest bridge in Portland. I couldn't believe it when she told me this. And she said it like she was reciting a grocery list. We were having dinner at her house with her family when she told me the story. I was stunned. And she was happy to tell it. No shame whatsoever. I was transfixed. How she had gone from what she described as "a crazy person begging law enforcement to let her leap into the dark abyss" to the gorgeous person sitting before me, I had no idea.

Laura taught me you could indeed go camping without psychedelic mushrooms, something I swore was not possible. But I had the time of my life on a camping trip with other members from that meeting, and we went rafting, too. I had no idea such "sober" activities even existed and that they could be so much fun. The following year, Laura, along with our best friend Stephanie and several thrill-seekers, decided to climb Mt. Adams for the hell of it, and our adventures continued.

When I had four years sober, Laura had surgery. It was a necessary surgery, but when I asked her about the pain medication, she assured me she had it all taken care of. Still, I felt a wave of concern. She had so much more sober time than I did, I assumed she had it under control. We were all warned about taking painkillers of any kind. Mark taught me so much about how my brain was affected by even a single painkiller, but when I spoke of it with Laura she convinced me that I was just overreacting.

One surgery turned into two, then three, four, and five. Each one came with a new set of prescriptions. When the necessary surgeries turned into plastic surgeries I felt the first inkling of trouble. It was something we talked about occasionally—how she would *never* have cosmetic surgery, but when this started, the uneasy feeling in my gut turned into something much more sinister. I had no idea what to do. Laura became hateful and ugly and began to turn on everyone. She turned into someone unrecognizable and though I knew it was her disease acting as a shape-shifter, morphing her into something I knew deep down she wasn't, there wasn't anything I could do—it had her by the throat. Her husband was in a full-blown panic; her sister came out from the East Coast and interventions were staged.

Then she turned a corner she could never recover from: she faked having cancer. By the time she disappeared, everyone knew her dark secret, and there wasn't anywhere left to hide. We knew she had gone to Mexico, but where was anyone's guess. She had plenty of money, so she could have been anywhere. She was discovered over a month after she died in what was described as "a most horrific scene." The room was littered with empty vodka bottles and enormous bottles of pills.

I was asked to speak at her funeral, and when her daughter turned to me after and cried, "Why her? Why couldn't she get this thing?" *Why couldn't she stay sober*—I had no answer. I just didn't know. Once again, I turned to the elephants. I spent even more time in the libraries and lost myself in their stories just as I had done as a kid. It was the only way I knew how to cope with anything if drugs and alcohol were no longer my option.

I went to the only other person I knew who could help besides my sponsor. Mark let me sit in his office while he worked; just being close to him made me feel sane and normal. Each time I visited, he would hand me another book to read about the science of alcoholism. I would pass the time waiting in his office while he was attending to another group. Sometimes I would hang out with Lowell in the front, and when Mark was finished he would take me to lunch and I would leave at peace. He helped me understand the insidiousness of the disease. That at any moment I could convince myself that I was fine, and just like that I could take a drink. *What would happen to me then?* He taught me about the progressiveness of the disease, that it continued to grow inside me even if I'm not drinking or using. That is why so many people die so quickly after a relapse, especially if they've been sober for a long time. They pick up as if they had been drinking that way all along, the same way Laura did.

Mark had been sober eighteen years and had worked as a drug counselor for twelve. He told me over and over again through the years to stay as close to the program as I could; I never knew what tornado may be right around the corner ready to blow my house down in an instant. I see now it was an ominous warning.

We went to dinner with his partner on a Tuesday. I had spent the afternoon in his office again and, as usual, felt light as a feather when we left. Two days later, I got a call from Lowell as I was driving down the freeway. The cadence of his voice instantly soothed me, but then he told me he had some very bad news.

"I'm sorry to have to tell you this, but Mark has … Mark is … "

"Mark is what Lowell? What's wrong?"

"He's dead."

I swerved and made my way to the side of the road before I let him continue.

"What do you mean he's dead? How?" I begged through my tears.

"Mark committed suicide." I dropped the phone and sobbed. Suicide … *suicide? How could that possibly even be true? How could he go by suicide?* There just seemed no way that it could possibly be.

But it was true. While mowing his lawn, he waved at his neighbor before he went into the garage and shot himself in the head. Just like that. When the neighbor finished mowing his own lawn, he wandered over to investigate Mark's still-idling mower; that's when he found him.

No one knew about Mark's severe depression. Not Lowell, not me, not any of his friends—no one except for his partner, and even he didn't know the full extent of it.

I spoke at Mark's funeral, too.

The loss of Mark so soon after Laura hit me incredibly hard. I couldn't breathe for what felt like months. If someone who was as rock solid as Mark was with eighteen years sober killed themselves, then what chance did I possibly have? Relapse suddenly seemed like much more of a possibility. And if I relapsed, just how far away was suicide, really? I was terrified I could suffer the same fate. I went to meetings every day, frightened of what would happen if I didn't. I talked to my sponsor, worked with new women, and went back to the stories of the elephants, but I was unsettled in a way I'd never been before.

It felt like my grief around the sudden loss of Mark so soon after Laura would consume me, and I realized the earthquake Mark warned me about only a few months earlier was now upon me rocking me all the way to the core.

∞

"Why don't you be our speaker?" he asked in a very rough, demanding, New York sort of way.

"No, I can't. There's no way. I wasn't even here on 9/11."

"Well that's a good thing because this doesn't have anything to do with 9/11. Are you or are you *NOT* an alcoholic?"

"Yes, I am but—"

"Do you have more than two years sober?"

"Yes."

"That's it then. Suck it up and do some service. *YOU'RE* our speaker." I ran to the bathroom and threw up.

When Carrie suggested we leave town for somewhere neither of us had ever been, I jumped at the chance. It had been a depressing year, and the timing couldn't have been better, since I had just quit my job as a leasing agent. Neither of us had ever been to New York. We wondered why the tickets we purchased were so cheap until we realized we would be in the heart of Manhattan for the one-year anniversary of 9/11.

On our first day, after we got checked into the "largest hostel in the world" (according to the website), we jumped on the subway. Unsure of where to go, we got off at the spot closest to the river. We immediately noticed each cobblestone street we turned down had another building under construction. When I mentioned this out loud, someone on the street pointed at one construction zone in particular. "That's where the towers stood."

We were right there and didn't even know it. As we got closer, we noticed an eerie silence interrupted only by the construction sounds around us. There was still a flag, battered and torn, hoisted atop a pile of rubble and tied to a massive, snarled piece of metal. I remember seeing that on TV.

Finally, we looked at our meeting schedule and noticed there was one right around the corner. It was a group that had a different meeting for each of us, perfect since we were looking forward to going to meetings in a new city.

Outside of the building was a row of black sedans lined up, drivers waiting. The meeting was larger than what I was used to and full of financial guys from Wall Street, which I didn't know at the time was only a block away.

Every day for a week, Carrie and I split off at the front door, finding our way to our own meetings, until the anniversary of 9/11 was upon us. That morning we met up with Tim, a friend of Carrie's, who'd been caught off guard by the first explosion as he walked to work in lower Manhattan on that fateful day. As the events of that morning began to unfold, he took pictures, trying to make sense of the chaos erupting around him. We retraced his steps as he held up a picture of each place where he'd stopped, revealing the landscape of only a year before. It was surreal.

We made our way down to the meeting through throngs of people from all over the world. The city buzzed to the sound of bagpipes and fighter jets roaring overhead. Since half of the streets were closed due to the president's arrival, we got to both of our meetings early.

When the gruff gentlemen insisted I be the speaker that day, I was in the midst of helping some guy make coffee before the meeting, lost in my own thoughts. As I made my way to the podium on top of the tiny raised stage, I shook in terror. If I thought the room was packed before, today it seemed ten times the size. It was standing-room only, and people just kept coming. Even though I heard alcoholism had run rampant through the firefighting community, I wasn't prepared for firefighters from all over the world to enter the room in groups of three or four. Then police officers began to arrive and the room looked like an event for the emergency response community.

There was a wall in the back of the room covered with pictures of faces from floor to ceiling. It didn't dawn on me that the faces on that wall were the members of that group who'd died in the towers until I saw the line of people tenderly touching the images of their friends before they took their seat. I would learn later there were sixty-three pictures on the wall for the sixty-three members of that group who'd died in the towers … *the average size of a herd of elephants.*

To my surprise, when the meeting was about to begin, a group of ten firefighters sitting in the front row introduced themselves as being from Hood River, Oregon, a short distance from Portland. Just when I think the world is so large, I am reminded once again of just how small it is.

I gazed at the back wall so I couldn't see the crowd and began to tell my story. I knew not to talk about 9/11 or the events of that day, and when the meeting was open for others to speak, not one person shared about it either.

After the meeting, I was approached by a German firefighter who'd acted as an interpreter for the men who came with him. He told me he was going to retell my story to the men he brought. Just being in the presence of people suffering from alcoholism made them feel better. I understood that. Each one squeezed me tighter than the next as they thanked me, "Danke, danke," in German. Then I heard the very same thing from a Japanese firefighter, who also had several firemen with him who didn't speak English either.

As Carrie and I silently walked down the street from the meeting, we heard a loud *swoosh* overhead. We looked up to see an enormous banner dropped from the fifteenth story of a building that read *The City of Hope.* We both stopped on that crowded sidewalk and just stared at it. Somehow looking at that sign and thinking about all of the stories I'd heard over the course of that week made the losses I felt with Mark and Laura pale in comparison. Being in a city dropped to her knees by unimaginable devastation gave me the hope and strength I needed to get through my own sadness. It felt like I had taken my first steps into the light as the darkness of the past few months began to lift.

Three months later, I took my place at the head table at Sunset to lead the meeting on my fifth sober anniversary. Halfway through the meeting, a gentleman I had never seen before stood up and explained he had traveled from the East Coast to visit his family. His group was the same meeting I had spoken at in New York three months earlier. He carried a five-year coin blessed by all the members of that group, many of whom I remained in touch with, all the way from that meeting in Manhattan.

When he gave me the coin and a massive hug, I completely lost it. It was hard to imagine a greater gift. I somehow made it through my most awful days in sobriety, and getting that coin made me realize just how grateful I was to be a part of a program I once totally despised. I carried that coin with me for the next several years as a reminder of one of my favorite passages in the first edition of the Big Book that reads:

"No matter how black the night, the stars are always shining."

CHAPTER 19

Warming blankets were put over the young, orphaned
elephants each morning, but each time a keeper tried
to put a red blanket over Edo, he ran away, screaming in panic, followed in hot pursuit by Dika, Eleanor, and one
of the keepers. Daphne knew the combination of the red blanket
and Edo's fear of a newly rescued sheep suggested it was the Maasai tribesmen he was most likely afraid of.

The Maasai people are the resident sheep and cattle herders
in the area of Kenya from which Edo was rescued. For thousands
of years, they coexisted peacefully with the elephants. Instead of
killing them, they held elephants in the highest regard; the Maasai
believed elephants possessed a soul as they did. The Maasai elders
spoke of stories passed down through generations that elephants
were once human themselves, and because of a shared human
trait, vanity, they were given beautiful white tusks to display as any
human would their finest jewels. In a historic twist of fate, it became
the vanity of humans, including the Maasai, that condemned elephants to their fate. Ivory brokers began recruiting Maasai warriors
to do their killing for them, paying what was, for a Maasai man,
an enormous sum of money. The solemn understanding between
elephants and the Maasai vanished like the setting sun.

As stories emerged about elephants acting fearfully whenever they came across the Maasai, it became clear that the trusted bond between the elephants and the Maasai that held for centuries had indeed been broken. Years after Edo's rescue, elephant researchers Dr. Lucy Bates and Dr. Karen McComb, collaborated with another woman whose work I deeply admired, famed elephant researcher Dr. Joyce Poole, while they conducted two revealing experiments with elephants and the Maasai in the same region where Edo was rescued. Dr. Bates wanted to see if it was merely the scent of the Maasai that elephants detected and therefore afraid of, or if it was the distinct color of red worn by the Maasai that the elephants reacted to.

The results of her research made me catch my breath.

In that series of experiments, Dr. Bates and her team discovered that a piece of cloth worn by a man from a tribe that rarely kills elephants caused the wild elephants to react with mild alarm. The group moved a slight distance away but as a whole remained relatively calm. However, a piece of cloth worn by a Maasai man caused the elephants to react with great fear, moving quickly to get as far from the cloth as they could.

Even more interesting was what happened when elephants were able to *see* the different colors of the cloths. Dr. Bates chose a white cloth, which had no significance, and a red cloth, which was the same color traditionally worn by the Maasai; neither cloth had been worn and was therefore completely free of human scent. The white cloth elicited nothing more than a playful response from the group of wild elephants. They tossed it around and played with it for a few minutes but showed no great interest in it. The red one, however, caused an entirely different reaction. Several members of the group acted aggressively toward the cloth, tusking at it and charging toward it.

"When there was a Maasai-associated object but no actual people, they took the opportunity to get angry," Dr. Bates concluded. It was merely the color that drew a reaction from the elephants.

Dr. Bates and her team discovered that elephants were indeed using their powerful sense of smell, as well as their vision, to determine the seriousness of the threat. This explained why Edo began shaking in terror whenever he saw the color red or the harmless sheep. To him, both of these likely indicated extreme danger.

Professor McComb decided to take her elephant experiment one step further. She wanted to see if elephants could also determine the differences between languages, specifically the language spoken by the Maasai and the language spoken by a less threatening tribe. Was it possible that elephants were actually *that* smart?

The experiment she, Dr. Graeme Shannon and her team conducted revealed something entirely novel. Reacting to voice recordings of a Maasai man and another man speaking the same sentence in their respective languages, elephants once again stunned everyone. They formed a defensive bunch and retreated in great haste when they heard the Maasai man talking. But when they heard the recording of the man from a tribe that rarely harmed elephants, they were more likely to put their trunks in the air to detect the scent, but they did not retreat as they did from the Maasai.

The researchers then wondered if gender also played a role, so they recorded a Maasai woman speaking the same sentence as the Maasai man. Since Maasai women rarely killed elephants, they wanted to see if this made a difference. *And it did.* The elephants didn't retreat at the voice of the woman the same way that they did at the man's. In the last part of their experiment, the researchers used a voice recording of a young Maasai boy's voice. Once again, the elephants reacted with less fear to the voice of the Maasai boy than they did to the voice of the Maasai man.

These experiments revealed that elephants were not only able to determine a threat based on scent, color, and language, but they could also distinguish between genders. I wondered how the young elephants were getting this information so early in life; Edo was only six months old when he was rescued. But Professor McComb explained to me that the young elephants were likely "strongly influenced by social learning." The adults were showing the younger ones what was most crucial for their survival, likely soon after they were born.

Edo would gradually adjust to the presence of the sheep, though he always made sure to put as much space between himself and them as he could. He would never, however, get over his fear of the color red.

∞

One of Mishak's first big tests came soon after the rescue of Edo and Dika in the early morning hours of a cold April day. A frantic call came in that a herd of elephants was surrounded in a field by an angry mob hell-bent on killing them all. As they descended on the terrified group, panic set in and elephants scattered in all directions. In the confusion, baby elephants were separated, and the mob set in to kill the easiest targets.

Someone raised an alarm signifying an urgent rescue. The men immediately stopped what they were doing and like a well-orchestrated army leaped into the back of waiting trucks. Milk, medicine, and supplies were furiously thrown at them by those who stayed behind as they sped to Wilson Airfield. Mishak had no idea what he was about to witness, but the chaos of the scene on the way to the airport suggested mayhem.

Mishak, along with the men, arrived at the most horrific scene they had ever witnessed. As he leapt out the back of a truck, Mishak saw a man with a machete chopping at what he thought was a large wooden log. As he got closer, he realized it was a dead baby elephant. He ran with the men to the far side of the field, where a small crowd of people surrounded two more baby elephants. They began pleading with them to stop. As the keepers argued with the men, Mishak and another keeper descended on the two lifeless gray forms lying in the heavy grass.

The tiny bull had been badly beaten over the head with a heavy club, and a basketball-sized lump formed on one side of his head. He was unconscious but alive. The young female was screaming and bleeding profusely, having been slashed by another machete, but she, too, was alive. The men got to work to stop her bleeding as a long negotiation took place. They looked for any other survivors but found none. Eventually the mob backed down and agreed to let the men take the young elephants.

The two three-month-old elephants, named Ndume and Malaika, were from a group of forest elephants locked inside the Imenti Forest. Their old migration route had been cut off by human settlement, leaving them imprisoned in a forest that couldn't support them. The only chance the herd had was to come out under the cover of darkness and forage for food in nearby fields.

The little gray form of unconscious Ndume was placed on a soft bed of hay with an IV hooked to his ear while they focused on treating and stitching Malaika's wounds. She stopped screaming as she realized the men were trying to help her, but then she began to shake violently. Shock set in and everyone grew more concerned. Eleanor entered through an adjoining stall that had a wall short enough she could easily reach over to touch and console her. Edo and Dika went straight into Ndume's stall and hovered over him during the chaos.

If the keepers were not able to control Malaika's shock, she would have little chance of survival. Mishak spoke gently to her and tried to get her to take some milk while Eleanor rumbled in the background.

"Come on, little angel," he coaxed. *Malaika* means "angel" in Swahili.

The sound of his voice seemed to calm her, and eventually she began to quiet. She inspected Eleanor's trunk, seemingly shocked that such a large elephant was surrounded by men. But Eleanor had the effect they'd seen countless times before. A few hours later, with her wounds properly bandaged, she watched as Edo and Dika took the milk that was offered to them in front of her as if to show her how it was done. When Mishak offered her a bottle, she drank it until it was empty, and everyone knew she'd survived the worst.

Malaika's stall looked like a hospital ward with all the bandages and tubing. Luckily the machete had missed the main tendons in her legs, which if cut would have prevented her from walking again, but the cuts she did have were deep and she needed constant medical attention.

The wild fear in Malaika's eyes was slowly replaced with sadness as her connection with Mishak grew stronger. Malaika stayed close to him, never letting him leave her side. Baby elephants are in constant touching contact with their mothers, and Mishak filled that role for her.

With such a severe head injury, Ndume was not expected to wake up, but a few days after their arrival, everyone was jolted awake by the unmistakable screams of a wild baby elephant. To their surprise, Ndume had awakened from his coma and begun climbing the wall of his stall to get to Malaika, who poked her trunk through a tiny slat to touch him. The lump on his head had shrunk considerably, a good sign, and he was let into Malaika's stall even though she was still covered in bandages. She, along with the other orphans, surrounded him in an attempt to comfort him.

After spending a few moments with Malaika, Ndume burst out of the stall and ran to one end of the compound, bellowing loudly. He then stopped and spread his ears wide as if he were listening for a signal from his lost family. The other orphans chased after him, but before they caught up, Ndume ran to the other end of the compound repeating the episode again and again. The orphans continued to try to coax him back to the stall, but Ndume only stopped when he collapsed in exhaustion. The keepers then collected him, put him on a blanket, and carried him back to his stall. Every few hours, he woke up and repeated the entire episode as the keepers waited again for his inevitable collapse. For days it continued as the keepers watched him run back and forth, until finally he just ran to the edge and stood completely still.

His ears no longer spread to listen for a call he seemed to finally understand wasn't coming. The keepers watched as his tiny trunk lay gently on the ground and his body slowly swayed from side-to-side. Malaika, bandaged and healing, left her stall and joined him in that spot. She, Dika, and Edo, laid their tiny trunks on him and comforted him in the way only another elephant can.

The elephant grieving process is similar to that in humans; no one knows how long it takes, and it can differ for each individual. Like Dika, Ndume and Malaika needed time to mourn the loss of their families. For weeks they stayed by themselves, always just outside the circle from the other orphans. Dika appeared to understand their depression and became exceptionally attentive to their needs. Eventually they turned a corner, and as each day passed, they seemed to pull a little further away from the horror they were rescued from. Ndume never showed any residual effects from his head injury, and in spite of her deep lacerations, Malaika healed so well one could scarcely tell she had ever been severely injured.

Nine years later, Ndume followed Edo and Dika to join a herd of wild elephants, but Malaika remained behind to become one of the matriarchs. With so many orphans to care for, including young Emily and Aitong, whose awful head injury caused her to walk in circles, Malaika was kept busy. During all that time, her bond with Mishak never wavered, remaining as strong as when he saved her life. The "little angel" was known as his first and favorite rescue.

CHAPTER 20

*F*or *years* I was the self-described "whitest white girl," and had tried numerous spray and airbrush tans, each time turning one weird shade of orange after the other. After I had an airbrush tan that gave me my first realistic looking suntan, a whole new world opened up to me. Getting the perfect tan, or even a tan at all, was something I'd always dreamed of. Even a whisper of sun burnt my skin to a crisp. I joked that my skin was so translucent you could see all the way through to the other side. Finally, after learning that it *was* possible to get a natural-looking airbrush tan, I decided to take matters into my own hands and buy my own airbrush tanning system. I thought if I could discover how to make my own skin look like a natural suntan, then it would surely be a hit for anyone as white as I was.

With little idea of what I was doing, I opened up my first airbrush tanning location in Portland's Pearl District, inside a booming salon called Amoré. It took nearly a year of experimentation before I figured out the *what* and the *why* of people turning orange, but eventually I did. Once I was able to produce the most realistic, perfect, airbrush tan, my business flourished beyond my wildest expectations.

A year later, I opened my second location in Lake Oswego, one of Portland's wealthiest suburbs, and began making more money than I'd ever dreamed. I had six years sober and purchased my first home in the Alberta Arts District, a trendy part of Portland. It was hard to believe my good fortune as I filled up my newly renovated, three-thousand-square-foot home with expensive furniture, artwork, and clothes.

Even though I was still sober, I stopped going to as many meetings, stopped working with as many sober women, and began to float further away from the program that had given me such a brilliant second chance. Without my even realizing it, the black hole that felt like it would consume me when I first got sober grew. Several years passed until I couldn't remember the last time I'd thought about the elephants. I was too busy building what I thought was an amazing career, accumulating the "things" I was sure would make me happy.

I had no idea that the life I built was hanging by a thread until one day everything came crashing down. The airbrush tanning industry, up to that point, had been largely unregulated. Two other airbrush tanning business owners and myself went to the Oregon Department of Cosmetology to begin the conversation in order to create a safe industry. They wanted us to have esthetician licenses, but we argued against that. Since our only trade was airbrush tanning, it made no sense that we had to spend five thousand dollars and five months in school to learn how to wax eyebrows and perform facials. We argued for regulation, but regulation that made sense.

Since there wasn't a beauty school in the state that taught airbrush tanning, I offered to institute a program. Eventually, the state board said the three of us would be grandfathered in since we already had existing businesses. Everyone else who started an airbrush tanning business after the first of the year would have to get an esthetician license. I checked in with the board in July to be safe so there would be no unexpected surprises. But I was wrong.

It is a strange feeling to be the last batter in a championship game with a full count and the bases loaded. The pressure of a situation like that is intense. It can be so overwhelming that even the most talented athletes crumble. I always had a solid batting record. Even though it was rare for a fastpitch pitcher to also be a good batter—I was. By studying the feet and hands of my opponent, I could usually tell what was coming before I ever stepped into the batter's box. In the pinch of the final inning of a championship game, I always knew my team could rely on me when my turn at bat arrived. My teammates would line the cyclone fence, screaming at the tops of their lungs—adrenaline pumping. The crowd would rise from their seats and I become even more focused on the task in front of me. The screaming around me replaced with only the sound of my breath as I slowly put one foot in the batter's box and stare down my opponent. I would read her every move before putting both feet in and hearing the umpire behind me yell, "Play ball!"

But this time, I could not read my opponent. The events that unfolded reminded me of the pressure of standing in that batter's box. I was given a shot at bat, but for the first time, as far back as I could remember, no matter how hard I studied her, I could not figure out what pitch she was going to throw next. And just like that—I choked.

In November of 2005, I was summoned to a meeting under the impression I would be given my license. The explanation given was the board had simply changed its mind, no one would be grandfathered in, and if I didn't go to school to get my license, I was operating as an illegal business. *Strike one.*

Then I found out the beauty schools had decided not to implement an airbrush tanning program in any of their schools. The spray-tan industry, in which a client stands in a booth and pushes a button that sprays them, was left completely unregulated. I was infuriated and knew I had been duped, but by then it was too late to get the license I needed to stay open. The deadline was December 31, less than two months away. *Strike two.*

A few days after the hearing, I received more bad news. The landlord where I consolidated both of my locations informed me they would not be able to provide insurance if I was not on site at all times, preventing me from hiring an employee to take over while I went to school. The $25,000 airbrush tanning booth I'd built for the space could not be taken apart and put back together in another location. If I wanted to move, I had to completely start over, and I simply did not have the money to do that. The walls began to close around me.

In the end, after I'd spoken with numerous attorneys, we all agreed that though it was incredibly unfair, it was not a battle we could win overnight, and with a massive mortgage and loans, it was one that I did not have the financial reserves to survive. After two months of fighting, no sleep, and the thought of total financial ruin, I was presented with only two choices: Drink or Let Go.

Strike three. The game was over.

That experience made me realize that *thinking* about losing everything is quite a bit different than *actually* losing everything. It was the *thinking* about losing everything that was the hard part. Actually losing it meant simply … handing over keys. And I did. I turned over the keys to my beautiful home, the keys to my car, and the keys to my business, and I did it surrounded by the very same women who helped me get sober. They stood beside me and propped me up when I didn't think I could take it anymore. I cried every single day.

To my amazement, the day after it was all over, after I had turned over every last thing I had to debt collectors, I didn't feel devastated. Instead, I felt only relief. With no idea what to do next, I launched myself back into my recovery program the same way I had when I first got sober. I started going to meetings every day and working with every newcomer alcoholic I could find.

The reality was that I wanted to stay sober more than anything. Losing everything at age thirty-three—with nearly nine years of sobriety—and moving back in with my parents was deeply embarrassing. Despite how far we had come and how hard I'd worked to repair my relationship with them, my ego was in control. It was so tightly wrapped around the things I owned and lost that now, for the second time in my recovery, I lost every single thing I owned. Just when I thought things couldn't possibly get any worse, the words of the woman I met in the shelter nine years earlier floated back into my head:

"Things can *always* get worse."

I knew the one thing that would add fuel to this fire was if I drank again—my life would likely be the next thing I would lose.

As I watched the alcoholic women I worked with heal, open up, become happy working members of society, and reach for their dreams, I became inspired to do the same. Slowly, that awful black hole began to shrink. A few months later, I found a good job, rented a home in a quaint area of town called Multnomah Village, and started to feel a sense of normalcy return.

Little did I know that another large wave was about to pound me again: the Great Recession hit in the beginning of 2007, and I was laid off from my fancy job along with the next two after that. The bills stacked up over that year, and my level of desperation increased. Then, out of the blue, a friend told me about a class I could take at the local community college in exchange for free health insurance for one year. It sounded too good to be true, but I signed up anyway. I had no idea that one simple act would put my life on a trajectory even I couldn't possibly imagine.

∞

In our first meeting, I realized we were a classroom of down-on-our-luck individuals, each with a personal story about loss due to the recession. One of our assignments midway through the semester was to meet with Casey Sims, the instructor and a college counselor, to find the best path back to work.

"So what do you want to do?" Casey asked as I took a seat in his office.

"I just want a job," I said, feeling nearly as overwhelmed as I had been a year earlier when I lost everything. I was distracted by an unopened bill covered in red writing by my front door. It was from the electric company, and I knew a secret date was hiding inside. The days of having power in my home were numbered.

"That's it?" Casey reminded me of Hulk Hogan without the muscles. He was tall, had kind eyes, a handlebar moustache that dipped below his chin, and he wore a flat, black hat like cab drivers wore.

"Pretty much." The office we were sitting in was small, and Casey's desk was covered in stacks of paper. I wondered how he knew where anything was. There was a guitar case propped up behind his desk and framed credentials on which I could vaguely see his name, hung in an uneven row across one wall.

"Come on, you can do better than that. What would you do if you could do anything?"

"I don't know. I just want to be able to pay my bills."

Casey prodded me with more questions I found myself unable to answer until he finally said, "I'll tell you what. I am giving you an assignment that I want you to bring back next week. Write down on a piece of paper what it is you wanted to be when you were eight years old."

"Seriously?" It was the stupidest idea I had ever heard.

"Yes, seriously."

Contemplating the assignment later, I was struck by just how hard that question was to answer. I hadn't thought about what I actually *wanted* to do for so long I nearly lost touch with my dreams, hopes, and desires. I'd worked what felt like a million jobs since getting sober: flower arranger, waiter, pasta maker, landscaper, property manager, leasing agent, business analyst, recruiter, entrepreneur—you name it, I tried it. Still, I sat there thinking about what it was that I *really* wanted, unable to put my finger on the one thing that had escaped me for so long.

But when it came time to put pen to paper, I wrote it down before I had even realized what I had written. There it was … staring back at me on that blank piece of paper, the one name that changed everything.

Eleanor.

CHAPTER 21

*A*s soon as I wrote the name Eleanor on that piece of paper, something inside me awakened. I ran to my attic and frantically rummaged through my old boxes for all the elephant research I'd collected over the years, piling it high on my dining room table. I couldn't wait to learn what had happened during my time away.

It had been so long since I looked at any of it. *Too long.* Suddenly, I was dying to pick up where I left off and find what happened to my elephant friends while I was busy being distracted by the accumulation of material things, which, I realize now, had very little importance to me compared to the elephants.

∞

Eleanor's life had gone into alarming upheaval, oddly mirroring my own. Kenya had been given its independence only a few years earlier, in 1963. All the positions previously held by English Kenyans were quickly filled with Kenyan Kenyans. David and Daphne received notice they were to move back to Nairobi, over two hundred miles from Tsavo. The move meant they would have to leave *all* of the orphans, including Eleanor, behind. I couldn't even imagine what hell that must have been. I wondered what Eleanor thought as they drove away, leaving her with the remaining orphans. *Did she know they weren't coming back?* I was deeply saddened as I learned what happened, but I flipped through the pages even faster, trying to absorb everything laid out in front of me.

David and Daphne were given a house on the edge of Nairobi National Park and allowed to receive regular updates as to what was happening back in Tsavo with their orphans. The new wardens in Tsavo, those that took over David's old position, noticed almost immediately how "tame" Eleanor was, and soon after the Sheldricks left she was trucked each day to one of the busy tourist roads to make some quick cash. I was so sad to learn that Eleanor's days in captivity were not all behind her. Poachers noticed almost immediately that the management of the park had changed and began re-entering with startling frequency. One day, more than sixty elephants were gunned down; the keepers ran to see if they recognized any of the victims. To their horror, they found one of their orphans, who'd been seen hanging out with a wild herd, was now one of the lifeless bodies strewn across the landscape.

Then, inside one of the many books laid open before me, I discovered a most interesting story from more than thirty years ago. It was not much as far as stories go, but it was one that meant everything to me. Two men were going from country to country with official papers, a grant of more than one hundred thousand dollars from the American Ford Foundation, and a need to kill elephants.

"It is for science," they said.

In order to do their work, they needed the eye lenses and uteruses of elephants. But there was another story unfolding like a coveted secret in between the pages of the one I was reading. David and Daphne knew what it was long before anyone else. The men were becoming quite rich going to each country with their

papers. The ivory from each elephant they were killing *in the name of science* disappeared.

In 1966, a messenger came with a warning that "the scientists" had wreaked havoc in neighboring Uganda and were headed to other countries with large populations of elephants. By the time they made their expected appearance in Kenya, which had the largest population of elephants in Africa at the time, the Sheldricks were ready.

It was no secret that elephants did enormous damage to the landscape—scientists feared the land would soon become a barren desert if elephants weren't removed as soon as possible. But David wasn't so sure. Though it was clear the landscape had gone through a massive transformation, he felt it better to take a "wait and see" approach instead of taking matters into his own hands. He had seen plenty of examples of man messing with Mother Nature only for the outcome to be far worse than if man had simply left the situation alone. After all, elephants had roamed the planet nearly as long as humans. It made him wonder what would happen if the *men* simply stayed out of it.

Initially the Sheldricks thought it was strange that the scientists needed to study eye lenses and uteruses of dead elephants when the identified problem was one of landscape. But the true motive revealed itself when, to their dismay, the Kenyan government allowed the men to kill three hundred elephants as a "sample study," in what would become Kenya's first elephant cull. Instead of allowing the people of the land on which the elephants were killed—or the local government—to take ownership of the ivory, Wildlife Services, a private enterprise, argued that since they did the killing, they should be the owners of the ivory ... and so it was.

This infuriated David and Daphne; they felt certain the money gained in the operation would lead to massive corruption. That fact was confirmed when the owner of Wildlife Services, Ian Parker—who'd been tasked with killing the three hundred elephants—showed up in a brand new Cessna 185 airplane, painted black with ominous orange wingtips. When David met him at the airfield, Ian nodded back to the airplane with a beaming smile on his face and said:

"Your elephants."

The Sheldricks knew this saga was likely only the beginning, and their worst fears were confirmed when the lead scientist, Dr. Laws, made a claim that he had identified ten different elephant populations in Kenya, something no one had proven and certainly not by someone who had never spent any time observing elephant populations there.

David had spent more than twenty years watching the ebb and flow of elephant populations and recognized they practiced what is called a fission-fusion society. One elephant or a group may be seen with one elephant herd on one day and then with an entirely different group more than twenty miles away the next. They constantly blended in between groups across incredibly long distances. The motive, however, for the scientist to insist on there being ten different populations, was that he would simply get to harvest the ivory of three thousand elephants instead of only three hundred.

There was only one way for David to go—his conscience could bear no other. He was the only one who could speak for the elephants that could not speak for themselves; this he knew. When the officials refused to listen, David did the only other thing he could think to do: he threatened to voice his concerns publicly. Kenyan government officials summoned him immediately, along with Dr. Laws and his team, to a government office in Nairobi.

David pointed out that the study could hardly be conclusive

without a botanist involved, since the original point was to determine the damage the elephants were inflicting on the landscape. In the end, it was David's passionate concern that made all the difference to the government officials. When Dr. Laws tried to pressure the decision-makers by threatening to leave the project altogether, the choice was easy. Dr. Laws and his team were kindly escorted out of the country, and the lives of those three thousand elephants were spared.

David was given the reins to the Tsavo Research Project and allowed to hire whomever he saw fit. He, along with Daphne and several of his colleagues, set up the Tsavo Research Committee with a clear intention that any scientific study done in the park from that point forward had to be relevant to the problems they faced in the park.

Dr. Phil Glover, a renowned botanist with extensive experience working in Africa, was chosen to lead the team. He went to work with a host of other scientists to determine once and for all the number of separate elephant populations within the park. He and David's first order of business was to radio-collar the elephants, which proved that David's theory about elephants living in a fission-fusion society was in fact the correct one. The female and male elephants they collared moved enormous distances due to food sources, rain, or simply because they felt like it. Years later, when scientists were finally able to use DNA as a way to determine elephant identities, it was proven just how difficult it was to settle on which family group was where.

Dr. Glover's work on the ecosystem in the areas of Tsavo that were most damaged by elephants showed something even more impressive. He focused on an area by the Galana River that had been literally leveled by the elephants. What was once expansive and unbearably thick underbrush had been reduced to a massive field of dirt, as the elephants had ripped out every tree as far as the eye could see. But as soon as the first rains hit, the field of dirt was suddenly replaced with long, lush grasses. With that transformation came a multitude of species including buffalo and lions, as well as the Oribi and Topi antelope, all of which depend solely on grasslands, and none of which had ever been seen in the region before.

Just as David thought, Mother Nature's plan was more perfect than any man could have devised. Had the elephants all been killed, as was proposed by those convinced by Dr. Laws and his colleagues, it seemed all of the animals, and therefore the region itself, would have suffered even more extensively, as there would have been no grasslands *and* no elephants.

Instead, David's ideas about elephants and the impact they had on the environment were correct. Mother Nature, however, proved in the years to come that though perfect in so many ways, she could also be unbelievably cruel.

By 1971, the region was in the grip of the worst drought in recorded history, and a staggering number of elephants died a slow and agonizing death. Each day, the number column in David's notebook recorded the deaths in ever higher numbers as he flew over Tsavo. It affected everyone who loved elephants, but none more so than David, who came face-to-face with the suffering on a daily basis. By the end of that year, when the rains finally came, ending the drought, Tsavo had lost nearly six thousand elephants … double what Dr. Laws wanted to kill in the first place.

An influx of ivory hit the market, not just from the elephants that died of natural causes due to the drought but from companies such as Wildlife Services, which were hired in other countries to kill large numbers of elephants. They quickly sold all the ivory they collected, whetting the appetite of everyone who wanted in on the action.

America's insatiable appetite for ivory was on an upswing. The land of liberty had held the top spot for ivory consumption for most of the nineteenth century. The rise of slavery brought ivory right along with it, destined for two sleepy Connecticut towns: Deep River and the aptly named Ivoryton. The ivory-carving shops employed most of the townspeople in one way or another, and like well-oiled machines they pumped out ivory combs for the Victorian age, knitting needles, billiard balls, and millions upon trillions of ivory piano keys.

But China would make her place in history known, overtaking the United States as the largest consumer of ivory in the twentieth century. The rich white American hunters never faded far from the picture, nor did the United States desire for white gold. Blaming China for all things ivory only made it easier for America to get away with slaughtering elephants on a massive scale.

Just as the drought in Kenya ended, poaching escalated to levels never seen before. Only this time the men who entered the park did so with sophisticated machine guns, and the elephants who had survived the drought were under attack all over again. David fought against them with everything he had, but in the end, his health could take no more.

By the time he realized the pains in his chest were indeed a massive heart attack, it was too late, and on June 13, 1977, exactly one month before my fifth birthday, another great warrior was laid to rest. David died the way most champions do—selfless and courageous. To me, David Sheldrick died the greatest hero. Reading the ending of his story made me feel as though he died yesterday: I was devastated and cried harder than I had in years.

He always believed it was his duty to let all wild creatures remain that way, and that humans had no business forsaking the future of any animal for the cheap thrill of watching the unnaturalness of one in a cage. Nor was he guilty of practicing what philosopher Peter Singer termed "speciesism," which values one species (such as man) over another. In his eyes, any animal had as much right to go about their life as he did. He had seen elephants suffer unspeakable cruelty at the hands of humans—Americans placed higher value on a tusk than on an elephant needing its face.

I sat at that table for hours reading through all of the material. *With one less protector defending the elephants, what on Earth would they do?* I could do nothing but cry. David was only fifty-seven when he died. *So incredibly young.* By the time my eyes reached the final page of that story, I was thirty-four.

I flipped through article after article, piecing more of the story together, frantically trying to find out what happened to Daphne and Eleanor after David's death.

With poaching reaching epic levels once again, the orphans just kept on coming, one-by-one, gently bringing Daphne back to life when she needed them the most. Eventually, in 1987, ten years after David's death, Daphne created the David Sheldrick Wildlife Trust as a way to continue David's legacy. Today, it is one of the largest non-profits in Kenya, and she, along with her keepers, have rescued and released more than two-hundred elephants (three average-size herds) back into the wild and saved hundreds of others that didn't make it that far.

Over the rest of that weekend I felt in some way that I betrayed my elephant friends by not learning the rest of their stories until then. I didn't know what I could do to help the ones that were left, but it seemed suddenly obvious—clear as a bell, in fact—what my next step would be.

CHAPTER 22

*W*ell, are you going to come in or what?" Casey said when he caught me standing outside his office door. I reluctantly entered and took a seat, my arm wrapped tightly around one of my elephant notebooks.

"Did you do the assignment?"

"Ummm … yeah."

"Let's see it."

But I froze. I just couldn't hand it over right away. The courage I felt so sure of when I walked into his office evaporated on the spot. This was the first time I was admitting to someone other than Laura one of my most treasured secrets: that I had always wanted to work with elephants—not in captivity, not in a zoo, but to get myself in a position to help the friends in Kenya I'd followed since I was eight years old. I felt so vulnerable I could hardly speak.

What if he laughed? What if he thought I was crazy?

But that isn't what happened. Instead, he simply looked at me for a second with an expression I couldn't read and began typing on his computer. His printer spit out a piece of paper he handed me. It said the yearly salary of an elephant researcher in Africa was sixty thousand dollars.

"Would that be enough for you to make if you followed your dream?"

"Sixty THOUSAND DOLLARS?" I couldn't believe what I was seeing. I didn't even know someone could get paid to do something so amazing, but this ... this was completely unexpected. It was *more* than enough.

"Well then you're going to need to get a science degree." He went back to his computer, typing.

"No, that's impossible. I can't do that."

"Why not?" He stopped typing and looked at me.

I felt my face flush. I had always been terrified of math. It felt as if I couldn't read, and I was constantly trying to hide that fact from everyone. I suspected that getting a science degree meant there would be an enormous amount of math involved—the sole reason I buried that dream, too.

"Because ... " I couldn't bring myself to share it. One secret was enough.

"Because—why?"

"Because ... ummm," I tried not to cry, which made me feel even more embarrassed "Because ... I ... can't ... do ... math."

Casey didn't flinch, smile, or look away. He was kind and silently gave me the space I needed to curl up next to my shame. Instead, he just handed me a Kleenex.

"Where do you think you are at in math?"

"What do you mean?"

"Like what grade level ... if you had to guess?"

"I don't know, probably like eighth grade math." Even saying it out loud I didn't quite believe it. I thought I *had* to be better at math than an eighth grader but figured it was best to aim low.

"Well, there's only one real way to tell for sure."

"What? How?"

"You have to take a math placement test."

I gave him every reason I could think of not to take it, but in the end, after what seemed like hours of negotiation, I agreed to take the test. I don't know what I expected. I had no intention of going back to school at age thirty-four. Surely I would be the oldest (and quite likely the dumbest) person on any campus. I didn't even know where to begin to even start that process, so I convinced myself this was just a stupid exercise and I would forget all about it as soon as it was over.

A few days later, I found myself back in Casey's office to hear the results of my test.

"OK, I've got good news and I've got bad news," he said.

"Hmmm ... give me the good news."

"Congratulations! You're not in eighth-grade math."

"Yes! I knew it! I knew I was smarter than an eighth grader." I jumped up and down. Something inside me felt like it was breaking open, and I felt smarter than ever.

"OK, are you ready for the bad news?"

I settled down, "Hit me."

"You're in fifth-grade math."

Everything stopped. I was completely speechless. I was stupider than I thought I was, not smarter. Only a complete dumbass would think otherwise.

"For FUCK'S sake," I wailed.

Before I could go on, Casey continued, "The only problem is that we don't have classes at the community-college level for fifth grade math, so what I can do is get you into an accelerated course to get you up to the eighth grade mark, and then I can enroll you in one of the classes here."

I explained that I didn't have a clue how to go back to school, but he signed me up for a financial aid workshop that weekend.

The following day, right after our class was over, he walked me to the admissions department and introduced me to a woman named Shirley. Once I completed my accelerated math class, Shirley would help me navigate the community college class schedule.

Still unconvinced that returning to school was the right choice, I explained everything to my new sponsor, Ann, who listened patiently as I explained the horrible turn of events.

"I just can't go back to school," I said.

"Why?"

"Because it will take me at least six years of straight math. I will be like forty years old by the time I graduate," I said, thinking she would surely agree. But she said something that stopped me in my tracks.

"How old will you be if you don't?"

She always had a way of saying things that made an enormous amount of sense, but that one—*that one* hit me hard.

How old would I be if I didn't go back to school? Who cares if I were forty, fifty, or even sixty? If it meant that one day I would wake up and be paid to do something I would gladly do for free, what did it matter what age I was? Hadn't I just spent a week devastated to learn about everything I had missed with the elephants, knowing there wasn't a damn thing I could do about it? What if there actually *was* something I could do?

The next day, I enrolled in my accelerated fifth-grade math class.

When I showed up the first day, I thought it was strange when I couldn't find any chairs for grown-ups. They were all made for tiny humans. Then I realized I was the only full grown human in the bunch. Even the teacher looked a day shy of seventeen. I ran away in a panic.

Back at Ann's, I told her what happened, and she did it again.

She put the entire situation into perspective for me, reminding me that in order for me to take a seat in that class full of tiny humans, I would need some humility. She reminded me that I spent the first nine months of my recovery in the same clothes, with no makeup or hair products. She reminded me that I had lived through a very humbling experience not just once but twice when I lost my airbrush tanning business. This ... well, this was cake.

Not exactly, I thought, but I could see her point.

Even though my math tutor was a seventh grader (literally), I learned more about math in that class from that seventh grader than I had in my entire time in school. By the end of that summer, I had turned the corner, gained some much-needed confidence, and decided to become a full-time student once again. It was my fourth try, having been kicked out of my three previous colleges, and even though I felt old and unqualified, I decided to just *DO* and not *THINK*.

I clipped out a picture of Eleanor, David, Daphne, and my two favorite keepers, Edwin and Mishak, and taped them to the inside cover of every book. I needed a constant reminder about what I was doing and why. It was clear that math did not come naturally to me, but I enjoyed learning about it, and when I hit that wall, as I frequently did, I looked at their pictures, dreamed of Africa, and found another math tutor.

Little did I know at the time that it would take two long years of straight math to even get into my first science class. I'm grateful that Casey didn't explain that to me in the beginning, as I don't know if I would have stayed. By the time I did enroll in my first biology class, I had two entire years of taking math every semester, including each summer, and that, by itself, made me feel like *anything* was possible.

CHAPTER 23

*A*fter many years, Daphne was finally able to persuade the new game wardens of Tsavo to allow her to manage the care and well-being of Eleanor once again. Daphne would not allow Eleanor to be taken anywhere against her will from that point forward and knew that if she couldn't be with her in Tsavo, she could at the very least give her back her freedom.

After David and Daphne were forced to leave Tsavo, Eleanor grew close with two wild elephants, Catherine and Diana. Together the two took care of Eleanor's orphans during the day while Eleanor was forced to beg for money along a roadside. Even after their own herd had moved on, Catherine and Diana remained with the orphans until Eleanor could return, which always amazed me. Daphne often wondered about where the two wild elephants came from and what their own stories must have been. The closeness they shared with Eleanor was obvious to everyone.

The three constantly worked together as one cohesive unit, raising the young elephants the same as three human nannies. One day a young orphan named Taru decided to stay out all night and accidentally got lost. Eleanor left the other orphans under the watchful eye of Catherine as she took off in the dead of night to look for him. The following morning she returned with Taru following close behind, the orphan squealing with excitement as he was reunited with the others. He seemed quite relieved to be back in the safety of the herd. How Eleanor knew where he was nobody understood. The humans had searched both by foot and by plane, but it was only the remarkable communication abilities of an elephant that were finally able to locate the terrified youngster.

Eventually, Eleanor began to show the telltale signs of pregnancy, and one day in 1996, at the age of 37, almost without warning, she walked away with Diana, leaving Catherine in charge of her orphans, and simply never returned. For months she remained close to the compound where the orphans could visit her when they were out on their daily walks, but she never returned to the stockades again. Over time she slowly got farther and farther away … until she was gone.

For thirty-three years she stayed behind, raising the orphans with Daphne never leaving when so many others did—never following when the wild herds must have beckoned her to join them. Everyone wondered if it was her pregnancy that made her want to leave. Daphne wondered if perhaps Eleanor questioned where all the orphans had come from and possibly feared that her own baby would be taken from her. Daphne, Mishak, Edwin, and the other keepers were all heartbroken to see her go, even though it had always been the plan, to release *all* the animals they cared for back into the wild—but Eleanor was by far the toughest elephant to let go.

Soon after Eleanor's departure, Catherine left too. To the surprise of no one, she was seen days later in the company of Eleanor and Diana. Malaika took her place as the head matriarch of the mini-herd, with Emily and Aitong as her trusted and faithful nannies. Malaika took her new role very seriously as she helped Daphne and the keepers take care of the newest orphans.

I scoured books, the internet, research papers, and magazine and newspaper articles for any news of an Eleanor sighting, but I found nothing over a span of many years. I wondered how Daphne must have felt. The poaching crisis, paired with another record drought, took a heavy toll on the country's elephants. If I wondered *how* and *if* Eleanor had survived, I could only imagine how concerned Daphne and the keepers must have been.

Ten years after her departure, in early 2006, Eleanor reappeared in the company not only of *three* wild-born babies, but Catherine and Diana as well. The keepers on duty were not the ones who raised her and therefore unable to recognize her. But they knew instantly by her behavior that she must have been an elephant raised by the Trust. Eleanor's family introduced themselves to the orphans in the daily mudbath in Voi, from which she'd disappeared. With Eleanor, was a ten-year-old, clearly the one she had been carrying when she left. There was also a five-year-old and, to everyone's delight, a tiny newborn, instantly adored by all of the orphans. The keepers took pictures of the entire event and alerted Daphne and Angela, Daphne's daughter, immediately, even though they were more than two hundred miles away in Nairobi. Daphne could hardly believe her eyes when she saw the footage of Eleanor, now in her late forties, with such a successful wild family. The fact that she had been able to navigate the wild world after living in captivity for so long shocked and amazed everyone.

Two years later Eleanor made another appearance, and this time Daphne jumped on a plane and hurried to Tsavo to see for herself. Even though Eleanor was a good distance away as the plane landed, she stopped what she was doing and stared in the direction of the landing strip. Her ears stood outstretched and wide as the keepers watched and wondered if Eleanor could possibly know it was Daphne in the distance. Suddenly, without warning, she began walking straight toward Daphne with her three wild-born babies, guarded by Catherine and Diana following close behind. Eleanor outstretched her trunk and rumbled long and deep when the two came face-to-face. There was no doubt in anyone's mind Eleanor remembered Daphne just as Daphne remembered Eleanor, and a most amazing reunion took place between the two.

I flipped between the pictures I had of Daphne and Eleanor in the 1950s and then of their reunion in the late 1990s, reflecting on how strong their bond still was. It was, quite simply, nothing short of spectacular.

∞

I raced across campus to make it in time. My backpack was full of heavy books, and I was completely out of breath by the time I found the classroom. I waited outside the room for a few moments until I could catch my breath. I checked my watch … 12:57. *I had three minutes to spare.*

I opened the door to what I thought would be a packed room but instead found it completely empty. I checked my phone to make sure I was in the right place and waited for the speaker to arrive. Five minutes later, I knew there must be a problem, and I went into the empty hallway to see if there was someone I could ask. Instead I saw the same flier taped to the wall that excited me so much a week earlier. After reading it a few times it suddenly jumped out at me. The talk I was so excited to attend was exactly … *one week earlier.*

"FUCK!" My voice echoed in the empty hallway as I dropped my heavy backpack on the floor.

"Can I help you?" Out popped a head a few doors down.

"Oh—um … " She had startled me, and I was instantly embarrassed by my sudden outburst "I missed the talk. I thought it was today, but it was a week ago and I missed it."

She came out of the room and walked towards me wearing a long rubber apron and heavy rubber gloves. As she got closer, so did the smell. "Was it the talk about the elephants?" she asked.

"Yes," I said breathing through my mouth. The smell was almost more than I could bear. I could hardly concentrate. "It's just that I didn't know there was anyone on campus who studied elephants and that's what I want to study and I totally screwed up the time," I said pointing at the flier on the wall.

She came and stood beside me, looking at the flier. "The talk was given by Matty Holdgate, and it was a really good talk." When she looked back at me, I was plugging my nose. I just couldn't take it anymore. "Oh," she said, backing away "I'm sorry, I didn't realize it was so bad. You just get used to it after awhile."

"Used to what?"

"Dead flesh. I'm Dr. Duffield, the head of the biology department, and we're dissecting a dead baby whale in the other room. Would you like to have a look?"

"No, thank you." I couldn't imagine anything more awful. I was so distracted by the smell that I nearly missed what she said. Dr. Duffield … *THE Dr. Duffield.* She was a living legend on the Portland State University campus and someone I had wanted to meet since I began taking classes there nearly two years earlier. I was instantly embarrassed that I hadn't known who she was moments earlier.

"Oh! You're Dr. Duffield!"

"Yes," she said "You can call me Deb."

I felt like a groupie meeting a rock star and told her of my passion to work with elephants.

"Then I think you should meet Matty."

"That would be great, but is that even possible?"

"Of course it is. I'm his PhD advisor." She handed me a card from her pocket "You just let me him know that I sent you and he will meet with you."

Again, I couldn't believe my luck. A few days later Matty agreed to meet with me, and only days into my junior year at college I was hired as a conservation research associate on a project that was slated to be the largest captive elephant project ever done in North America, with teams of researchers spread across the United States. Our group of three included Matty Holdgate, Dr. David Shepherdson, and me, and our subjects of study were the sleep patterns of captive elephants (both African and Asian) as well as how far elephants moved in captivity. Matty had already collected data on more than one hundred zoo elephants across the United States and Canada. It was my job to prepare all of the raw data for analysis.

A year into the project—having worked hundreds of hours alongside Matty in our office at the Oregon Zoo—he surprised me when he told me that he and Dr. Shepherdson had determined on their preliminary analysis that the sleep portion of the study (the part I had been working on all year) had revealed nothing particularly fascinating. Instead they wanted me to focus on something else. But I *had* noticed something. What it was for certain I wasn't sure, but I convinced Matty to let me continue working on the rest of the raw data over the long three-day weekend. After that, I agreed to return it all, unfinished or otherwise, and not to pursue it any further. Matty decided to run one final analysis on whatever amount of finished data I brought to him after those three days, and that would be the end of it.

I barely slept over that weekend. The amount of data I had left to go through was enormous, but I had completed every last bit by the third day. Bleary-eyed and jacked up on thirty-seven pots of coffee, I handed over everything I had. Later that afternoon I received an urgent text to meet Matty on campus after my last class. He was beaming as he told me that the data had in fact showed something quite peculiar, just as I'd suspected. The Asian elephants in our study were sleeping much longer than captive African elephants. It was quite strange, because until then there had never been any difference identified in the sleep patterns between the two species. We had no idea what it meant. But as we consulted other researchers, we came up with numerous possibilities, the most interesting of which was that African elephants had not been held in captivity as long as Asian elephants due in part to their sheer size. An African elephant is larger than a wooly mammoth and significantly larger than an Asian elephant. Perhaps, we thought, Asian elephants were depressed since they tended to sleep more when separated from family members than African elephants did. In other words, they were simply more used to it. The discussion seemed endless, but the project was no longer abandoned, instead moving full-steam ahead.

At the end of that week I met Matty in our office at the zoo when he told me he had another surprise for me. He said he had spoken to Dr. Shepherdson, and they agreed that since I had worked so hard on the project, they would like to give me appropriate credit. He slid a letter across the table, which read in part:

" ... we have invited Debbie to contribute to writing up the results and being a co-author on the resulting publication."

I was beyond thrilled. To be included on a scientific research paper as an undergraduate is one of the highest honors a baby scientist could hope for. During the previous year, Matty had worked on the elephant project to get his master's degree in biology. However, Dr. Shepherdson suggested that he skip ahead to his PhD because the data we had accumulated was worthy of a much larger degree. Just as I thought my part of the project was ending, Matty asked that I continue working for him and Dr. Shepherdson for another year.

The truth was that I loved the work, but my classes were getting increasingly harder and my time even shorter. The pay varied from semester to semester and was never something I could count on, so I had to work another job on top of everything else. Against my own better judgment I agreed to continue working on the project for another year.

A few months before the end of that second year, just as Matty was finishing up his PhD, he asked to speak to me in his office. What he said to me next became a blur of frustration and anger. He explained that since he and Dr. Shepherdson had consulted so many other scientists, they all wanted to be included as authors on the papers the three of us had worked on. Now there were too many "authors" for my name to be included as one of them. I could barely understand what he was saying. Two years of my life flashed before me. Two years of working side-by-side with Matty, spending hours upon countless hours, all for ... *nothing*. No one else on that project had spent the amount of time that Matty and I did on that research, no matter what their titles were or how many degrees landed behind their names.

Matty explained that it wasn't for nothing. He would mention my contribution to the research in the back of each scientific paper as well as in his PhD thesis. As the tears welled up in my eyes, I felt the distinctive sting of a slap.

I went to Deb, who was now my mentor and told her what happened. I could see her mouth tighten as I told her the story. I'd spent many hours with her too over the course of that year, and she knew first-hand how hard I'd worked.

"How can I possibly call myself a conservation research scientist now?" I asked.

"How can you not?" she said.

"What do you mean?"

"The conditions for calling yourself a conservation research scientist are a) if you have been hired and paid under that title, which you *have,* and b) if you have a science degree, which you *will have* shortly. So that's it then: you *are* a conservation research scientist, whether or not they put your name on any of those papers."

The truth is my relationship with Matty was never the same again. No matter how hard I tried to let it go and move on, my resentment against him grew. It took countless hours of work with my sponsor to finally find peace around that situation, but in the end it ruined what I previously considered a precious friendship.

CHAPTER 24

Sitting in a science classroom, I suddenly realized I had zoned out during the lecture. I became distracted by the pencil sharpener bolted to the front of my desk. There was no using pens during classes like this: since the amount of writing and note-taking was enormous, pencils (and lots of them) were required.

A memory flooded back from my past of an instructor commenting on the amount of pencil shavings covering my desk. After a cocaine binge the night before, I began chewing up my pencils like a beaver chewing down a small tree. My desk was covered in wood particles, and I was already half-way through the third one. That was over twenty years ago.

How did I make it this far? I was in my sixth year of college and getting straight A's, working harder than I had at anything in a long time. My eyes hurt on a daily basis from so much reading, and I was convinced I was killing more brain cells than I was creating. *But I loved it.* Every. Single. Second of it. I loved learning about things I'd never even considered. It felt as if I had only been allowed one television channel, but being in school was like having unlimited access to thousands.

The unmistakable sound of a whale song flooded the room, which was draped in skeletons of marine mammals. The largest was that of a baby blue whale that hung above our heads as a constant reminder of what we were studying.

The putrid smell of rotting flesh yanked me out of my trance and drew my attention to the far side of the room. Dr. Duffield and her lab assistants wheeled out four enormous mounds on gurneys covered in black plastic. Today was the first day of the mandatory lab that went with the lecture. I hadn't bothered to investigate what the lab was when registering for the class. As we were handed heavy rubber aprons with matching rubber boots, eye goggles, nose plugs, and gloves, I began to wonder just what exactly I had signed up for.

The black plastic was pulled from one of the mounds, and my eyes widened. I shoved a huge glob of Vick's up my nose to deal with the stench as the shock set in. I was then handed a small, sharp paring knife while I stared at an incredibly large dead sea lion, which I was apparently expected to dissect from head to toe.

No way, I thought to myself. *No Freaking WAY!* I always considered myself even-keeled when dealing with blood, but this was something else entirely. *Would I throw up? Would I pass out?* We were given instructions on how to cut, where to begin, and what samples to collect. The eight of us were given the task of finding out what, exactly, killed them.

An hour later, I was knee deep in entrails, and I knew my life had taken another unexpected turn. I loved every single minute of this, too. Who knew that I would find something as disgusting as an animal necropsy this invigorating? But it told the most remarkable story. Each necropsy I performed was a journey through the life and death of that animal. You could tell how many babies it'd had and whether it had good or poor nutrition. There were diseases to identify and old shark-attack wounds miraculously healed.

Each time we traced the final moments of a sea lion's life, we found bullets inside each magnificent creature—bullets from angry fisherman littering their lifeless bodies. The death of a sea lion rarely told a different story. The death of an elephant rarely told a different story, either. With each metal clink in the tray, I thought about the researchers in Kenya doing the same thing with their specimens ... the elephants. On opposite sides of the world, we cradled the bodies of endangered species in our laps as we unraveled the final devastating moments of their lives. It was a constant reminder of what I was doing in that marine mammal biology class: learning how to tell the story of life through death.

∞

My eyes really began to bother me, and I had a constant headache during my final month of school. Although my vision had always been perfect, I thought I had better get an eye exam to see what was going on.

I was grateful a Portland State University nurse navigator helped me find an eye doctor just a block off campus. Dr. Gradin put me through a series of eye tests, and as I waited for the eye drops to dilate my pupils, I heard him in the next room speaking to another patient.

Wait ... what? Was he speaking Swahili?

It is the language spoken throughout Kenya and most of Eastern Africa, and I was in my second year of studying Swahili, so I understood bits and pieces of what he was saying. By the time Dr. Gradin returned, I was blind as a bat.

"Were you just speaking Swahili?" I asked.

"*Ndiyo. Nasema Kiswahili. We we je?*"

"*Kidogo* ... just a little. I'm trying to learn," I said "Did you live in Africa?"

"Yes. Nairobi, Kenya, for many years. I went there with my wife on a mission to work in the eye institute to help fix the eyes of children in orphanages. We loved it so much that we ended up staying for seven years and adopted two children."

I wished I could see him as he was telling me this, but he was just a multi-colored blob. Before I could ask any questions, he continued.

"I had some pretty remarkable experiences while I was there, not the least of which was being asked to work on an elephant, of all things."

I felt a cold chill wrap itself around my entire body.

"A colleague and I were asked by a group called the David Sheldrick Wildlife Trust to look at the eyes of a baby elephant they rescued. It was a poor little thing, but we did surgery on him. No one thought the little guy would survive, let alone ever see again, but he did. We went back, and he was happy as could be."

I cried in disbelief at what I was hearing.

"Are you OK?" He gently touched my arm. "Are you in pain?"

"No. No, I'm fine, I mean, I can't see anything, but it's not my eyes. You were the doctor who worked on Ndololo, the orphaned blind elephant. It was you … and … and … Dr. Schwende … Shende … "

"Schwendemann."

"Yes, from the Kikuyu Eye Hospital."

"Yes," he gasped. "That's right. How could you possibly know that?"

"I study elephants. I study the elephants rescued by the David Sheldrick Wildlife Trust. I know everything about Ndololo. He was rescued at just one-month-old, blind in both eyes. His mother had given up all hope and was in the process of burying him with dirt and leaves when he was rescued. When the keepers arrived, she simply stepped aside and let them have him as if she knew they were going to try and help him. They thought he had been spit in the eyes by a cobra, but you and Dr. Schwendemann thought it was most likely genetic."

"Wow. That's all true, although I didn't know the circumstances behind his rescue. That's actually quite … amazing."

Even though I couldn't see him, I could tell he was shocked.

"Do you know what happened to him?" he asked.

"He formed an incredibly tight bond with a keeper named Edwin Lusichi. In fact, he became one of Edwin's favorite elephants."

"Yes," he laughed softly. "I remember Edwin."

"Ndololo followed him everywhere, and his eyes cleared up considerably. He seemed to be able to see light and shapes and everyone thought he would recover completely. You guys did such an amazing job with him."

"I'm glad to hear he's thriving. It was touch-and-go with that little guy, I remember that."

"Unfortunately, he didn't make it. He came down with an infection in his small intestine and died in his sleep completely without warning a few months after his eyes cleared up. It stunned everyone. Edwin and the other keepers were devastated because he was such a gentle, loving elephant. They only found out his cause of death after they did a necropsy."

We sat in the eye exam room and talked about the elephants until my eyes were clear enough to go outside. He couldn't find anything wrong with my eyes other than the fact that I was doing an enormous amount of reading and studying.

When Dr. Gradin told his wife about our remarkable meeting,

she sent me an email with the names of several of their friends in Nairobi and at the Kikuyu Eye Institute so that when I was finally able to go to Kenya, I could contact them if I got into any trouble.

I couldn't even begin to estimate how many eye doctors there were in the city of Portland, but what were the chances I got the opportunity to meet the one who I not only read about years earlier, but who lived in the same city I did? What were the chances that he would have an African client in the next room with whom he was speaking Swahili loud enough for me to hear?

∞

"Go get the elephants for her," Edwin yelled. He knew that if they didn't bring in other elephants to communicate with her, Loisaba would die from severe shock. Edwin also knew they had to act fast since the elephants were far away.

"There," another man yelled from high atop a rock.

"What is he saying?" shouted Edwin.

"The elephants are already coming," replied one of the keepers. "They know she is here."

Edwin climbed to the top of a fence to get a better look. Soon he could see three reddish-brown backs bobbing up and down as they quickly made their way through the underbrush to the stockades. Emily, Aitong, and another young elephant named Mweiga each had their trunks raised in the air as they descended on the compound. Edwin looked back toward Loisaba, who, locked in her own trauma, rhythmically rocked back and forth, tears streaming down her face.

"Open the gates," he bellowed.

Loisaba, severely injured during a poacher's attack on her mother, had a perfectly round bullet hole in one ear, nearly four inches sliced off the tip of her trunk, and she was a strange color of shock-induced green. She was mean and incredibly angry. It was clear she was deeply traumatized upon her arrival and on a mission to kill any man who dared get near her, something easily done by a two-year-old elephant. Only the most athletic keepers were allowed in her stall as she relentlessly charged them.

Two keepers ran to allow the three elephants into Loisaba's stall, and they rushed in, startling her in the process. Emily and Aitong brushed up on either side of Loisaba, rumbling gently while Mweiga hung back and allowed the two older females to use their abilities to calm her down.

The keepers jumped up on the fence next to Edwin and watched the remarkable scene unfold. Loisaba instantly calmed down in the presence of the three elephants. Mweiga slowly reached forward and began inspecting Loisaba's wounds with her trunk. Emily placed her trunk lovingly over Loisaba's back and continued rumbling gently. Edwin wondered what they were saying in their silent transmissions. But the immediate transformation of Loisaba was obvious. Tears continued to flow down her face, but her whole demeanor had softened. One of the keepers accidentally lost his balance, slipping off the fence, but caught himself before falling into the stall.

The noise and sudden movement shocked Loisaba back into the moment, and she screamed, wildly chasing the man as the keepers quickly dragged him out of Loisaba's "kill" range.

"Let's get down and let them be," Edwin said, and the men retreated, leaving the door of Loisaba's stall open so the elephants could go whenever they chose. The trio stayed with her from that point forward.

Loisaba still tried to kill any keeper who got near her, but

Emily was finally able to convince her to take her milk bottle between the slats of a stockade. When a keeper laid a blanket over the top, blocking Loisaba's view of the man on the other side, she calmed down and reluctantly accepted the nourishment.

The keepers knew that Loisaba's trunk injury was devastating. African elephants have two finger-like structures at the tip of their trunks. They can do as much with the two "fingers" as any human can with their thumb and pointer finger. Daphne first became aware of this when Samson and Fatuma figured out how to turn on the water spigots and hose themselves off whenever they chose. Once David accidentally dropped a shilling, the size of a penny, and Samson delicately picked it up off the ground and handed it back to him, stunning David with his dexterity. The keepers also knew that Loisaba would likely never be able to gather the amount of food required for a growing elephant without the use of those two fingers. It was an enormous disability, and one that was becoming disturbingly common among many of the elephants they rescued.

Malaika spread her wings as the new matriarch after Eleanor left, mothering the orphans as Eleanor had and adopting each traumatized survivor, giving them reason to live again. This included Loisaba, named after the ranch from which she was rescued, the place Loisaba witnessed her mother's killing as poachers destroyed her mother's face for her tusks while she was still alive.

Each morning, a long, single-file line of elephants walked through the bush, followed by Mishak and a group of keepers. Malaika was trailed by her favorite nannies, Emily and Aitong and led the group wherever she chose. The keepers never knew where they would go or what wild herds they would mingle with; Malaika just seemed to have an understanding about this each morning when they left.

During the day, the keepers sat high on the rocks overlooking the scene. Lions were nearly always present, and one should never get close to an unpredictable wild elephant. If there were trouble, the men could radio for help and were always available should any of the newer orphans need their presence, which happened often. The still milk-dependent elephants always seemed to know when it was time for their midday feeding and began lining up before the jeeps, loaded with milk, arrived.

In the evening, when the men packed their belongings and climbed down from the rocks, the young elephants unwound themselves from the wild herds and followed the men back to the safety of the stockades. They seemed to understand that being out at night before they were big enough to thwart off a lion attack was unwise. So they followed Malaika once again back to the stockades in the evening where each was tucked in for the night before another day of wild adventure.

∞

I had studied Edwin nearly as long as I had studied the elephants he saved, gleaning tidbits here and there about his life history the same as I had with the elephants I followed. Parts of his story emerged over the years in various documentaries, television series (including several appearances on *60 Minutes*), films, and radio programs around the world, and I recorded every last detail I could find.

Ten years after Mishak came to work for the Trust, Edwin became the head keeper in charge of the men. Both Daphne and Angela made sure each rescue ran as smoothly as possible.

Located in Nairobi, he rescued and raised the youngest elephant orphans until they were two years old. Then he, along with several keepers, prepared and accompanied each group of two-year-olds for their journey to Voi, where the young elephants would spend the next several years intermingling with the older orphans and wild herds of elephants before going back into the wild themselves.

I thought back to Edwin's own story, similar in many ways to my own, and though we were nearly the same age, our upbringing couldn't have been more different. Nonetheless, I was struck that, although oceans apart, two young kids on separate ends of the Earth were irritating their mothers in the same way, rescuing every young creature they came across.

∞

"Mama! Mama!" young Edwin yelled as he ran toward his village. Cradled in his arm he carried a tiny ball of fur.

Juliet stepped outside of the mud house. It was full of heavy, dark smoke, a reminder of their last meal. Food was scarce, and her husband, Totesta, the local Catholic bishop, was forced to find work in Nairobi, a more than eight-hour bus ride from their village. Feeding her six children was always a struggle, but somehow she managed. She bent down to stretch her tired back when she heard Edwin yelling from the end of the road.

"*Nini tatizo, mwana?*" What's wrong, son?

By the time Edwin reached her, he was out of breath. He gently lowered his arm revealing the subject of the alarm. Two tiny bunny ears popped up, exposing the reason behind his urgency. The young rabbit had been attacked, suffered from a badly broken leg and had a deep gash along its back.

"*Anaumiza, mama,*" She's hurt, mama.

Juliet quietly rolled her eyes. *One more mouth to feed.* But she knew there was no sense in arguing with Edwin. He had been saving animals as long as he could walk, and now, at seven, he showed no signs of slowing down. I was also seven when I rescued my rabbit, Petie, and the coincidence between our stories struck me. As Juliet led Edwin past the cows and the chickens behind the house, she went into the small barn and grabbed a handful of hay to use as a cushion for the injured rabbit while Edwin wrapped the leg with twine and a stick so the bone could heal. Her other son, Walter, had discovered an empty weaver bird's nest on the ground earlier that morning and left it in the barn. Weaver birds build extraordinary nests woven from reed, palm fronds, and grass. She grabbed it, as it was large enough to hold the injured rabbit.

A cat's meow broke the silence as a small feline wound its way around Juliet's leg. As soon as Edwin put the rabbit down, he picked up the cat. *Another rescue.* Juliet looked around: mixed in between the cows, chickens, and goats were an odd assortment of animals, from random cats and dogs to a duck Edwin found with a broken wing. Juliet made it clear to him they had nothing extra to feed his mini-orphanage, but Edwin insisted on bringing them all home anyway. She watched him at each meal as he separated his own food into small portions for his growing brood, leaving himself the smallest on the plate.

Edwin loved school, but it wasn't something his family could afford. In Kenya a child can only go to school if they have the necessary fees to pay for a uniform, but Edwin's parents were far from making that kind of money. Juliet heard of an organization called Compassion International, a Christian child sponsorship ministry, and they selected Edwin as a candidate. He was the first one in his family who could attend school, and this changed his life. He was excited to learn English, study math, read, and ... write. It was something his mother had always wanted for herself when she was growing up, but the opportunity never presented itself. Each child learns his or her tribal language when they are born, and then Swahili is spoken as the national language between several countries and most of the tribes. English is taught mostly in school, up until the eighth grade, a remnant and reminder of English rule.

It was Edwin's dream to follow in his father's footsteps and become a bishop. He studied theology for many years, but getting paid enough to survive was another story, and eventually he too moved to Nairobi in order to find work. A friend loaned him a camera, and he discovered he was quite good at taking and selling pictures of tourists. Soon he was able to afford to rent a small unit behind his sister's apartment building, where she worked as a hair dresser in the town of Ongata Rongai; a suburb of Nairobi. That's when I realized Edwin had some hustler in him, too. He may not have used his talents in the same ways I used mine, but I appreciated his ability to think and act on his toes. And like my own destiny, it was a random twist of fate on what appeared to be a normal working day that changed … *everything.*

Edwin was on his way home from a long day of taking pictures in Nairobi. Traffic was awful, and he wondered why they were inching forward at the pace of a snail when a sign on the side of the road caught his attention. *What was it?* he thought. He read it several times before something clicked.

A former boss and friend of his father's, Josphat Ngonyo, heard about Edwin's compassion for animals and asked Totesta to invite him for a visit where he now worked, though at the time Edwin had no idea why. When Totesta shared this with Edwin, he didn't think anything of it—he was too busy selling photographs—but when he noticed he was sitting directly across from the sign where Josphat worked, he pulled his car out of the standstill line of traffic and up a long road that appeared to disappear into Nairobi National Park. Anything was better than sitting in his car for the next several hours.

He parked his car next to several large transport trucks and walked toward a group of small buildings. As he got closer, he realized there were groups of tiny stalls, smaller than any he had seen for cattle. He was wondering what they were for when a man approached.

"*Jambo* ... *'bari gani,*" The man reached out to shake Edwin's hand.

"*Nzuri,* I'm fine, thank you. I'm here to see Josphat Ngonyo, is this where he works?"

"*Ndiyo,* he's down in the field waiting for them." The man pointed. Edwin wondered who *them* was and followed in the direction of the man's gesture.

As he rounded a corner of the path, he suddenly heard strange screaming sounds. There was a small group of men standing on the edge of the field as Edwin approached. He looked in the direction the men were facing, and in the distance he saw a small group of baby elephants emerging from the forest one-by-one and running toward the men. Edwin had never seen an elephant before but knew they could be incredibly dangerous. It was startling to see how calm the group of men appeared to be.

"Edwin!" yelled Josphat who waved in the distance as he handed an enormous bottle he was holding to one of the men he was standing next to. He calmly walked up to Edwin and embraced him.

"I'm glad you came. I told Totesta to tell you to visit and now here you are!"

"*Asante sana*—thank you for inviting me."

"Come with me. I want you to meet my friends." But instead of introducing him to the other men, he walked Edwin straight into the tiny herd of elephants. Edwin had never seen anything like it. Men with wheelbarrows delivered enormous bottles of milk to the men in the field as they fed two to each young elephant. The elephants screamed, rumbled, and shoved past one another, but the men seemed at ease, laughing and pointing out certain characteristics and behavior of some of the young elephants.

Cautiously, Edwin looked back toward the forest. "Where are their mothers?"

"*We* are their mothers now," said Josphat as he handed Edwin a bottle of milk to feed one of the orphans. As the young elephant sucked away at the bottle in Edwin's hand, Josphat explained how they had created a new family for victims of poaching. Edwin could hardly believe what he was hearing and seeing. Even after spending such a short time with the young elephants, he too could see the differences between each one. One appeared more reserved and shy, and another appeared to be incredibly playful, mock-charging the men as they mock-charged back at him, sending the youngster into what appeared to be fits of ecstasy and sending the men into a frenzy of laughter.

Over the course of the next several hours, Josphat explained everything to Edwin as he showed him the entire compound—the David Sheldrick Wildlife Trust—and at the end of that meeting, Josphat introduced him to Daphne Sheldrick, with whom Edwin had an instant connection.

Years later Edwin was asked about his first meeting with an elephant. He paused for a moment and said, "It felt like I had been touched by an angel."

I knew exactly what he meant.

CHAPTER 25

*Y*ou should use the money you've saved for a car and buy a plane ticket to Africa instead," Leslie said one afternoon over coffee "I have a *VERY* strong feeling about this, Debbie Ethell."

Whenever Leslie used my first and last name together, I knew she meant business. She was one of my two best friends, along with Stephanie. We became close during the year after Mark's and Laura's deaths. I met her at Sunset, and she was one of those people that made me wonder how I ever lived without her.

Leslie was my rock through school. She made me promise that *when*—not *if*— I wanted to quit, when I was ready to finally throw in the towel, I was to call her first, no matter what.

"Promise, Debbie Ethell."

So I made that promise. And I did call her many times, wanting to quit. One time I couldn't memorize all the information I needed to in order to get through an intense zoology class. She met me in a park and quizzed me on my note cards for hours. When we were done, I didn't want to quit anymore. Another time, I had an awful chemistry professor who made me feel worthless and stupid—as if I needed any encouragement in those categories. After listening to me bawl my head off for an hour, she suggested I meet with a college counselor to see about alternatives. I hadn't even thought of that. I was able to switch out of that class for another I excelled at, and I forgot about quitting for at least another month.

When my car broke down, she picked me up and took me to class, and after I donated the piece of junk when it wouldn't run anymore, she not only helped me move to a new apartment on a bus line, she also paid for my bus passes until I could afford them on my own.

Leslie had always wanted to go back to school but convinced herself it was too late. I think that's why she worked so hard with me; she couldn't bear the thought of seeing me fail, because it would feel like she failed. Whatever her intentions, I have no doubt that I never would have graduated had it not been for her.

I saved all my money for two years to buy another car once I was out of school, but Leslie's words got me thinking. Dr. Duffield convinced me that the large amount of research I had collected on the elephants in Kenya might be useful to the David Sheldrick Wildlife Trust. So I emailed them. And when I heard nothing, I emailed them again. I did this over and over for a year until Leslie suggested I go there myself and meet them in person. The thought hadn't occurred to me, since I had never traveled anywhere.

I found numerous people who had been to the Trust headquarters in Nairobi, but none of them had actually met the Sheldricks or anyone high up in the organization. When I finally found someone who did, they insisted that since the David Sheldrick Wildlife Trust was one of the largest non-profit organization's in Kenya, I had about as much chance meeting with Daphne or Angela Sheldrick as I would meeting Oprah Winfrey. The situation felt hopeless, but once again, Leslie convinced me otherwise. She suggested I do more research and find out all the information I could, from the price of a plane ticket to where I would stay, before I made my final decision.

Her advice led me to contact a travel agent. I didn't even know how to book an international plane ticket, but since I had recently completed a calculus class and now had nearly six straight years of math under my belt, I had a newfound confidence. If I could get through *that*, I could get through *anything*.

The travel agent turned out to be a weaselly kid I didn't like. After an exhaustive search, the cheapest Nairobi hotel he could find was over a hundred and fifty dollars per night. My entire budget, including food and transportation, was one hundred dollars a day. I thought there must be other travel agents, but when I searched for them, only one other name popped up. So I called her and explained everything I wanted to do. She was not familiar with the David Sheldrick Wildlife Trust but said she would do some research and get back to me.

The travel agent called me back with some surprising information. She had located a phone number for the Trust in Indiana and already had a long conversation with the girl who answered the phone. *Indiana?* In all the years I'd spent rummaging around their website, I'd never found such a number and was completely shocked by this new information. The travel agent was given a referral to a woman who had visited the Trust many times over the years. She thought she might be a good contact for me.

The woman turned out to be an amazing resource and gave me the contact information of the place she stayed each time she went, as well as a driver she used. She sent me information on everything I needed to know. My cottage rental, including a driver, was less than one hundred dollars per day, which allowed me enough for food. I couldn't believe my luck. When I asked if she had ever met anyone connected with the organization, she responded that she had not. She said she had tried, but it was extremely difficult to meet them. She also had many friends who visited regularly, and none of them had met the Sheldricks either. That was discouraging, and I mentioned this to Leslie when we spoke later that evening.

"She doesn't know the hand that guides you," she said, borrowing a quote from the televangelist Joel Osteen "You have no idea what God has in store for you until you go there and see for yourself."

She reminded me of all the things that had already happened. Joel spoke about having faith when it seemed like nothing was happening, and that "God was either getting them ready for you or getting you ready for them." Neither of us was religious, but we both loved Joel Osteen and listened faithfully to his weekly sermons. It was his message of hope that constantly grabbed our attention.

Looking back at my past, I was always a hustler. I could find drugs no matter what city I was in, no matter what time of day or night. When I was particularly desperate, I lost all fear of the people I had to deal with and the parts of town where I had to go. I was a great thief, too. When push came to shove, I always had the ability to find what I needed. Why was this any different? All I had to do was to show up and *hustle* the opportunity. If it was meant to be, then a path would reveal itself. Or at least I hoped so.

"You need to use that money you saved to buy a car and buy your plane ticket to Africa" Leslie repeated, "this is your chance. This is your shot. I can *feel* it."

The only caveat was that as soon as I was ready to make the purchase, I was to call her at work so she could hear the "click" of my mouse. She wanted to hear the "click" of my dream coming true.

A few days later, I was ready. There was no fork in my road. The decision was obvious. Even though I would be lying if I said I felt no fear, the pull in my gut each time I thought about *actually* going to Africa was simply too strong to ignore. I pulled up the Delta website and called Leslie at work with my finger hanging precariously over the mouse and my forehead covered in sweat. *I was doing this.* I looked at all the faces staring back at me, the faces of those that had given me so much inspiration throughout the years: Daphne, David, Eleanor, Mishak, and Edwin ... each one pasted on the wall above my computer, I made the "click."

Leslie sobbed as soon as she heard the sound. Together we sat on the phone crying until I said, "Oh God, what just happened?"

"Oh, sweetheart," she said, sniffling "Your life has just changed forever. With one 'click,' your life has just changed forever."

∞

After that first visit, Edwin continued to go to the David Sheldrick Wildlife Trust almost daily, and each time Josphat taught him something new about elephants, their behavior, or the challenges they faced living in the wild. Edwin was mesmerized, absorbing everything he could. He looked forward to his visits with Josphat more than anything else.

One day he received an urgent phone call.

"Edwin, can you come right away?" Josphat asked in a tone Edwin hadn't heard from him before. He had just set up his camera in downtown Nairobi for another day of taking pictures but immediately packed everything up after getting the disturbing call.

Josphat was waiting for him in the parking lot when Edwin arrived.

"Thank you for coming on such short notice! We are short-handed today: one of our keepers did not show up, can you fill in for him? We need you to go right away."

"Of course," said Edwin, having no idea what he was getting himself into. "Where are we going?"

"You go with those men in that jeep," he pointed. "I have to stay, but I will be here when you get back. Go, quickly!"

Edwin jumped into the back of the jeep with the other men, many of whom he had met before except for one. He was very tall, Edwin could see, and had a quiet demeanor. He didn't seem rushed and frenzied like some of the other men: instead he moved with calm precision. It was clear they looked to him for guidance. When he spoke he had the deepest voice Edwin ever heard.

"*Jambo wewe ni rafiki wa Josphat?*"

"Yes, I am friends with Josphat."

"He doesn't speak English, you have to speak Wakamba or Swahili," said a man named Pom who introduced himself earlier. Edwin nodded and repeated his response in Swahili.

"*Jina langu ni Mishak,*" the man introduced himself.

On the ride Mishak explained what Edwin's duties would be and gave a brief description of the call Daphne received about the baby elephant they were on their way to rescue. Edwin had absolutely no idea what to expect, but Mishak told him to stay close to him, so he did.

Edwin watched as the veterinarian, Dr. Rottcher, opened a medical bag and began organizing his supplies. There was tubing, rope, syringes, and a bunch of medical equipment Edwin couldn't fully see. They pulled into Wilson airfield, and everyone began loading the supplies from the jeep onto a plane. While everyone got into the plane, Edwin hung back. He had never been on a plane before and wasn't sure if he was supposed to join.

Mishak said something to Pom that Edwin couldn't hear over the noise of the engine.

"Come on," Pom waved, "you too!"

An hour later they arrived in Mweiga, landing just a few miles from the coffee plantation where David Sheldrick was raised. Edwin didn't know this at the time, but I had to wonder if David *had* known, what must he have thought? I mean, what were the chances—that one of the greatest elephant keepers the Trust had ever known did his very first rescue on the land on which David was raised, roamed around, and fell in love with elephants himself? Kenya is roughly the size of the state of Texas, so they could have gone anywhere, but to be in Mweiga, of all places. I could barely wrap my mind around the irony of it. And Edwin was brought there by Mishak, a Wakamba man, teaching him the ropes. If there was any way to see David's legacy recognized, I thought to myself—*this was it.*

They were escorted to the local police station. Edwin could see no sign of an elephant but followed Mishak as he was told. After a brief discussion, the men were led into a back room where Edwin could see several people huddled around a small cage. Dr. Rottcher went straight to work as he hovered over the small elephant, inserting a tube into its ear. As Edwin got a better look, he could see the young elephant was unconscious: in fact he wondered if it was even alive.

The local villagers who escorted them to the police station told them what happened. Like Ndume and Malaika, the young elephant was from a small refugee population in Laikipia. With their migration route completely cut off by human settlement, they too were locked in a forest that couldn't support them. Mishak took a deep breath as he listened to another tragic story of a baby elephant attacked by humans when discovered outside the forest boundary. Edwin watched the young elephant as details of the attack were relayed. The young female was covered in deep puncture wounds Dr. Rottcher covered in a green clay paste. How the little elephant got away from the angry mob nobody seemed to know, but luckily she made it to the safety of the police station before collapsing—likely from the pain or the severe trauma she must have endured.

They named her Thoma, after Thomason Falls, where she was found. On the flight back, Edwin watched her intently. He noticed her long eyelashes and how each breath seemed stronger than the last. Her feet were so small Edwin wondered how old she was. As if on cue, Mishak raised two fingers and said she was about two months old.

Thoma was brought into one of the tiny stalls and placed on a soft bed of hay while Dr. Rottcher continued his work. Edwin waited outside the stall until the commotion of the new arrival settled down. He was just about to leave when Mishak called him over. He explained that Thoma needed someone to stay with her now, round-the-clock.

Edwin didn't realize elephants suffered from horrible night-mares—especially those who, like Thoma, had been through a particularly traumatic event. Not only would she require regular milk feedings throughout the night since she was still so young, Thoma would also need someone there to comfort her when, and *if,* she woke up. And because of so many puncture wounds, the young elephant would likely also suffer from an infection that could kill her all by itself. Mishak insisted he would be in the adjoining stall with another young rescue named Mpala if Edwin needed anything.

Edwin spent the next three days and nights with Thoma, who did wake up, paced, screamed, mourned the loss of her family,

suffered from terrible night tremors and infection, and, to everyone's surprise ... *survived*. Mishak stayed with Edwin and taught
him everything he knew about caring for the young elephants, and
the two became lifelong friends. It took a long time for Thoma
to trust another human being, but Edwin took the place of her
mother, and the bond between them was just as strong.

Edwin's life was never the same after Thoma's rescue, and he
knew it was the one thing he was born to do. Since it was obvious
to Daphne that Edwin also had a very special connection with
the elephants, he was given a permanent position as an elephant
keeper at the Trust. Mishak spent countless nights telling him the
most remarkable stories of elephant survival, and Edwin was in
awe of his ability to save even the worst cases. Mishak had a gift
with the elephants so precious, Edwin often wondered if he was
touched by an angel too.

"But what about your dream to become a bishop?" Juliet asked
Edwin one evening after he told her he had accepted a full-time
position as a keeper.

"It's OK Mama, I've simply traded one post of God for
another."

∞

Mishak spent most of his time in Voi with the older orphans,
helping them integrate back into the wild while Edwin was in
charge of the youngest rescues at the orphanage in Nairobi. When
a new group of young orphans was being transported to Voi,
Edwin always went along not only to offer comfort and support
to the young orphans during the journey but also to make sure
they integrated with the older orphans when they arrived. The
young elephants formed tight bonds with each other, but they

still looked up to their keepers for emotional support. The keepers learned the hard way that if a bond was broken between the men and the elephants too early, the elephants would sink into another devastating depression, which many did not survive. Having a keeper stay with the young elephants twenty-four hours a day for *years* became the routine.

Once Edwin and his team pulled into Voi with the newest group of two-year-olds, they spent the next several hours getting them integrated into their new surroundings. Mishak was out in the field with the other keepers and the older orphans by the time they arrived. Edwin was stocking one of the stalls with food when the call came in that Loisaba, the poaching victim shot in the ear with her trunk partially cut off, was on her way to the Voi stockades. He quickly quit what he was doing to get another stall ready for her.

Later that evening, the keepers sat down to dinner and recounted to Edwin and Mishak what they witnessed earlier in the afternoon before Loisaba arrived. Edwin listened intently. Even though he'd only worked at the Trust for just over a year, he had learned the perceptive powers of elephants were so shocking—so powerful—he never tired of hearing about them.

"Malaika raised her trunk first," said one of the keepers. "I looked in the direction to where her trunk was pointed. I saw nothing but a few orphans and wild elephants. Then I climbed higher for a better look, and I noticed Emily and Aitong walking away, back in the direction we had just come. I wondered what they were doing," he said, waving his hands.

The distress call from the headquarters in Nairobi that signaled the rescue of Loisaba came in after the early-morning keepers had already left with the elephants for the day. They had no way of knowing that an elephant rescue was underway, but it appeared the elephants somehow did.

"Then I looked back to Malaika, who still had her trunk high in the air," he said, raising his hand over his head. "And Mweiga starts walking as fast as she can toward Emily and Aitong. I think something is wrong, but none of the other elephants moved. They just kept on doing what they were doing. But then I noticed that Emily and Aitong stopped. When Mweiga caught up to them, they began walking together, the three of them, back toward the stockades. They waited for her. And they knew. They knew Lois-aba was here." The men all nodded their heads in agreement.

"Why only those three?" asked the newest keeper.

"Because Malaika is the head matriarch now," Mishak said in Swahili. "Emily and Aitong are the favored nannies, or next in line to be matriarchs themselves. Mweiga has been spending a lot of time with them. Maybe she called out to them or they called her, we don't know. Obviously, it seemed that Malaika knew what was going on the whole time, since she was the only one with her trunk raised in the air."

The new keeper could hardly believe what he was hearing, "So you think they are 'speaking' to one another, and that's how they knew?"

"We don't think," said Edwin before getting up to leave. "We *know*."

The shocked keeper looked to the rest of the men, but they had all gone back to eating and laughing. No one looked even remotely surprised by what Mishak and Edwin had just revealed.

"Don't worry," said Mishak "You will see it for yourself." He patted the shocked man's shoulder as got up to leave, joining Edwin. The two continued the conversation deep into the night.

Even though Edwin was heading back to Nairobi in the morning, he never tired of hearing Mishak's remarkable stories.

The elephants had traveled farther out into the bush that day than on previous days, Mishak told him. Emily, Aitong, and Mweiga walked several miles, and it took well over an hour to get back to the stockades. By the time an unconscious Loisaba had been taken out of the truck to have her wounds inspected by the vets, the trio of elephants were already halfway back to greet her in the stockades. *How on Earth had they known she was coming?* Edwin gave up doing the math in his head. It was just nothing short of incredible, what they were able to do.

CHAPTER 26

*G*raduation was upon me before I knew it. When I told my parents I wasn't interested in "walking" down the graduation aisle, my father was furious. I was surprised when he went on to explain that he would literally disown me if I didn't. This was as important to them as anything I had ever done. Leslie freaked out, too, when I told her.

"How dare you, Debbie Ethell! Do you have any idea how hard I worked to make this happen?" She had a point.

Then my Uncle James called and asked if he and my Aunt Trish could come; they lived in California. When I told them I didn't want them to pay all that money *just* to come see me graduate, my uncle said, "This is a really big deal. It's a dream I've always had for myself, so to see you accomplish something as great as a college degree is something we wouldn't want to miss." I agreed to let them come, embarrassed by all the attention.

I began to realize just how significant it actually was. I started back in fifth-grade math, but by taking classes every semester for nearly six years, I had ascended through statistics and calculus—more than enough math to get my science degree and higher than I ever thought possible for myself. One of my most enjoyable classes turned out to be physics, something the old me could never have imagined.

On graduation day, my sister was well into her second day of hard labor with my parents' first grandchild. I was at the hospital with her the night before with the rest of my family. No one slept, but we were all so excited about a new baby and the crazy alcoholic finally making something out of her life on the same day, we didn't even notice how exhausted we were.

I made it to the auditorium with only moments to spare. A stranger in the line next to me helped me frantically get dressed in my cap and gown as we entered the auditorium. In all the chaos, I'd forgotten my phone, and realized I had no idea where my family was. I didn't know if they could see me, and all I could do was scan the crowd over and over again.

I didn't realize they had seen me enter the room on the jumbotron screen, so they knew right where I was and watched as I scanned the crowd for them. Just as I was about to feel sorry for myself, I turned to look at the top of the auditorium and saw them all going wild. Their screams seemed to fill the massive room. I leapt to my feet and waved like a madwoman, and my parents, with James, Trish, and Leslie, lost it. I laughed and cried at the same time, so grateful I hadn't followed my own instinct and skipped what would become one of the happiest moments in my life.

∞

Mishak was watching a new group of orphans playing with some babies in a wild herd when he noticed a large bull elephant approach from a distance. He could clearly see the bull "walking with purpose," which meant he headed straight for the group of orphaned elephants without veering in any direction. Mishak knew it must be one of the orphans they raised, but the bull was still too distant to identify.

"What is it?" asked the keeper sharing the rock with Mishak. The newest recruit, he still had a hard time believing the stories about elephants and their behavior.

"It is your opportunity," Mishak said.

"For what?"

"To witness the return of one of our orphans."

"It's Edo!" one of the men called out as Mishak climbed higher for a better look. He recognized him instantly and thought it unusual for Edo to be alone, without his two best friends, Ndume and Dika. The park was in full bloom after a recent rain—a time when Edo should have been gorging himself with his friends in the lusher parts of the park.

The men watched Edo walk directly over to Malaika, who gave him an especially exuberant greeting, as she always did whenever he appeared.

"When is the last time you saw him?" asked the new keeper.

"Well over a year now," said Mishak, watching Edo and Malaika with intensity.

The bond between Edo and Malaika remained as strong as it had been before he, Ndume, and Dika went off into the wild together. Mishak always found it interesting that none of "the boys," as they called them, tried to mate with Malaika, even when she was in estrous. In the wild, bulls never mate with their sisters, but it made one wonder if the satellite orphan families acted any differently. What was even more interesting was that Edo and Dika introduced Malaika to an enormous wild bull they did see mate with her, though it made them nervous because she was only nine years old at the time. The wild bull befriended the three grown orphans in the wild and was with them the last time they made an appearance.

It is unusual for an elephant to get pregnant so young, though it does happen occasionally. Elephants, like humans, tend to give birth in their late teens or early twenties. It is not unusual for a mature female in her fifties or even sixties to give birth, but nine is a bit young to get pregnant.

Edo gently touched Malaika's belly with his trunk. She had just turned 11. Everyone knew she was pregnant, but as Mishak watched Edo's peculiar behavior, he knew it was official—Malaika was in labor. *Was it only a coincidence that Edo just happened to show up, or had he known somehow? Had Malaika sent him a communication through long-distance infrasound?*

"It's time," Mishak shouted, his excitement clear to everyone within ear shot. "Malaika is in labor!"

The men cheered and whistled from their rock perches. Since her arrival, Malaika had been a beloved elephant: kind, gentle, and incredibly patient. Favored among the men, everyone was excited at the prospect of an orphan—one with no chance of survival before they rescued her—giving birth and completing the cycle of life.

Three days later, when they were out with the orphans again, Mishak was startled by someone yelling in the distance.

"Ndume is coming!" a keeper yelled. Soon, the familiar outline of Ndume emerged from the dense underbrush. Whenever a bull with tusks as large as Ndume's made an appearance, everyone was relieved. For the time being, he'd survived the poaching onslaught and was safe.

Mishak watched Ndume exhibit the same behavior Edo had days earlier. He went straight to Malaika and began gently touching her belly with his trunk. Mishak ignored the first whisper of concern. *It is not uncommon for elephants to be in labor over several days*, he told himself, but his intuition nagged him.

The following day, as Mishak watched Edo, Ndume, and Malaika, another yell penetrated the African landscape.

"Dika," yelled one of the keepers "It's Dika!"

What should have been a joyous celebration, the three "boys" back together, instead sent a shiver down Mishak's spine. He instantly knew something was very wrong. The three bull elephants, not seen together in over two years and individually in at least one, were now all together and displaying the same strange behavior, touching Malaika's belly.

Mishak leapt off the rock and sprinted full-speed back to the stockades to call the veterinarians. The next day, a team of vets flew out to inspect Malaika, and Mishak's worst fear was confirmed; the baby was wedged in Malaika's birth canal. Mishak, along with Edo, Dika, and Ndume, stayed with Malaika.

Mishak talked to her the same as he did when she had been at death's door eleven years earlier. He did everything he could to comfort her. If it were true that he did have some sort of magic to heal elephants, he silently begged whoever was listening to bless him now. Edo, Ndume, and Dika remained at the compound, and two of Malaika's adopted orphans, Loisaba and a little bull named Lewa, stayed by her side as the days turned into a week. Loisaba had developed an especially strong attachment to Malaika after her arrival nearly six months earlier.

Each time Malaika laid down, Lewa got down on his knees and tried desperately to pry her back up. Then he gently laid his head on her stomach, almost as though he were listening to the baby she was carrying. Mishak had never seen the elephants act this way. They wouldn't come into the safety of the stockades with the other orphans at night. They refused to leave her side, staying outside with Mishak, who grew more concerned by the hour.

Several off-duty keepers came not only to help with the situation, but also to support Mishak, who slept little and ate less. They set up a makeshift camp next to Malaika and kept constant vigil as more vets around the country were consulted.

By the eighth day of her labor, reality set in. The vets made one last desperate attempt to extract the baby. But unfortunately they discovered it had already died of a broken neck from being wedged so tight, likely days earlier. They tied a chain to the dead baby's foot, and the five men pulled with all their strength, but it wouldn't budge. Then they decided to make a small incision to see if they could widen the opening, but nothing worked. Finally, the gravity of the situation began to sink in. There was nothing more they could do; Malaika was simply too young to give birth to a baby that size.

On the afternoon of the ninth day, as the gun was loaded, Loisaba gingerly approached Malaika, who had been unconscious for some time. She gently touched Malaika's face with her trunk, and Malaika suddenly opened her eyes as if to say goodbye. Then Mishak approached and knelt down by her face with tears streaming down his own. No one knows what he said, and he has not spoken of it since, but when he got up, he gently touched her face and whispered, "Goodbye, my little angel."

Mishak walked as far as he could from Malaika, the orphans trailing behind, as the keepers said their final goodbyes one-by-one.

Then a gunshot shattered the air.

At that very moment, Loisaba ran deep into the bush screaming, the trauma of losing her mother to gunshots still fresh in her mind. Several of the keepers ran after her. As Mishak sat on the ground, exhausted and devastated, several orphans surrounded him, tightly huddled together, and touched his face gently with their trunks. As each new tear fell, there was another trunk to wipe it away.

By nightfall, the keepers in search of Loisaba were unable to locate her and forced to return. They prayed she would make it through the night, since she was still small enough for a lion to attack. The keepers slept outside in shifts whenever an elephant got lost or didn't come home, much like a concerned mother waits up for a wayward teen.

The following morning, near dawn, a keeper sleeping on a lawn chair awoke to the sound of breaking branches and the sight of two massive, reddish-brown forms emerging from the dense underbrush. He could see Edo with Ndume and, right there wedged between them, little Loisaba. The keeper ran to wake up the men, and a bleary-eyed Mishak approached the bulls, who extended their trunks to him while another keeper ran to get milk for Loisaba. Suddenly, Emily and Aitong came running out of the stockades and surrounded Loisaba, just as they had when she'd first arrived. Without Malaika as the matriarch, they were now "on duty."

Lewa, Malaika's other adopted orphan, never returned to the safety of the stockades again but instead remained just outside the compound. No one knows why. Seemingly understanding that the young bull needed his protection, Dika remained close to him throughout that first night, while Edo and Ndume disappeared to look for Loisaba.

Edo, Dika, and Ndume remained behind for several weeks after Malaika died, and they seemed especially protective over Lewa, who was still too small to be left on his own and would still be milk-dependent for some time. Each day, as the milk trucks arrived with nourishment for the youngsters, Lewa left the protection of the bulls and joined in for his share. Ndume and Dika enjoyed spending the following days with the youngsters in the mudbaths. And just like Samson so many years earlier, they laid down and the let the youngsters crawl all over them, enjoying it as much as the young elephants did.

Bull elephants are not typically part of the parenting process; that is something left to the matriarch and the nannies. One day from high atop a rock, the keepers noticed Ndume, Dika, and Edo standing together as a distant wild herd that had been lingering in the area for the past few weeks began to move off. Ndume and Dika turned and went with them, leaving Edo behind with Lewa by his side. What surprised everyone was that Edo seemed to understand that Lewa had adopted him as his surrogate parent. Instead of leaving with Ndume and Dika to join the others in the wild, he remained behind to watch over Lewa. Edo's behavior was perplexing. No one had ever seen a bull elephant show so much compassion. One had to wonder if it was the close bond that Edo shared with Malaika throughout her life that may have had something to do with it. How could we possibly know?

Each morning Edo and Lewa waited just outside the gates to the compound for everyone to get up for the first milk feeding. During the day they mixed in with the wild herds and the orphans, but Lewa remained outside with Edo each evening, and Edo protected him like a watchful parent. Loisaba often joined up with them, as well. The three kept themselves just apart from the other elephants. Lewa and Loisaba grieved together over the loss of Malaika while Edo kept a vigilant eye on the pair.

Everyone thought surely Edo would only stay back for a week, maybe two, but true to elephant form, he did something no one had ever seen or expected. He stayed with Lewa, keeping him on

his milk-feeding schedule, for *two entire years* until he was fully weaned. For those two years, he brought Lewa back to the safety of the keepers for his twice-daily milk feedings, proving once again just how little is understood about the majesty and complexity of bull elephants.

Then one day, just like Ndume and Dika, Edo and Lewa disappeared with a wild herd. Months later, a soaring plane spotted Lewa with Dika and a group of female elephants far below. How they'd found one another again no one knew, but one thing was certain: the compassion shared between those bull elephants was unmistakable.

∞

Aitong adopted Loisaba after Malaika died, and Loisaba became as close to her as she had been to Malaika. I always wondered if their severe injuries made their bond so strong: Loisaba with the base of her trunk cut off, and Aitong with a head injury that left her walking in circles for months. The other elephants, just as aware of Loisaba's disability as they had been of Aitong's, helped her with food gathering as often as they could. Emily and Aitong slid right into the role of matriarchs after Malaika's passing. For the next several years, Loisaba remained faithfully by Aitong's side.

One day a spotter plane saw the group on the outskirts of the compound. Emily and Aitong's small herd had grown. They no longer came into the stockades at night but instead stayed on the outer edges of the park, ready to accept any new orphans or wild wanderers wanting to join their herd. The keepers had seen Edo mate with both Aitong and Emily; now each had young calves of their own. Loisaba took her role as a nanny to Aitong's newborn baby quite seriously. The pilot immediately noticed a problem.

He recognized Loisaba but noticed she hung back from the rest as though she couldn't keep up. He radioed the keepers, and men were immediately dispatched to the scene to investigate.

When they inspected Loisaba, they found no obvious sign of injury, but it was clear something was wrong. Loisaba's movements were much slower than usual, including her pace. They wondered if she had been bitten by a poisonous snake, something common in the park. Before they could get her back to the compound to examine her further, she collapsed. A short time later, with three keepers by her side and surrounded by her herd, she died.

For the first few moments, Emily and Aitong sniffed her lifeless body with their trunks, and then Aitong got down on one knee to nudge Loisaba back up. The keepers stepped back as Aitong repeatedly tried to lift her. Emily rumbled to her, and the other elephants inspected Loisaba gently with their trunks, but Aitong's will to get Loisaba up only grew stronger. She became even more frantic, as though unable to accept that her faithful friend was gone. Finally, after several failed attempts, she simply stopped. The other elephants stepped back, allowing Emily to comfort her friend, and when it became clear that Loisaba wouldn't be getting back up, Emily touched Aitong gently with her trunk as she rocked slowly back and forth. The keepers knew Aitong would mourn the loss of her friend for a long time.

Loisaba was only thirteen years old when she died, but at least the keepers felt comfort in knowing she had been given a second chance at a life that never would have been possible without them. And she didn't die alone, but among the men and the elephants she loved and who loved her. A necropsy later revealed her cause of death was tuberculosis, which angered everyone.

Tuberculosis was just one of the many reasons conservationists worked so hard to keep cattle from grazing inside the protected parks where elephants lived. It was one of several diseases that easily jumped from cattle to elephants, and just one more thing they were up against.

Emily, Aitong, and the rest of their herd were spotted numerous times over the next several years lingering in the spot where Loisaba died. It's a shared trait between humans and elephants—neither of us *ever* forgets a loved one.

CHAPTER 27

noticed the moment I stepped off the plane that Kenya smelled like a campfire. I loved that smell. Standing there in the dead of night on a tarmac in Nairobi, the sweet smell of flowers mixed with campfire gave me an instant jolt of déjà vu. I literally felt as though I had been there before. As we flew in, it was announced that the airport had just burned down. Something about hearing that greatly excited me. I was in a foreign country, and the airport just burned down—it was already turning out to be an *amazing* adventure.

Two days before I left, a bomb had gone off on the outskirts of Nairobi. I waited anxiously as the embassies began issuing stronger and stronger warnings to foreigners in Kenya. Then England mandated everyone who was English leave Kenya immediately. I waited for the same instruction for US citizens, but one never came.

"Mom, don't you think a city is the safest just *after* a bomb goes off?" I argued with her.

"You cannot be serious," she said.

I decided not to share with my parents the whole airport-burning-down thing until after I got back. They didn't need one more thing to worry them.

"Look at the size of those hawks," I said to the Kenyan gentleman standing next to me. We'd met on the plane and he'd told me all about his family on the flight from Amsterdam. Right when we were about to get off, his wife gave me their card and told me to contact them if I got into any trouble. I didn't know if it was an ominous warning or if they were just being nice. We had to wait in a long line for buses to take us to a makeshift baggage facility. I stared up at the lights, fascinated by the enormous birds as they flew through the light.

"Those aren't hawks," he giggled.

"Well ... what are they?" I said, looking up.

"Bats," said his wife.

Goddammit I love Kenya, I thought. Bats as big as hawks ... such a thing had never even remotely occurred to me.

It felt good to drop my enormous backpack. The plan I'd made with Leslie was that I was going to take all of my research with me. That way, if I got an opportunity to show it someone, anyone, then I would have it readily available. I hadn't anticipated just how heavy it was all going to be and began to second-guess myself. Now that I was standing on the tarmac in Nairobi, there was no going back.

Each day there is an hour-long viewing session at the Trust in which visitors are permitted to visit the youngest baby elephants at their noon mudbath. My hope was that I would get an opportunity to meet someone there and show them my research. I heard it could get quite crowded, but I simply had no other options.

Eleanor, Edo, and so many of the elephants I'd followed were actually located about two hundred miles away in Voi. I wanted so badly to go there but couldn't afford another plane ticket. I decided that for this trip my sole purpose was to meet Angela Sheldrick, David and Daphne's youngest daughter and current CEO of the Trust. I already knew this was going to be next to impossible. Leslie promised to listen to Joel Osteen every day I was gone to get as much mojo for me as possible.

The summer of my junior year, I'd decided not to take any classes other than math so I could have the time to finish logging all the data about each rescued elephant's life history. It was a database I created and subsequently intended to present to someone at the Trust if and when an opportunity presented itself. What I discovered in the data about the elephant behavior I was reading about completely blew me away. I had no idea if anyone else was looking at it the way I was. The Trust database was organized by year, but mine was all organized *by elephant*. It took what must have been hundreds of hours to do it this way, but I now had more than four hundred elephants in my database. This allowed me to look at the entire life history of one elephant neatly archived in one place. Each time that elephant was mentioned in a scientific paper, an article, a book, another database, or a YouTube video, it was all archived. When I looked at it like that, I could see the whole picture of that elephant's life, not just bits and pieces criss-crossed between years.

It looked as though the elephants were making choices based solely on their emotions. I saw them returning repeatedly to the keepers when they were injured or dying, seemingly knowing that the men who raised them would work tirelessly to save them over and over again. Even more remarkably, I also saw wild elephants doing the exact same thing. This suggested the orphans who had gone back into the wild were communicating with them, their wild friends. I saw female elephants walk many miles to give birth with a specific keeper, many times in the company of wild elephants that had joined their herd. This always made me wonder what the wild elephants were thinking in light of the threat man posed.

Everyone in my circle had heard these stories because I simply couldn't stop talking about them. They were some of the best stories any of us ever heard. I also began to ask people if they had heard of the David Sheldrick Wildlife Trust, but rarely met anyone who had. Once, when Leslie and I were bored, we spent the afternoon asking random strangers in a busy area of Northwest Portland if they had ever heard of them. Very few had. When I finally found someone, I asked them the second part: "Do you know who David Sheldrick was?" To this day, I have never met a single person who knew the great conservationist he was, and I consider *that* one of the biggest travesties of all.

I knew for several years the only real way I could tell this story was in the form of an on-going television series. It was simply too long and complicated to tell it in a two-hour documentary. Personally, I was done with sappy documentaries about elephants. Either they showed them all being killed, which would take months of therapy to try and un-see, or they did a fantastic job of outlining the problem, getting me all worked up with no solution in sight and leaving me feeling even more frustrated. A two-hour documentary could not even begin to scratch the surface. Since I worked in the television industry once, I sought out individuals who I could talk to about my idea. A friend of a friend knew one of the business partners of Oliver Stone, and he agreed to meet me. When he said, "This is like 'Old Yeller' on crack," I knew I was on to something.

But I had never been to Africa, and I had never met the elephants I wanted so badly to teach people about, both of which were sticking points in nearly every conversation. Leslie reminded me that if nothing else, when I returned I would at least be able to say that, *YES*, I had been to Africa, and *YES*, I had met the elephants I wanted the rest of the world to meet.

Now I just had to find a way to convince Angela Sheldrick, but in order to do so I would have to meet her first.

∞

By the time I gathered my bags in the makeshift terminal and made my way outside to look for my driver, it was nearly 3:00 a.m. My flight was supposed to have arrived at 10:30 p.m., but the fire delayed things. I knew there was a slim chance my driver would still be waiting, which was confirmed by the sea of blank faces staring back at me, holding placards with names not matching my own. I did not have a Plan B. I was warned to never use certain cabs, but I was so tired I forgot which ones. Then I saw a man in full uniform holding a machine gun. That's when the fact that I was halfway across the world really hit me.

After walking back and forth in front of the hundreds of waiting drivers, I heard the faint sound of my name.

"Debbie ... Debbie ... "

I was sure my mind was playing tricks, but then I heard it again. I followed the voice all the way to the end of the line and saw a very young man looking down at his phone. He was playing a game while reciting my name out loud. The placard with my name leaned against a nearby post. A wave of gratitude washed over me, knowing he must have waited for hours.

"Are you saying Debbie?"

He looked up in surprise. "Debbie? Debbie! Debbie Ethell ... is it you?" Then he flashed the picture I sent to him on his phone. I liked him instantly; he had the biggest smile I had ever seen, and I nearly crushed him with a hug. And then I learned his name was Edwin too. I knew instantly it was a sign. Friendly, talkative, and easygoing, he loaded my bags into his car and we began the journey to my new home for the next eight days. As we left the airport, we passed more uniforms and more machine guns.

"Do those guys always carry machine guns?" I asked.

"No, it's not usually like this. It's because of the bombing. Damn Al-Shabaab. But don't worry, Nairobi is the safest city on the planet right after it gets bombed."

"I just said that to my mother before I got on the plane," I laughed.

"So where do you want to go while you are here? I will take you anywhere you want to go," he said.

"I need to go to the David Sheldrick Wildlife Trust that has the baby elephants."

"Oh yes, I am very familiar with the Sheldricks. Very familiar. But that's it? No place else?"

"Yes, there is another place. I will get the address for you."

"No problem, I will find it for you. So you love elephants, huh?"

"Yes, I need to meet someone there ... or a few people, actually."

"Who?"

"Well, to start with, Angela Sheldrick ... "

He made a clicking sound with his tongue, shaking his head. "Does she know you are coming?"

"No."

"Then she will be very hard for you to meet. I take people who want to meet her all the time, but I've never known a visitor who has met her."

Leslie's words flashed in my head: "*They don't know the hand that guides you.*"

"Who else?" he asked.

"Edwin Lusichi and Mishak Nzimbi."

He laughed.

"You know my name is Edwin, right?"

"Yes! That's crazy isn't it? I mean, what are the chances?"

"I'm laughing because I am named after him."

"You were named after *the* Edwin Lusichi?" Then it dawned on me: this was now a very famous organization in Kenya, and there were probably lots of young men named after him.

It was as if Edwin had read my mind. "I am not named after him because he is famous," he said. "I am named after him because he is very close friends with my family. I know him quite well. I can introduce you."

I was almost too stunned to talk. "You ... you ... know him? You can introduce me?"

"Yes, first thing tomorrow. I will introduce you. You will love him."

I was too tired to cry. The second shock came when I checked into what was the most beautiful cottage I had ever seen. After I put my bags down, I stared at the beautiful bed covered in mosquito netting and the exquisite bathroom. I imagined it was as nice as any four-star hotel, but having never stayed in one, I had nothing to compare. It was simply more beautiful than anyplace I had *ever* stayed ... in America.

CHAPTER 28

The younger Edwin had barely pulled into the parking lot the following morning before I opened the door of his car, startling him. Although I was exhausted from the long flight, I'd barely slept; the very thought of meeting Edwin, someone I had looked up to for so long, made me incredibly nervous. I had my backpack full of research along with a tiny notebook with his tattered picture and that of Mishak, Eleanor, and Daphne. They were the same pictures I had taped inside all my schoolbooks. It seemed appropriate those pictures should be with me when, and if, I got an opportunity to meet any of them.

As we drove up the long, winding road leading us to the Trust, I began to record everything with my new camera, wanting to get every last second on film. There were baboons and warthogs everywhere, and I wondered if the warthogs were any relation to those I'd read about. Daphne had raised an entire family of them at the compound.

A small group of people stood beside a rope at the entrance to a group of low-lying buildings as we pulled into the parking lot. When I opened my door, I heard a loud thud and a squeal.

"Oh, sorry," I yelled.

"What happened?" asked Edwin as he came around to my side of the car.

"I just hit a wartie."

"A what? What's a wartie?"

"One of those warthogs over there. I just hit one with my car door by accident."

Edwin laughed hysterically, so hard he couldn't stand, as he waved me away with his hand. I didn't know what had gotten into him until he explained that he had never heard anyone call a warthog that before. From that point forward, he only referred to warthogs as "warties," laughing hilariously each time he said it and referring to me as a "crazy, crazy American."

I followed him as he walked through the group of people and lifted the rope for me. The crowd became silent, as if wondering who we were, as we walked in like we owned the place. We continued past a group of tiny stalls, then increasingly larger ones. I could see people mixing a substance in buckets in a shed.

"Milk station," Edwin said. I nodded.

According to young Edwin, he had contacted the older Edwin that morning and told him he was bringing someone to meet him, which was why we were allowed to enter the compound before everyone else. I still couldn't believe I was *actually* this close to meeting the one and only Edwin Lusichi.

We entered a small office, and there he was. He rose from his desk as he heard us approaching and came over to give me a hug. I fell apart, then tried to pull myself together.

Edwin told me the story about the Trust and what they did, unaware that I already knew everything about them. As he spoke, I noticed a picture of him and Tom Cruise on a wall I suddenly realized was covered with pictures of Edwin posing with what seemed like every celebrity on the planet. There was Natalie

Portman, Colin Firth, Gisele Bündchen, and some of the most powerful politicians in the world.

"Tell him what you told me," the younger Edwin said. "You're not going to believe this," he added, nodding to his namesake.

So I told him part of my story, the same story I'd already told the younger Edwin on our long drive from the airport the previous night. At first he listened patiently, but as I continued, his eyes grew wider. Occasionally, he looked back to the younger Edwin, who nodded. It was clear the younger Edwin had been right when he'd said, "Edwin is going to be very, very surprised when he hears what you just told me."

The moment I had been waiting for presented itself, and I began to tell the Edwins about the little blind elephant named Ndololo. I could see the older Edwin stop breathing as I continued. When I told him about how I met Dr. Gradin, the eye doctor who treated Ndololo, and showed him my notebook with his business card taped inside, it had the exact effect I hoped. He was totally speechless.

"Show him what's in your backpack," young Edwin said.

I dropped two giant notebooks on his desk. Then, I opened to the story of Ndololo, and he read it to the end. He began slowly flipping the pages, seeing one story after another of elephants he had raised and loved. Finally, he looked up.

"You have done remarkable work. Everything I have read so far is ... remarkable. I want to know so much more. Can you come back this evening for the night milk feed?"

If he had asked me to stay all day, I would have. Instead, I promised I would bring all of my research back with me that evening. Once we got back into the car, Edwin asked me where I wanted to go. I handed him an address.

"This is a hospital, no?" he asked.

"Yes, it is … kind of. It's a treatment center actually."

"Do you need a treatment?" he asked.

"No, but I want to meet the people who are in there." On the way over, I told him about my own alcoholism and explained what a meeting was. Before leaving Portland, I had looked up a meeting only a few miles from the elephant orphanage.

When we pulled up to the building, there was a circle of people in a cabana surrounded by palm trees. It was beautiful. I could see stacks of literature confirming I was in the right place, so Edwin waited in the car while I joined the circle. I was immediately drawn to the laughter I heard in the back of the cabana. When I turned around, I saw three older men, full of life, giggling about something like a bunch of schoolgirls. It made me smile—alcoholics are some of the quickest people to laugh, even when our lives have completely fallen apart. English was spoken everywhere, so, thankfully, language was never a barrier, and as the meeting progressed, it was clear there were people from all over the world, some accidentally stuck in Kenya, some working in Nairobi, and the rest simply alcoholic Kenyans who couldn't quit drinking any more than I could at first. It was clear that alcoholism reared its ugly head here, too, ripping families apart like a tornado. Hospitals overflowed with drug addicts, and treatment centers, a fairly new thing, began to pop up all over.

When we returned to the Trust a few hours later, the older Edwin greeted me like an old friend. There were about thirty visitors at the milk feed, and they all seemed to wonder who I was, since it appeared Edwin and I were old friends, which shocked me as much as it did anyone else. I could never have predicted I would not only get to meet the man I so deeply admired, but to have him be so kind was simply beyond my wildest expectations. I secretly wished I could disappear and relay every detail back to Leslie. Just thinking about her screaming when she heard what happened made me smile.

Edwin was giving a small talk to a group of people when we walked in. As soon as he was finished, we were told to stand off to the side, just before the baby elephants emerged from the bush, where they had been with their keepers since the noon mudbath. One-by-one they appeared, walking single file from around a bend. I recognized only one, who had been rescued with severely sunburned ears, but I was looking for little Mbegu. I had no idea if she'd survived the injuries inflicted on her a month earlier, but I secretly prayed she did. Reality began to set in as I realized she wasn't among the group.

∞

One month before I landed in Kenya, the keepers received an urgent call about an elephant that had just killed a woman. The Kenya Wildlife Service was called in, and they shot the female elephant after determining she was dangerously aggressive. Then they realized she had a tiny newborn calf—the likely reason for her behavior. The villagers wanted only retaliation and began stabbing the defenseless baby with spears until another villager stepped in to stop the attack. It was his friend who made the rescue call to the Trust keepers, who sprang into action and raced to get to the baby.

Once again, the reception of the keepers was anything but welcoming. The dead woman's family was devastated, furious and wanted revenge, begging to kill the tiny elephant. The keepers negotiated with the family while Edwin and another keeper sought to examine the injured baby. They found her in shock, as was often the case. The baby elephant, one of the smallest Edwin had ever seen, had run into an empty schoolroom where several young students stoned her until she collapsed. It was a miracle she'd survived, though it was clear by her tiny size that she was still in danger. She barely opened her eyes as they approached her.

She had multiple stab wounds across her body, and although the cuts appeared superficial, they knew infection could easily set in. Edwin also knew she was bruised and battered by rocks, causing injuries not obvious to the naked eye. Mishak laid a blanket across her shaking body and gently spoke to her while Edwin inserted an IV drip into one of her ears for the long flight home. Dr. Rottcher had taken Edwin under his wing and taught him how to insert IV tubes into the ears of baby elephants. Though Dr. Rottcher was always on call for the most serious injuries, Edwin was now in charge of the simple medical procedures. Finally the men outside ended their lengthy negotiation with the angry villagers and were allowed to leave, taking the baby elephant with them.

She was placed in a stall next to another remarkable survivor, a young female named Ashaka, rescued one year earlier from a muddy water hole. As they laid the baby down on a fresh bed of hay in the next stall, Edwin and Mishak assessed her.

"How old do you think she is?" asked one of the keepers gathered around her stall.

"She's quite young," said a thoughtful Edwin "Maybe only six or seven weeks at most, but she is very, very small."

"She is a *kidogo mbegu*," said Mishak "But the smallest seeds make the most beautiful flowers." He flashed a brilliant smile to the other keepers who nodded in return.

The men all looked back at the tiny mound as Edwin and

the vets went to work, covering her stab wounds with green clay, hoping to stave off infection. They named her Mbegu, which translates to "seed" in English, and faithful Mishak took his place by her side, working his magic once again to slowly nurse her back to health.

∞

As all the visitors went from one stall to the next, watching the elephants take their milk for the evening, Edwin asked me more questions about my notebooks and the residents that lived inside.

"Would you like to take them with you so you can read about the elephants for yourself?" I asked.

"Yes, please. I would love that," he said with a beaming smile.

Then I told him I really wanted to meet Angela Sheldrick. He shook his head and explained it would be extremely difficult. She was incredibly busy, and if she didn't have an appointment with me, it would be nearly impossible. I told him I would be there every day for the next week, and if there was any possibility to let me know. He promised he would.

Just before we left, something caught my eye. I saw the outline of a man in a stall that I hadn't seen when we entered.

"Which elephant is over there?" I asked one of the keepers in another stall.

"She is a very young elephant who is healing from serious wounds. She was speared many times by some angry villagers and is very sick with infection."

Was it even possible? I walked over to the stall unnoticed by the man inside. A rubber tube hooked to a saline bag stretched from a tiny mound on the floor covered by a blanket. As she moved, part of the blanket fell away, and I could see several distinct green patches across her back and legs. She was the tiniest elephant I had ever seen, and I knew instantly it was Mbegu, and she had survived.

Suddenly a man appeared out of the dark shadows, and I felt the second wave of goosebumps creep across my skin.

"*Jambo*," he said with a voice so deep I knew it *must* be him.

"How is Mbegu?" I asked. He seemed a bit taken aback that I knew who she was.

"She is healing," he said, "but I think her chances are good."

The little elephant moved again, and the man spoke quietly to her while he covered her again with the blanket.

"Are you Mishak?" I asked.

"Yes," he said, leaning against the door of the stall. It took me a moment to catch my breath.

"Mishak Nzimbi?"

"How do you know me?" he asked.

"I have followed you and your work for many years." I told him everything I knew about him, from the fact that he was from the Wakamba tribe to his first interaction with Eleanor and the orphans. I told him how touched I was when he stayed with Malaika for the nine long days of her labor and how precious I knew "the boys," Edo, Ndume, and Dika, were to him. He listened intently as I told him everything.

I hadn't noticed that all the visitors were gone and a small group of keepers, including both Edwins, had gathered around us. Then I realized the younger Edwin was speaking to them quietly in Swahili, filling in additional details to some of them about what I was saying.

"*Ni nani?*" Mishak asked the younger Edwin, wondering who I was.

"She has studied your elephants for a long time," he answered, pointing to one of my notebooks the older Edwin and a few keepers were huddled around flipping pages.

"Does she know that I am also a powerful warrior?" joked one of the keepers who leapt upon a fence, startling a baboon that screamed in displeasure. Everyone broke into laughter and began playfully punching the keeper. When I looked back to Mishak, he broke into the brightest smile I had ever seen. It was time for us to go.

As we left, Mishak asked, "*Tuonane kesho?*"

"*Ndiyo, tuonane kesho,*" I said. *Yes, I would see him tomorrow.*

I couldn't believe that in one day alone I'd gotten to meet not just one but two of my heroes. I thought we were off to a *very* good start as I went back to my cottage. That night, I slept harder than I had in years.

The next morning, I woke up to a *rap, rap, rap*. Through the mosquito netting on my majestic bed, I saw a small monkey knocking on my window. I decided instantly that I liked this version of an alarm clock so much better than the old one. I went straight to my computer to send Leslie a message that her prayers were working.

CHAPTER 29

$\mathcal{E}$do, Ndume, and Dika returned to the stockades many times over the next several years for various reasons. One day all three appeared: Edo and Ndume acted as guards, or sentries, to a wounded Dika who had a snare embedded in his ankle. Once he was treated by the keepers, the three disappeared back into the dense underbrush almost immediately. It was clear they weren't there for a friendly visit but a medical one.

Twice Ndume returned to the stockades in Voi with poisoned arrows in his body. Each time Dika was by his side, guarding him. Luckily for Ndume, the poison was old and weak, and he recovered rather quickly, but I saw this episode repeated over and over again. The bulls always seemed to look out for one another. The strong bonds they made in the orphanage lasted for as long as any of them had been in the wild. Bull elephants were proving to be *anything but* the loners scientists previously thought.

There was one story, however, that stood out from all the rest for me. It was a story so remarkable it shocks me even when I read it now.

Irima, a young poaching victim, was found emaciated and starving but thankfully took the milk offered to him rather quickly, something the keepers all agreed was a good sign. Emily and Aitong were thrilled to have another newcomer to take care of and instantly devoted themselves to him.

A few days after his arrival, they were all out in the bush as they normally were when the keepers heard a commotion. From high up on the rocks, they saw a small group of wild females charging and acting aggressively toward Emily and Aitong. Much larger and older than the two, their ears were flared, and the temporal glands on the sides of their faces wept, suggesting they were under an enormous amount of stress. Eventually the keepers realized what was happening. The wild females were trying to get in between Irima, Emily, and Aitong. After watching in disbelief, they realized the two older females were in fact trying to kidnap the young baby. Emily and Aitong did everything they could to stop them, but because they were so much smaller than the wild females, there was little they could do. The standoff lasted for over an hour, but in the end the wild females left with Irima.

The keepers called for backup to follow the wild females in hopes of re-rescuing Irima at some point. They could tell there were no lactating females in the wild group, and Irima was still very much milk-dependent. Having only had a few days of nourishment after arriving so emaciated, everyone knew time was of the essence for Irima. The keepers wondered if the wild females were actually his own family, perhaps his aunts. He was a poaching victim, and they knew his mother had been killed, but the wild elephants could have come back for him the same way Sobo's family had for her all those years ago.

Sadly, they lost track of him when his female escorts went outside the boundaries of the park over seventy miles away. A search plane was sent up, but the elephants had disappeared. No one was more heart broken than Emily and Aitong. The keepers watched the two as they stood in the very spot he was taken day after day, trunks raised in the air, trying to detect any scent of him. In the evenings, they were reluctant to join the others in the stockades, and it took much persuading by the men to get them to follow. Without milk, everyone knew Irima had little, if any, chance of survival. All they could do was pray for a miracle.

A few days later, Mishak and the keepers watched as Emily and Aitong took their same position on the spot Irima was taken, trunks raised high in the air, when suddenly they began trumpeting and rumbling loudly. Mishak stood high on a rock to get a better look. Far in the distance, a large bull approached, walking purposefully in their direction, and he knew instantly it had to be one of their own. But he was too far away to identify. Then he realized there wasn't one bull but two walking side-by-side. One of the keepers called out, but Mishak waited anxiously in silence to see what was about to unfold, assuming one of the bulls was hurt or in trouble.

But the two bulls didn't walk in the direction of the keepers: instead they walked straight toward Emily and Aitong. As the bulls got closer, Mishak recognized them as Edo and Ndume. Emily and Aitong were getting more excited than the keepers had ever seen them, which seemed odd at the time. Usually the girls were excited when Edo or Ndume made an appearance, but this was something different.

Suddenly, a little gray blob appeared from between the legs of the massive bodies of Edo and Ndume. *It was Irima.* The keepers could hardly believe their eyes. Emily and Aitong's screams scared all the birds out of a nearby tree as they surrounded the young elephant. Mishak leapt off his rock, running toward the scene as he shouted into his radio to get milk out to Irima as quickly as possible.

Edo and Ndume hung around for a few days while everyone tried to absorb the stunning events. At that time, Edo hadn't been seen in over a year and Ndume in nearly two. Mishak often wondered how they knew where Irima was. *So did I.* Did they know he was a newly rescued orphan? How had they taken him away from the wild females? When Emily and Aitong stood on the spot Irima was kidnapped each day, were they sending infrasonic signals, letting all the elephants in the area know? How in the hell did something like that happen? It is just one of thousands of examples in my already overflowing notebooks of how little is truly understood about elephant behavior.

I want to know the answers to these questions before it is too late.

∞

Early the next morning, my second day in Nairobi, my driver, Edwin, took me back to the elephant orphanage. This time, when we entered, several of the keepers approached him speaking Swahili, which was odd. When Swahili was the only language spoken, it was usually because they realized I only spoke English, even though I could understand more Swahili than I could speak.

"They all want to know what you know about them," young Edwin explained.

"What do you mean?" I was confused.

"You knew so much about Edwin and Mishak. They want to know what you know about them." I looked at several smiling faces and wondered what they must think.

Of course, there were several keepers I knew nothing about, but I shared the information I had with those I did. Some of them wanted to know about specific elephants, and I shared the elephant stories I had with them. Watching their faces light up like children with unopened pieces of candy as they heard what happened to their elephants made my heart flutter.

During the noon mudbath hour, Mishak came over and said, "*Jambo*, Debbie, *'bari gani?*" Just the fact that Mishak even knew who I was startled me.

"*Nzuri sana*, I'm fine, thank you." Little Mbegu was glued to his side. "How is Mbegu doing today?" I asked.

"*Ana njaa*, she's hungry. It's a good sign," he said, looking down at her. "Every flower needs food to blossom."

I loved that analogy. It reminded me of looking at an alcoholic newcomer. A seed has to go through a very dark phase before it can bloom. My father taught me this years ago. If you left a seed on the windowsill, in the light, it died. Before that seed could show all its beauty and color, it must stay far beneath the soil, in complete darkness, as it harnesses all of its energy to push toward the sky and show everyone just how brilliant and spectacular it can be. Just like an alcoholic whose found recovery. Just like Mbegu. Just like me.

Later, after all the visitors left, I spoke to the keeper Edwin in his office. He told me that he read as much as he could from my elephant notebook the night before and enjoyed reading about so many of his friends. He told me again how impressed he was at the time and energy I spent collecting all the data.

"Come to the orphanage early tomorrow. Angela has several meetings set up with people, but I think she will want to see this. I will ask if she can see you, but I can't make any promises. You will just have to wait to see if she has an opening."

My heart stopped. I knew this was it, the opportunity I prayed so hard for. I just needed a bit more luck. Then all my hard work and preparation could take me down the home stretch. As I walked back to the car with the younger Edwin, I was struck that he was just as excited as I was about this most recent development. I thought to myself just how much fun it was to be able to share this experience with him, and I was incredibly grateful to have him with me.

"OK, so where are we going?" he asked when we got into the car.

"Back to the meeting at the treatment center please."

$$\infty$$

Paul was a Maasai man who didn't wear the traditional red *shuka* that so distinguished the Maasai from everyone else. Instead, he looked like an accountant in a nice pair of trousers and a button-down shirt. He was close friends with a Somali man named Mshalé and a Samburu man named Igbé. The three of them together reminded me of the three stooges, and it had been their laughter that caught my attention in the back of the room the day before.

They were constantly laughing, poking and making fun of one another. Igbé had a very tiny head, and this fact was apparently brought up often. Mshalé, on the other hand, had a very long head with very crooked teeth, so that became the thing Igbé focused on when they made fun of one another. But Paul had a normal-sized head with perfect straight white teeth. I couldn't believe how beautiful the teeth were in Kenya, and yet no one I had known or spoken to had ever been to a dentist.

After the meeting, a group of us was outside smoking when I said to Paul, "It is so great to see you all together, laughing the way you do." It was no secret that on the outside these three groups of people did not get along.

"Out there we three are enemies. But in here, we are the best of friends," Mshalé interjected, holding in a drag of his cigarette. And just like that, Igbé made some stupid joke and the three of them laughed so hard I found myself staring in awe. They morphed into children on a playground with hardly a care in the world, instead of three grown men locked inside a treatment center with, what I learned later, no outside life to go back to. Their stories were tragic and similar to my own in many ways: their families had had enough—they'd lost everything, as many of us do, and there were shameful secrets I detected in the painful undertones an alcoholic has when sharing an event from his past.

The program of recovery is one of those rare entities in which shields are left at the door and no religion, no politics, no tribe … nothing intrudes. It is all left outside. Once inside that treatment center, it's just alcoholism, pure and simple. And no matter where you are from or how high your rank in the community, in those rooms it simply doesn't exist. We all speak the same language. I had experienced a million examples of this over the years.

After the meeting, Paul ran after me. "You know I want to help my people," he said. Paul lived in one of the most beautiful regions of Kenya called the Maasai Mara and worked as a teacher.

"They are in a terrible, terrible way," he said. Apparently, alcoholism had her claws wrapped around the Maasai communities in the most horrible way.

"Do they have meetings out there?" I asked.

"Yes, they do, but they need more."

"Where are they? I mean … how do you find them?" It wasn't like there were addresses where some of the Maasai communities were. They lived nomadic, cattle-herding lifestyles with tiny villages spread across enormous stretches of land.

"They have them in tents at the stopping points." I learned that a 'stopping point' was a place where several of the herders planned to meet up. It was a place they cooked meals and connected with each other after living a solitary existence herding cattle for weeks at a time.

Hearing this reminded me of just how alike we all were. Whether we were brought to meetings by a car and driver, or whether we were a nomadic cattle herder living on the Maasai Mara, at the end of the day we were all just humans being ... human.

CHAPTER 30

I sat up most of the night and pored over my research in preparation for my meeting with Angela, even though it wasn't a "for sure" deal. I followed advice given so many times before and acted *as if* the meeting was definitely taking place. By the time Edwin pulled into his parking spot, I was waiting with coffee in hand, silent as we drove up the winding road to the compound. My stomach was in knots. Of course, it was possible Angela would say no and refuse to meet with me. More than possible ... *it was likely.* Unfortunately, Daphne had taken ill and traveled to South Africa for medical treatment, so there was no possibility of seeing her. I had only this one chance.

They don't know the hand that guides you. I said Leslie's words over and over until we parked the car. Edwin Lusichi left me on a bench outside his office while he went to find Angela. As soon as I sat down, feeling like I was about to throw up, I noticed something happening in one of the elephant stalls.

It was full of people. There were tubes and blankets, vets bent over something on the ground, and men running back and forth— to where I couldn't see. Everyone seemed to be talking at once when I realized that the little elephant they were all hovering over must be dying. It looked like a triage unit in an emergency room, only we weren't in a hospital, and these men weren't frantically trying to save the life of a human, but that of a baby elephant. A few keepers huddled tightly together outside the stall. Then, after a few minutes of talking and shouting, everything fell silent.

People began slowly packing things up and leaving until a keeper suddenly ran out of the stall toward the back of the compound, then stopped and crouched low to the ground. Two of the keepers went over and sat on the ground next to him. It took me a moment to realize the keeper was crying and his friends were consoling him. I wondered how any of these men did what they did, day after day, elephant after elephant.

Then a wheelbarrow came out of the stall with a tiny mound covered by a blanket. A small lifeless elephant foot dangled over the edge. As soon as the man pushing the wheelbarrow got close to the elephant's keeper, the keeper jumped up, shoved the man aside, and took the wheelbarrow himself, his two friends following close behind. I wondered where they buried the dead babies since poaching had gone insane. I watched them disappear into the bush.

"She will see you after the noon mudbath," Edwin said, startling me back to reality.

Too stunned to answer, I sat for a moment, taking it in. I was here, in Kenya, about to do what everyone told me was impossible. Then, I looked back to Edwin.

He flashed his perfect white smile and said, "Don't worry, you'll do fine. You have David and Eleanor on your side."

∞

It was a bright, sunny day with hundreds of visitors, more than I had seen at the other mudbaths. Then I noticed the film crews. They seemed to be everywhere, filming from every vantage point.

As I got closer, I saw BBC and National Geographic stickers on the cameras and actually recognized someone from several documentaries I had seen set in Africa. Watching all of them work intimidated me. How could Angela possibly even consider my idea when I'm standing right next to some of the most significant documentary producers of animal conservation in the world? The thought of it made me even more nauseous; I needed to calm down. I decided to sit in the shade and meditate until my meeting with Angela.

After everyone had gone, Edwin pointed to a bench and told me to wait for her. Ten minutes passed, then twenty. I started to sweat. One of many machine-gun-toting police officers came over and asked what I was doing there. I told him I had a meeting with Angela.

"You have a meeting with Angela?" he asked, smiling slightly.

"Yes, I was told to wait for her right here."

He got on his radio and spoke in Swahili.

"Come with me," he said. *It must have been Angela he was speaking to,* I thought. He led me down one winding path after another until we arrived at a building with two offices. I heard arguing as soon as I entered. The two people in front of me quietly listened to the commotion going on behind a closed door.

"Please, we just want to share our idea—"

"Do you have an appointment?" said a young woman in a beautiful accent.

"No, but—"

"Then you can't see her."

On they went back and forth. The Machine Gun received a call on his radio and told me to stay put before he left.

As I listened, I realized it wasn't Angela to whom they were speaking, but a gatekeeper. It sounded like there were about five individuals, all arguing and speaking at the same time, not taking "no" for an answer.

Soon, the disgruntled party was rushed out of the office, and the two individuals in front of me were whisked in. I started to panic. This line clearly wasn't for people waiting to meet Angela, but for rejects. *Another test.* I had to think quickly as a bead of sweat trickled down my back.

What was I going to say? How was I going to get past this?

Even though Edwin said Angela would meet with me, whoever was behind that door wasn't letting anyone in. I wondered if Angela was already looking for me on the bench while I lingered here.

I closed my eyes as I pictured myself in the batter's circle feeling the pressure of the situation rise around me. I pictured the girl at bat in front of me being struck out as I listened to the two people in line before me arguing with the gatekeeper behind that closed door.

The crowd was on their feet, screaming at the top of their lungs, but as I looked into the stands it wasn't a sea of strangers looking back at me but all of my friends and ancestors. Clinging to the cyclone fence were my grandmothers Pearl and Frances, my Auntie Ella, uncles Roy and Rolly and my favorite cousin Johnnie, who had died earlier that year of a drug overdose.

Laura's unmistakable scream drew my attention as she stood next to my dearest Leo, who passed away of a methadone overdose not long after Laura. Right behind the umpire where I could see him the clearest was Mark, standing tall and proud, his arms crossed over his chest and one hand touching his mouth the way he used to when he was about to say something brilliant. He nodded in my direction as I made my way to batter's box. This was it—it was my turn. And just like that, the screams faded away until I could hear only the sound of my breath as I put one foot in the batter's box and sized up my opponent.

Suddenly, the front door slammed open, yanking me out of my trance, and a large group of people entered the tiny office, pressing me tighter against the wall. I recognized them as the BBC film crew from the mudbath.

"Are you waiting in line?" one of them snapped as he started to shove past me.

"Yes, but I haven't—" Before I could finish, he pushed past me to open the door, and I felt my last shred of hope slip away.

Then the door to the office flew open, and the BBC film crew began shouting questions as the previous group was whisked out. In all the confusion, I didn't notice the nice-looking blonde girl until I turned to find her right in my face.

"What business do you have here?" It was so sudden, so rude, I couldn't breathe for a second. Then I realized everyone talks this way in Kenya. It isn't rude to them, only direct.

Somehow I knew exactly what to say, and words I hadn't prepared flowed out.

"I'm a student and just graduated a few days ago. I've been working on a research project for the past twenty years with the elephants here. I brought it all with me to show Angela. I have an appointment with her." She doubted that—I could see it in her eyes as she looked me up and down. I unzipped my backpack bulging with its two enormous notebooks.

"You have an appointment with Angela?"

"Yes, I met with Edwin, and he told her I was here. She told Edwin that I was to wait for her on the bench after the noon mudbath. I brought everything with me all the way from Oregon just to show her. See?" I said, grabbing one of my notebooks.

She stared at me, and I stopped breathing. Then she got on the radio and spoke to someone in Swahili.

I wished I'd paid better attention in my Swahili classes.

"Ok, wait here for Alexandra."

The BBC crew stopped talking, and the room grew eerily quiet. When the woman gestured for them to enter the office, they rushed past me, barking like a pack of starving dogs. Then the door closed and I was alone again. I leaned against the wall, exhaled a huge breath, and looked at the ceiling. The stress was enormous, but I wasn't finished yet. I had just had made it past the first gatekeeper, but there were bound to be more, and I had to keep my wits about me.

Then another woman appeared in the open doorway and said, "Follow me."

She led me down the series of walking paths the Machine Gun had taken me down earlier. Each building was covered in winding vines unlike anything I'd ever seen. Only a small, narrow path wound between each vine-covered building, reminding me of something I had seen in *Lord of the Rings*. I could only make out a few feet in front of me until another building appeared. I wasn't sure if this meant I was meeting Angela or if I was about to be put to another test.

The woman approached a door and told me to wait outside. I knelt, ripped open my backpack, and took a long drink of water before taking out my two notebooks to show whoever was about to appear, but one got stuck in the zipper. I was trying to release it when two shoes came into focus on the ground before me.

"What business do you have with me?" I knew instantly it was Angela.

I abandoned my effort to free the notebook and jumped up with only one notebook in hand while quickly reciting everything I had just said to the first gatekeeper. Angela was tiny, not at all what I expected. She had piercing eyes and thick, long, flowing brown hair. She wore jeans with a western belt buckle, the cool kind that belonged in a Calvin Klein ad. I was easily taller, but she looked fierce standing in front me with her arms crossed. No question: I was terrified.

As I explained the research I had collected on the elephants her organization rescued, I opened the notebook and began to flip through the pages. She lowered the glasses that had been holding back her beautiful hair and took hold of the notebook for herself. I took a moment to gather myself as she flipped through the pages.

After a moment, she asked, "What is this, exactly?"

"It is the life history of every elephant you—or the Trust, I mean—has ever rescued. Only it isn't spread out all over the place; instead, I organized and collected information on every elephant and put it into a database. This way, you can see every significant event in that elephant's life all in one place—a big picture of its entire life."

As I spoke, she flipped through the pages faster, which made me more nervous. I took another deep breath and continued.

"I've followed these elephants since I was eight years old."

She kept flipping.

"Since the beginning, starting with Samson and Fatuma and, of course, my favorites, Eleanor, Emily, and Aitong. And I picked up their stories after they went back into the wild, like here, with Edo." I reached over and flipped to the back of Edo's story for her to see.

"I need to have a better look at this." She paused, and I held my breath again. "Debbie, come with me." She took off down another hobbit trail.

I snatched my backpack with my other notebook still wedged in the zipper and raced after her. She was fast, darting from one trail to the next; I had to jog to keep up. As we rounded a corner, I recognized the people that were begging to see Angela but weren't given that opportunity, the previous batters that struck out right before me. They were waiting to ambush her, but she saw them and simply waved them away.

"No, I don't have time right now. Thank you. Follow me, Debbie."

They stopped midsentence, looking like frozen statues with their hands still in the air, and we whisked past.

Then we entered the same office I had just come from. I could hear the commotion of the BBC film crew still arguing with the young woman on the other side of the closed door.

"Have a seat there." Angela pointed at a corner desk, opened the door to all of the yelling, and said, "OK, everyone out, I'm sorry but I can't—I have a meeting. Everyone out PLEASE! Come on, Jes, I need you to see this."

One by one, the exasperated BBC film crew left the office, each one staring at me. Embarrassed, I kept my head down, knowing I had to focus. Then Angela closed the door. I had to get back in my zone. That's when I realized I was literally shaking, and both Angela and Jes could see it. But a voice deep inside screamed, *Who cares if they know I'm terrified? I'm COMPLETELY freaking out right now. This is the biggest opportunity of my life.* Once I allowed myself to just feel the fear, I calmed down, and the meeting got underway.

I told them everything: how it all began, how I had gone back to school, and how I wanted to tell these stories. They asked many questions about specific elephants from long ago, and I knew about every single one. When they asked how I recalled so much,

I explained that they had become my friends over the years, so it was like reciting the past of a childhood friend. Then we talked about David and his incredible work as a conservationist. I had also brought several of his research papers with me; I showed them my favorite parts.

Finally, Angela said, "I wish Mom was here. She would have loved to meet you." I could hardly make out the words as she said them. Then I had to pinch the inside of my thigh to prevent myself from going into complete shock.

Dr. Duffield was right; the research I collected on their elephants was very valuable to them. Then things took a serious turn.

"OK," Angela said gravely as she crossed her arms and leaned back in her chair. "How much do you want for it?"

"For what?" I was confused.

"All of this research—how much?"

It took me a second to process the thought that she would assume I wanted money for the research. Then, I understood her tone.

"Nothing ... I mean ... it's yours ... you can have it. I didn't do it for the money."

"You don't want *anything* for it?" she gasped.

"Well ... there is one thing," I said, looking from her to Jes. *It was now or never.*

"I'm listening."

"I want to be able to tell these stories the way I see them in my head. I want to tell David's story and the history of the elephants. People need to know all the things the elephants are up against, from snares to poisoned arrows, not to mention all the extraordinary ways they're surviving. Each one of these stories is more fascinating than the next. And they need to *know* the elephants

the way that I have come to know them. We need more people in the U.S. to understand the great work you do here, because I ask people all the time if they have ever heard of you, and they haven't. I want to help with that. If we are going to make any sort of impact, we have to touch the heart of the people with the stories, not statistics. In my opinion, everyone is exhausted by the statistics. I want to focus on how the United States, not China, contributes to the poaching epidemic. Everyone is talking about how China is decimating the elephant populations, but no one is talking about the United States being a close second."

"So how do you propose doing this?"

"In the form of a television series," I said.

"Really? Do you know how many times I get propositioned by people like you that want to film a series?"

It was do or die. The ball coming at me was a perfect pitch. It was a full count and I had no choice but to swing with everything I had. I heard the familiar crack as the bat made impact.

"For a show like this? Using the stories of the elephants weaved in with the stories of the people?" I argued.

Angela looked at Jes for a moment before flipping the page to another elephant story before she said, "No. No one has ever pitched us a show like this, have they, Jes."

"We've never had anyone in here even want to talk about the United States' involvement in the poaching crisis," Jes said.

"Debbie, if you could do a show like this, what would you want from us? I mean, there are a lot of restrictions as to what you could or could not film."

For the next hour, we talked about possibilities. I told her what I wanted, and after nearly every item she said, "I think that would be fine." If I had dreamed a perfect dream, it simply *could not* have gone any better. We talked about David and his extraordinary passion and commitment, and she revealed memories I had never heard. Then I shared stories about the elephants that had gone back into the wild. They wondered if many of them were still alive, and I was able to flip to the page of that story and tell them the last time that particular elephant had been spotted. It was like magic.

Finally, she said, "I have to tell you that your passion for the elephants is undeniable. We are interested in helping you any way we can, but you've got quite a lot of work to do on your end, don't you? I mean, you don't have a film crew or a production company, do you?"

"No," I said, "But there were at least three other film crews today who you turned away. I have a great idea, and that is the hardest part, don't you think?"

They agreed.

I could hear the roar of the crowd, my friends and relatives, rising from their seats as I rounded first base, and the sound of my breath was replaced by their screams.

Then Angela said something I never expected. "Well, if you want to film Eleanor, and the older orphans such as Edo, Ndume, and Dika, and Mom and Dad's old house, then you need to go to Voi. Do you have plans to go there while you are here?"

"No, not on this trip."

"What are your plans for the rest of your stay?

"It was only to meet you."

"How long are you here for?"

"Five more days."

"Would you like to go to Voi? You have plenty of time."

"Yes! Are you kidding? I would die to go Voi."

"Well, maybe that can be arranged, can't it, Jes?"

I sat in stunned silence as Angela called Joseph Sauni, the head keeper in Voi, and told him I would be coming. I knew all about Joseph, too. Arrangements were made for a visit to Voi, and since I would be leaving that evening, I needed to get back to my cottage and pack my things for a most unexpected journey.

I floated out of her office and into the empty parking lot where my driver, Edwin, waited. He was parked on the far side. There was only one other vehicle, a Range Rover, and as I got closer, I saw several people standing beside it, smoking. Then I saw the BBC sign on the door and instantly recognized the film crew that was asked to leave during my meeting with Angela. As soon as I got close, the group went silent and stared at me as I walked by.

"Hello," I said.

"Hello," they said in unison. It sounded like a Gregorian chant, hanging in the air, like the cigarette smoke swirling high above their heads.

When I got into the car, Edwin told me they had asked all about me, wanting to know who I was and where I was from.

"I'm nobody," I laughed.

"Oh no, that's not true," he said clicking his tongue.

"What did you tell them?"

"I told them you were BIG—HUGE in America—and I convinced them, I think." He was serious.

I laughed so hard I could barely breathe. Then, the laughter turned into sobs as the stress of the entire day hit me. I couldn't stop crying. I made Edwin wait until we got out of the compound before he pulled to the side of a road, and then I told him absolutely everything. He laughed and cried right along with me. When I told him we were going to Voi, he screamed so loud a goat herder scolded us for scaring his herd. Then he called Edwin Lusichi to tell him the good news.

He handed the phone to me and Edwin said, "It's about time you get to meet the friends you know so well on paper."

I had hit a home run.

CHAPTER 31

We walked for about two miles along a steep hill. It was hot, much hotter than Nairobi. In the distance, something high on a rock caught my eye. As we got closer, I realized it was a hyrax, a small, furry creature that resembles a jack rabbit, only with smaller ears and two small tusks. They are one of the closest living relatives to the African elephant. I had only seen the back side of one, since they were all incredibly shy. But this one stood on his hind legs, in full view, and then sat back down again, repeating this behavior over and over.

"Look at that hyrax. What is he doing?" I asked Fred, a keeper who walked in front of me. He stopped and looked up.

"Oh … Cheerio my good friend," he said, waving to the hyrax "That one we raised," he added before continuing on.

It really did appear as though the hyrax was trying to get our attention, and I laughed, imagining Fred bottle-feeding that little thing every two hours. The keepers continued to follow David's philosophy and carried out his mission, rescuing any animal they came across, whether orphaned or injured. David used to get irritated with the scientists pleading with him to allow nature to take its own course. He felt strongly, as did I, that since so many animals were in peril *because* of humans, the very least we could do as a species is try to help the lucky few we came across. No one would know if they left a hyrax to die. But these men were as compassionate about animals as anyone I had ever known. A life was a life. No matter how small.

I could hear them long before I could see them, the low familiar rumbling sounds of elephants. As we rounded a corner, I looked up, and it appeared as if the entire hillside suddenly came to life. All of the big rocks began to move, then I realized the red features on the hillside weren't rocks, but individual elephants. First one elephant moved toward us, then another, then an entire group all at once.

It's difficult to explain what it feels like to be surrounded by a group of large elephants. Something deep inside tells you to be very afraid. At that very moment, I saw her, an elephant named Lesanju. She stood out because of her badly cut ears, and I recognized her instantly. She, along with an elephant named Lempauté, were the matriarchs of this miniature orphan herd now. On my journey to Voi I secretly wished I would see them both.

Lesanju was rescued in 2006 by a Samburu herdsman after she fell down a deep well. The man who rescued her dug the well for his cattle and was stunned to find an abandoned baby elephant swimming at the bottom the following morning. Imprints on the ground suggested her family had tried to free her, but she was too far below ground for even the largest elephants to help. The tribesman could tell she was exhausted and wondered how many hours she must have tread water waiting for help to arrive.

The first miracle was the fact that she had been spotted by the cattle herder before she drowned. The second was the fact that it was a Samburu man who rescued her. The Samburu were not usually sympathetic toward elephants. In recognition of the baby's bravery, she was named after the man's brother, the chief of the tribe, who had recently died.

After the cattle herder and several of his friends pulled Lesanju out of the well, he marked her as his own by slicing her ears in the same specific pattern he used to mark his cattle. Each cattle herder cuts a unique pattern into the ears of his cows as a way to recognize them if they get lost or stolen. But the man did not realize he was giving Lesanju an enormous disability by cutting off more than half of each ear. An elephant's ear is essential to regulate body temperature, with dozens of intertwining blood vessels running through them. All of the blood in an elephant's body is shunted through the paper-thin membrane of the ear before it is re-circulated back into the body. When the weather is hot, an elephant flaps its ears, which act like a fan, allowing the air to cool the blood in the ear before it gets pumped back into the body. And when the temperature drops, elephants press their ears tightly against their head. Behind each ear is a ball of blood vessels that act as a heater, warming up anything that touches it, thereby warming the blood and raising its body temperature. Without its ears, an elephant has no ability to regulate its own body temperature.

The moment I recognized Lesanju, several of the elephants put their trunks into their mouths, sucked water out of their stomachs and began to spray her. Somehow they knew she was overheating and sprayed her to keep her cool. I stood there in awe, thinking there must be an understanding among the group that without the full use of her ears, she was unable to cool herself down. I wondered if she had just sent a silent signal, or how the group seemed to know what she needed all at the same time.

Even more touching was the reaction of the Samburu man once he learned he was the one responsible for Lesanju's disability. Every year after her rescue, that same man traveled by foot from the northern part of Kenya to the southern region, all the way to Voi, so he could see Lesanju again and "beg for her forgiveness."

Lesanju extended her trunk to me and I blew in it, an elephant's handshake. *She will remember your scent forever,* I could hear David say. Then another elephant approached. I knew it must be Lempauté, since the two rarely separated. Lempauté was rescued in the same region as Lesanju, though she arrived with both ears intact. I've often wondered if the two knew each other before they were rescued since they seemed to have a connection from the moment they first met. Lesanju and Lempauté were now the matriarchs of the young herd in Voi, just like Emily and Aitong were so many years ago.

∞

A radio call came in and everyone chattered wildly. A plane had spotted an orphaned elephant in need of rescue. Once again, I couldn't believe my luck. We separated ourselves from the orphaned herd and ran back to the compound, where two loaded jeeps waited for us. The effort was highly coordinated, with milk, medical supplies, and several men piled high on the back of each jeep. We took off in different directions as the tense pilot shouted details over the radio. As my jeep climbed a large hill, we retrieved our binoculars.

Another radio call came in; the pilot had spotted an injured lioness with two cubs trailing behind. She had fought with a porcupine, and her body was completely covered in massive quills, something she could not survive without intervention. We saw a slight poof of dust rise from a road far below our perch—the other jeep was already heading in that direction. We were ordered to stay on course and look for the baby elephant.

The pilot soon radioed that the elephant had ducked into an area he couldn't see; we would have to wait until it came out. After searching for more than an hour, we decided to turn back to help the other jeep with the injured lioness until the young elephant revealed itself.

Just as we came around a bend, we spotted a waterhole with another of the Trust's jeeps parked near the edge, the men looking at something inside. As we edged closer, we could see what appeared to be two dead zebras stuck in the mud. But just as we were about to pull away, I saw one of them move its head.

"One of them is alive," I yelled.

I had never seen quicksand and wasn't even sure it was a real thing. But it *was* real and incredibly dangerous. The mud had a strange texture with a long, elastic quality, more like rubbery putty than mud. It was obvious that once you got stuck, there was little chance of freeing yourself without help.

For several hours, the men worked to free the zebra. A zebra covered in mud so black I could barely make out a single stripe. As I watched the scene, I thought back to the zebra of my past.

∞

I woke to the sound of blaring techno music. Everything around me was purple. I had passed out in a round purple Naugahyde booth in a dance club. There were flashing purple lights and pulsating music but no people ... anywhere. It took me several minutes to get my bearings. I had no idea where I was or how long I'd been there. I made my way to the outside, where the bright sun blinded me as soon as I opened the door. I stood there for a moment while my eyes and my pounding head adjusted as something moved right next to me.

It was a zebra. I thought for sure that my eyes were playing tricks on me, but as the image slowly came into focus, it was definitely a living, breathing zebra standing right in front of me. I just could not comprehend what was happening or where I was. Most of the evening was a total blank, and I decided to sit down to try and sort out what little I did remember. I wondered if this was indeed Africa. But that didn't even make any sense, although I had no idea how I could possibly be staring at a real-life zebra.

"Debbie!" Matt burst out laughing hysterically as he leaned on the back of Cruz. *Matt and Cruz ... thank goodness.* I could see they were wasted as they approached.

"Where am I?" I asked.

"Mexico, baby," said Cruz, one of my best friends from Taft College. When Matt had driven down from Portland, he and Cruz had hit it off immediately, and somewhere along the line it was suggested we head to Tijuana.

Just then, the two of them stopped cold and stared at the zebra. They burst out laughing again, pointing out the zebra was, in fact, only a painted donkey. We saw several more on the way home.

Matt had been my best drinking friend for a long time. We'd met in Portland nearly twenty years earlier when he'd moved out from Virginia. I recognized him immediately as someone who drank like I did. He never questioned how much I had or why I always wanted more. He was right there with me, drink for drink. But as the years passed, his appetite for harder drugs increased. A few years after our trip to Mexico, a group of his friends asked me to participate in an intervention for him. Once he discovered crack cocaine, little else mattered.

His family all flew out from Virginia, as did his best friends from college. We all went to dinner the night before the intervention, and I got terribly drunk. The whole thing was depressing. I didn't know what to do if I lost my best drinking friend. I was ashamed to admit that my thoughts were not about Matt's well-being, but about my lack of a social life without him.

The following day, we all met up at 5:00 a.m. to surprise Matt, the best time for a "sneak attack," according to the intervention counselor they had flown up from California. One of his friends blocked in his car while the rest of us barged into his apartment. He stared at us in complete shock. He hadn't seen his family for a very long time, and they commented on his ghost-like appearance.

After Matt calmed down, we told him how his drinking and using affected us, one by one. But when it was my turn to talk, he sat and watched me closely from across the room before he said, "You, of all people, have absolutely *no* right to be here."

I knew he was right, but I justified my behavior by the fact that I *only* used cocaine and alcohol and sometimes a little pot and psychedelic mushrooms. I had never even tried crack cocaine. In my mind, he had clearly crossed some invisible line while I was still mostly focused on alcohol. But somewhere deep down, I knew he was absolutely right, and I was ashamed.

In the end, Matt agreed to check into rehab, and his college best friends drove him to the nearest treatment center. But one month later, after everyone had gone, Matt was found passed out in a park with another crack pipe in his hand. After he was evicted from his apartment, he sold everything he had to pay for the drugs he needed to survive and became one more homeless person sleeping on a bench in a park across the street from where he used to live. Over time, we heard less and less from him, until there was nothing.

Eventually I decided to move San Francisco, and the weekend before I left I heard the devastating news: Matt was dead. I didn't know the circumstances, nor did I want to, but hearing it was still devastating. I cut off all ties with that group of friends and just left. But his words haunted me for years.

You of all people have no right to be here.

One year later, I got sober.

∞

It was a Sunday when I got the call. I had moved back to Portland seven years earlier and was running my airbrush tanning business. My business cell phone rang, and for some reason I answered it, which I never did on my days off.

"Illumination Tans Airbrush Tanning," I said.

"Yes, I—I—ah … I'm looking for Debbie Ethell." It was a familiar voice.

"This is she. Who is this?"

"This is Matt … Matt Johnson."

I froze. It simply couldn't be. "No way. Matt Johnson is dead." But his voice sounded frighteningly familiar.

"It's me. I'm alive. I heard that someone said I was dead, but I'm not."

"Oh my god." I began to cry. "Matt! Where have you been? What happened to you?"

"There are so many things I want—I need—to tell you, but first, I—I … have to do something. I need to make what's called an amends with you, because I'm in this program and I'm working these things called the twelve steps, and I need to make an amends with you."

I could not believe what I was hearing. I knew exactly what he meant.

"Wait—you're sober?"

"Yes, I'm sober. And I need to tell you. Please let me finish, because it's hard. But I need to tell you how sorry I am for what I said to you at my intervention. When I said that *you of all people have no right to be here* ... I've always felt so bad for saying that to you, and I want to tell you that you were right. I was in a really, really bad place, and I needed help."

I sat in stunned silence. In total shock, I asked, "How much time do you have now?"

"I have nine months sober—today actually," he laughed.

"I am so proud of you Matt," I said as I cried "And I need to tell you something. I'm sober, too. Did you know that? I'm sober, too."

"What did you say? You're sober too?"

"Yes ... when I came back from California."

"How long ago was that? How much time do you have?"

"Seven years."

"I have nine months and you have seven years. What are the chances of the two of us ever getting clean?" he laughed.

God, how I missed him. I jumped into my car and drove across town that evening to watch him take his nine-month coin. And I not only got to meet his incredible sponsor, Jim, but I got to meet his girlfriend, Kristin. Throughout our friendship, I'd hated most of Matt's girlfriends. I thought he had awful taste in women, so when he told me he wanted to introduce me to one, I braced myself. But I *adored* her. She was everything I could have hoped for him. And just like that, Matt and Kristin became an enormous part of my life.

Six months later, I had them over to my house for dinner. As we ate, Kristin looked over to Matt and said they had something to tell me.

I waited.

"We. Are. ENGAGED!" Kristin yelled as she showed me her ring. The three of us jumped up and down, wildly screaming—it was such a happy moment.

"But wait," Matt said, "that's not it."

"What?" I asked "You're pregnant?"

Matt rolled his eyes and laughed, "No, we're not pregnant. Kristin, you tell her."

"We were thinking about *where* we wanted to get married ..." she trailed off and looked at Matt.

Then Matt said, "And more importantly, we were thinking about *who* we wanted to marry us ..." then he looked back to Kristin.

"It's YOU," screamed Kristin "We want YOU to marry us!" I was so stunned I couldn't speak. "Honestly, Debbie, I had heard so much about you from Matt that from the moment I met you, I knew you were the only person who could marry us." I couldn't believe what they were saying. *They wanted me to marry them.*

One year later, I walked into the Old Portland Church in downtown Portland with my "ordination" certificate in hand for Matt and Kristin's dress rehearsal. I was nervous because I hadn't seen Matt's family since his intervention a million years before. The same group of people who had flown out for the intervention all came for his wedding.

The door slammed behind me, startling everyone huddled together in the middle of the large room. They all went silent.

"Hi. I'm ... um ... I'm Debbie ... the ... the one who's marrying them." I didn't recognize anyone.

Suddenly, this tiny, beautiful woman walked through the middle of the group, right up to me, and grabbed my face in her hands. "There you are. How nice it is to see you again," said Matt's mother as she warmly embraced me. Matt's family and college roommates, the same seven that were at his intervention, surrounded me, each giving me a hug bigger than the last. They told me how they'd worried about me, and how shocked they were to learn I was sober, too.

The following day, as I stood at the podium surrounded by Kristin, Matt, and their families, as well as my own parents and Leslie—I felt pure joy. It was one of the few times in my life I was able to experience it in real time, at the exact moment it happened.

Matt had just celebrated his seventh year of sobriety by the time I made it to Africa. We'd met up at a meeting a few weeks before I left so he could show me pictures of his new life—that life so different from our past. He and Kristin had bought a beautiful home and had a six-year-old daughter who had never seen Matt drink or use.

∞

Staring at a real zebra in Africa, not a fake one in Mexico, I was struck by how vastly different my own life had become. My old life of painted zebras and the alcohol that went with it was gone. Now I was finally staring at a real zebra, another life the keepers would work tirelessly to save, and living in a world beyond my wildest dreams.

Finally, the keepers were able to free the zebra from the quicksand. He ran a few paces before he stopped and stared back at us. Joseph waved, bidding him farewell, but the zebra stayed right where he was. I wondered what he must have been thinking when Joseph yelled out, "You're welcome," laughing as he said it.

It looked like he was thanking us. A group of zebras had gathered in the distance, and they were calling to him. He walked a few more paces, then turned and stared back at us again. We all watched as he finally turned and headed back to be with his own family.

The other jeep located the lioness and successfully removed most of the porcupine quills. We received a call shortly after we'd freed the zebra; they had just released her. Then it struck me that these men had just worked several long, hard hours to free a zebra that would likely be eaten by the lion. But that was never the point. *A life was a life. No matter how small,* I thought as I looked up at the sky.

∞

Back at the compound, I walked to the top of Mazinga Hill. There were keepers sitting on large rocks keeping an eye on the elephants below, the same rocks they stood on when they saw Irima kidnapped, and then saw Edo and Ndume return him. I found my way up a trail to an outcrop of rocks, retracing David's footsteps, the same rocks he'd climbed all those years before when he'd marveled at the monumental task of transforming the barren wasteland into one of the most beautiful landscapes anyone could possibly imagine.

Standing on that flat rock overlooking the grass plains of Kenya dotted with acacia trees, watching zebras, giraffes and elephants roaming below, I knew God had been right there with me all along. When I thought my life was over, it was, in fact, just beginning. I have never been a religious person and am not one today, but I know that something remarkable transported me from the courtrooms of my past to this veranda overlooking *Heaven*.

I felt something poke me from my pocket, and I pulled out a page ripped from one of my meditation books, *The Book of Runes*. It read:

The nature of your passage depends on the quality of your attitude,
the clarity of your intention and the steadfastness of your will.
Do not attempt to go beyond where you haven't yet begun.
Be still, collect yourself, and wait on
the Will of Heaven.

I closed my eyes and felt the hot sun on my face as the wind whipped my hair. I had dreamed of this sensation for so long, and now that I was finally experiencing it in real life, it felt just as I imagined it would. I stood on that rock for a long time overlooking David and Daphne's first home in Tsavo, wondering how many of the animals that passed by were ancestors of those they'd raised. I stared at the waterhole in which Sobo was finally reunited with her family and felt grateful that the reunion with my own had been just as spectacular. From where I was standing, I could see the bright flowers I'd laid on Malaika's grave earlier in the afternoon and wondered where Eleanor, Edo, Ndume, and Dika were at that very moment. I said one final prayer to each of them, including David, wherever he was, hoping to cement that moment in my mind forever.

I was struck suddenly by the thought that every perfect, awful moment of my life up until that point had led me to the exact place I was standing. And every one of the people I'd encountered along the way were leading me toward something I couldn't see or imagine—each with their hands wrapped tightly around my own, leading me toward my destiny, leading me toward the Sunlight of the Spirit. Never in my wildest dreams did I truly think I would make it this far, but there was an awakening in that moment, and I knew I was *exactly* where I was supposed to be.

EPILOGUE

Several significant events happened upon my return from Kenya. The first was the surprise that my entire family, including extended members from Minnesota, were waiting for me when I got off the plane. They cried as they hugged me nearly to death. They knew this was a lifelong dream accomplished. And when I got to sit down and tell them the events that unfolded while I was there, we ran through every box of tissues in the house. It was another precious moment.

A few months later, I received an opportunity to pitch my idea for a television series to Vulcan Productions, one of Paul Allen's companies. As one of the founders of Microsoft, he'd put more money and effort into stopping the African poaching crisis than nearly any other individual. It became the second scariest meeting of my life, after the meeting with Angela in Kenya, and unfortunately I left myself in the waiting room on that one. My fear got the better of me. After I'd presented my idea, they said that *if* I was willing to turn my show into a children's series and air it only in China, they would consider it. It was clear we were not on the same page. Actually, I found the idea stunningly absurd.

Then they said something I found even more interesting.

"The people in the United States are just *not* that interested in helping elephants." Apparently based on the fact that their

documentaries weren't getting the viewership they'd hoped.

Before I could stop myself, I blurted, "It's because you're not inspiring anyone. No one wants to see one more documentary full of statistics that mean nothing to the person watching. People in the United States have no perspective on elephants. It is our job to teach them."

Needless to say, my words didn't go over well, and the meeting ended. After thinking about it for a long time, Leslie finally talked me into starting my own nonprofit as a way of teaching people everything I could about elephants while there was still time. I began meeting Jason for coffee on a regular basis, since he had started several successful nonprofits. I knew I wanted to name it The KOTA Foundation for Elephants, which stood for Keepers of the Ark, because it is what I believe we all are. We have the power to let elephants go extinct, or we have the power to save them. Also, the name is borrowed from a book by the same name, *Keepers of the Ark* by R.J. (Ray) Ryan, that I'd read during my last year of college. When I finally got the opportunity to speak with Ray, he was thrilled that a passion project of his had inspired a passion project of mine.

There was only one person I wanted to work hand-in-hand with on the foundation, and that was Jason. He was always fighting for the underdog. Elephants soon became something he wanted to fight for as much as I did, so he became the first President of The KOTA Foundation for Elephants.

I started speaking to small groups at first, but as word got out about my presentations, larger crowds came. I was right. People in the United States were as deeply passionate about elephants as I thought they were. The problem was that they simply didn't know that much about them. So it became my mission to teach them everything I could, from the evolving science to the stories of the individuals I continue to follow.

∞

Edo was spotted in Voi just a few weeks after I left. I was thrilled. Ndume was last seen in 2016 by fellow conservationists Mark Deeble and Vicky Stone. When they noticed a large bull who didn't seem disturbed by their presence out in the bush, they contacted the David Sheldrick Wildlife Trust. Mishak and Edwin went down to see if they recognized him, and they did. He hadn't been seen in nearly ten years. Mark wrote about their emotional reunion in a blog called *Ndume: The Story of an Elephant.*

Eleanor was last spotted in 2015, and though she has previously disappeared for long periods of time, I would be lying if I said I'm not nervous. I often wonder about the ivory that people display in their homes. Do they know who it belonged to? What if it came from the tusks of Eleanor or Dika? Dika hasn't been seen in years, either. Are the owners of that ivory aware of the remarkable and intricate stories of the individuals that owned it originally? It is for this reason that my foundation fought to ban the sale of ivory in the state of Oregon, and why we're working just as hard with other states to do the same. So far, only seven of the fifty states have passed similar laws. That is not nearly enough.

Between 2011 and 2017, over 115,000 elephants were killed in Kenya. The tragedy lies in knowing that the original number of living, breathing elephants was 135,000. Just like it was in 1980. Today there are fewer than twenty thousand elephants left in Kenya, which once had the largest elephant population in the world. Once again, we will be lucky to have any left in the next decade, and that is why I sleep so little.

In April of 2016, Richard Leakey came out of retirement at the age of seventy-two, once again taking the helm of the Kenya Wildlife Service, the same position he'd held in 1989 during the first poaching crisis. On April 30, 2017, he orchestrated the largest ivory burn in history, again with the entire world watching. Many may not realize that it was a last-ditch effort to try something, *anything*, to make the poaching stop, and again I sat up in the middle of the night watching it burn.

President Kenyatta said to the massive crowd, "For us, ivory is worthless unless it is on our elephants … " He stood next to Richard Leakey, who had just given his own impassioned speech. He went on, "There's a passing of judgment from some that we're doing the wrong thing because Kenya is a poor country, and we could use the 150 million-odd dollars that they claim the ivory is worth to develop our nation. But I would rather wait for the judgment of future generations, who I am sure will appreciate the decision we have taken today."

And just like that, they did it again. President Kenyatta and Richard Leakey torched more than 105 tons of ivory in a repeat of the 1989 ivory burn. They destroyed every last piece in Kenya's stockpile. Within hours, French minister Segolene Royal announced her decision to adopt a near total ivory ban in France, while the European Union and the United States stayed conspicuously quiet. Slowly, over the rest of that year, the price of ivory steadily dropped, and awareness of the plight of elephants steadily rose. *There is still hope.*

But it is hope tempered by the corrosive effects of money. Ivory trafficking has mimicked the illegal drug trade in many ways. Assassinations, conspiracy, and suspicious links to highly placed government officials continue to undermine conservation efforts. However, it is the thousands of small-time traders in the United States who contribute most to America's status behind China as number two in the illicit ivory trade.

∞

The year after my return from Kenya, both of my best friends, Leslie and Stephanie, were diagnosed with the same deadly form of breast cancer, and my entire world came crashing down. I spent my days in chemo appointments, making food, cleaning their houses, and telling them the most inspiring elephant stories I knew.

At the end of that year, Stephanie thankfully made it into the clear, and they could find no sign of cancer anywhere. But Leslie's spread throughout her tiny body. Even though we fought like hell against a fate we knew was coming, we laughed equally as hard. At each medical appointment, she would introduce me to the nursing staff.

"This is my best friend Debbie Ethell, and she is a fucking miracle!"

It was in my grief over losing her that I finally began to write this book, a book she tried to get me to write for years. I never could have dreamed she would become one of the angels guarding over me, yet here we are. Now, as I continue my path, I feel her with me, whispering to me when I want to quit and making me promise, once again, to *never give up*.

When I look into the eyes of a newly orphaned elephant suffering enormous trauma, it reminds me of the eyes of a newcomer alcoholic. Deeply hurt, both physically and mentally, and confused, angry, sad, ashamed—I see the parallel. I call them butterflies because they go through a metamorphosis so extraordinary it seems almost impossible.

Watching a young elephant begin to trust its keeper, make friends, and begin to show who they truly are is something I wish everyone could witness. They come in like a cocoon, shut down and closed off from the world by unspeakable tragedy, and they leave like a butterfly, spreading their brilliantly colored wings, readying themselves to fly toward the sunlight, the same way alcoholics who get sober do.

Each time I sit across the table from another terrified, angry butterfly, I think of the elephants. And when I watch the alcoholic woman spread her beautiful wings, get her children and family back, and reintegrate into a society that was so unbelievably cruel, I am reminded once again of just how precious and wonderful life can be.

ACKNOWLEDGEMENTS

*T*here are so many people I would like to thank for propping me up (sometimes literally) along this journey. I have to start with my amazing family. My mom, Sandra, for believing I was a writer long before anyone else did—for painting the beautiful cover of this book—and for her kindness, love, and support. My dad, Ray, for always taking my late-night phone calls, guiding me through one crisis after the next, and for always believing in me when it sometimes felt like no one else did. *You both stood by me even after I made your lives a living hell, and I will always love you for that.*

My sister—*my rock*—Carrie. She is the only one who can still make me laugh harder than anyone else. *No one has ever supported me as unconditionally as you have—love, love, love you forever for that.* Two sweet boys, Sam and Charlie: From the first moment Sam opened his eyes and looked at me, I knew my life had changed forever. I cannot wait to see what the future holds for you. You have inherited your mother's gift for making me laugh. Thank you, Charlie, for giving me honest feedback and for bringing your lovely mother, Carol, into all of our lives.

I owe a HUGE shout out to Dave Lutz—I will forever be grateful that you never sleep and always take my calls into the wee hours of the morning. Our friendship spanning the better part of twenty-five years has been a lifeline for me. Pennie Trumbull, aka *Pennie Lane*, who I met on the same night I met Dave: thank you for planting the seed for this book at one of your infamous dinner parties with the ladies, Kris, Gretchen, and Kelly. Two fateful nights I will not soon forget.

My many dear friends who have walked beside me on the road to recovery: Matt Johnson—what a journey we have gone through, from best drinking friends to a life of recovery. Wow. All I can say is—*W-O-W*. Ann M., where would I be today if you didn't put things into such simple perspective for me? Thank you for giving me so much of your time and for letting me have a space in your home. Stephanie M. ... I can hardly say thank you to you without crying. We have been through so much together, and you've been with me nearly every step of the way. Thank you for always giving me the space to be exactly who I am and never judging me for it. And thank you for the laughter ... *always thank you for the laughter!*

I have to thank Yvonne W. and Shelly P. for taking my hand in those early first days and teaching me how to live a life free of all mind-altering substances. Yvonne—you've always been like a second mother to me, and no matter where you are, I will never forget you. And Carol M., for teaching me how to be a working member of society with double-digit sobriety.

The rest of my recovery family includes: Herb K., Jim & Tina W., Bob H., Barbara B., Pat J., Phil E., Ed W., Melinda P., Jo D., Teri S., Steve W., Lara N., Tom B., and Debra L. I love the hell out of all you guys!

Bob Lee for being so kind, generous, and safe. I owe an enormous debt of gratitude to you and often wonder where I might be if you hadn't brought me into your home.

Thelma (Linda P.) you have inspired me more than you know with your wit, your humor, and your wisdom. *You and Lola …* you are the Thelma to my Louise.

Hugh Lacey—you were my first real friend in a very long time and have continued to be ever since. You have protected me, defended me, and fought for me. I love you like family.

Devorah Maddox, Justine Light, Kirsten Milliken, Fred & Leila Brown, Erik Berkey—you each own a piece of my story, and I have no doubt divine intervention put you in my life for a reason.

My fellow warriors for elephants: Edwin Lusichi, Mishak Nzimbi, Ray Ryan, Dr. Deb Duffield, Dr. Lucy Bates, Dr. Karen McComb, Dr. Joyce Poole, Cynthia Moss, Dr. Richard Byrne, Dereck and Beverly Joubert, Dr. Caitlin O'Connell-Rodwell and one of the most amazing animal-rights lawyers I know—Stephen Wise—and one of his fellow worker bees: Lauren Choplin. I raise my glass (of water) to each of you.

Casey Sims—where I would be if you didn't remind me of what I wanted to be when I grow up? I will always be grateful you asked me that question and helped me navigate my way back to school.

I have to thank my editors Kristen Steenbeeke and Mark Merrill for taking me through this process and humbling me every step of the way. Kristen, your wit and humor made the process an enjoyable one, and Mark, you brought the book into a new dimension and I learned just how much I hate the semicolon— *full stop*.

I also need to thank David and Daphne Sheldrick. Thank you for writing down your thoughts, your words, and your discoveries and leaving your work in a place where a kid growing up about as far away from Africa as you could get could find it. Everything you did continues to inspire me.

I owe the largest debt of gratitude to Bill Wilson and Dr. Bob. Without your foresight into the eyes of addiction—well, let's just say the ending of this book would have been quite different. You not only saved my life but those of just about everyone I know. Thank you for creating a pathway that has allowed me to follow my true will.

And lastly—Eleanor, Edo, Ndume, Dika, Emily, and my dearest Aitong—where would I be without each of you? You have all inspired me more than any human, seen me through my darkest hours, and given me the courage to keep moving forward. Now that I am finally in a position to help, I will never stop working against the forces trying to end you. When I close my eyes, I picture all of you roaming below Mazinga Hill, wild and free—I whisper a mantra that brings you closer to me:

for the elephants,
for the elephants,
For the Elephants ...

ABOUT THE AUTHOR

DEBBIE ETHELL is the executive director of The KOTA Foundation for Elephants and a conservation research scientist. Her blogs and articles have been featured in both national and international publications including *Grapevine, Mother Nature Network,* and *Africa Geographic* as well as several scientific research publications. She lives in Portland, Oregon. This is Debbie's first book, the first in a three-part *Will of Heaven* series. You can visit her foundation's website to learn more about elephants at kotafoundation.org.

Debbie Ethell is available for select readings and lectures. To inquire about a possible appearance, please contact the Alberta Pearl Publishers author page at authors@albertapearl.com.

Alberta Pearl Publishing
albertapearl.com

47725167R00166

Made in the USA
Middletown, DE
09 June 2019